Still Life

Samuel F. Pickering, Jr.

Still Life

University Press of New England

Hanover and London

University Press of New England

Brandeis University
Brown University
Clark University
University of Connecticut
Dartmouth College

University of New Hampshire
University of Rhode Island
Tufts University
University of Vermont
Wesleyan University

© 1990 by University Press of New England

All rights reserved. Except for brief quotation in critical articles or reviews, this book, or parts thereof, must not be reproduced in any form without permission in writing from the publisher. For further information contact University Press of New England, Hanover, NH 03755.

The author and publisher gratefully acknowledge the following publications in which essays in this volume first appeared: *Virginia Quarterly Review,* "Politics"; *Negative Capability,* "Canned Stuff"; *The Bread Loaf Anthology of Contemporary American Essays,* "Faith of the Father"; *Kenyon Review,* "These Essays, My Life"; *Chariton Review,* "Still Life"; *Northeast Magazine* of *The Hartford Courant,* "Celebrity"; *Texas Review,* "Selecting a Past"; *Chattahoochee Review,* "Back From the Edge."

Printed in the United States of America

∞

Library of Congress Cataloging-in-Publication Data
Pickering, Samuel F., 1941–
Still life / Samuel F. Pickering, Jr.
p.   cm.
ISBN 0–87451–515–7 (alk. paper)
I. Title
AC8.P673   1990
081—dc20   89-28605
                                                                              CIP

5   4   3   2   1

For that other and better Sam Pickering,
my father, with respect and love.

Contents

Still Life

Politics

After finishing the commercial course at the high school in Orphan's Friend, Stewards Tissler left Jackson County and moving to Carthage began selling tickets for the Louisville and Nashville Railroad. Diligent and able, Stewards was determined not to rust away on a country siding, and within a few years he steamed up the tracks to Louisville. Once there he shoveled more hard ambition into his firebox and keeping the throttle open and the side rods pounding, married carefully and well and eventually became vice-president in charge of freight operations. Although Stewards sometimes alluded to Tennessee, attributing his success, as he typically stated in an address before the United Daughters of the Confederacy, to the thick red clay he felt between his toes as a child, two decades rolled by before he returned to Orphan's Friend. Then he went back for just an afternoon and the funeral of his uncle Mordecai Bickings. Having scrubbed Jackson County off his feet, Stewards was uncomfortable and didn't know what to say to people he had long since pushed out of thought and, he believed, out of memory. At Mordecai's grave Stewards recognized Isom Legg, coal agent for Orphan's Friend and the nearby towns of Bone, Flint Hill, Buckeye, and Lassiter's Cross Roads. Legg's twin boys had been in Stewards's class in high school, and although Stewards had not liked them, he felt obliged to ask about them. "Mr. Legg," he said, "it's good to see you looking so hale and hearty. I want to know about Amon and Lusk. What's Lusk doing now?" "Oh," said Legg, "Lusk is down to Nashville in politics." "Well, that's mighty fine," Stewards replied beaming bland approval, "and how's Amon doing?" "Amon," Legg said, turning aside and spitting over a tombstone, "Amon ain't worth a damn neither."

Few members of my family have been involved in things political. Whether concern over character or distrust of partisanship has kept us far from ballot and position, I am uncertain. Whatever the truth,

I

however, the only Pickering to hold public office was appointed. In
1881–82 my great grandfather William Blackstone Pickering was
chief clerk of the Tennessee legislature. About the same time another
great grandfather "Bud" Griffin was killed in a brawl in Franklin,
Tennessee. With a reputation unsullied by politics, Griffin was a
drinker and a philanderer, and it seems probable that matters fleshly,
not political, lay behind his death. Still, Griffin was outspoken, and
some rash proposal of his might have raised consciousness so much
that it provoked a permanent veto. A splattering of Griffin courses
through me, and once or twice an occasional statement of mine has
warmed the blood of the politically active. On my remarking that
I thought de Gaulle a great Frenchman, a man across the table from
me at a seated dinner jumped up and shaking his fist, shouted, "You
Communist; burn your draft card. Carry a protest sign. Move to
Russia."

In retrospect, the man's response was not surprising. He was a
dentist, and I have never met a liberal dentist. The steamy rank air
of bicuspids and molars, root canals and plaque, is not intellectually
bracing. Patterns of work influence patterns of thought, and the
mind confined by day to the narrow world between gum and epiglot-
tis is not likely to pay lip service to the broad view at night. Still,
the dentist may have been more correct than he knew. Although I
have never carried a sign in a demonstration, I have liberal leanings.
On May Day I tie a strand of red yarn around my left arm as protest
against incomes policy at home and foreign policy abroad. Of course
I'm not politically consistent, and I stagger to the right as much as
I totter to the left. I am tired, for example, of hearing the American
Civil Liberties Union give high reasons for being on the low side. I
believe in capital punishment, not simply for murderers but sundry
types of malefactors, lawyers, developers, even folks who cheat on
their income tax. People who drive faster than the speed limit pro-
voke me to the edge of reason, and I think whipping posts should
be constructed every quarter mile or so on the shoulders of public
roads. Instead of wasting time writing tickets police ought to jerk
speeders out of their cars, strap them to posts, and flog the tar out
of them.

Irritating me almost as much as speeders are foreigners who
come to this country and spend affluent days criticizing everything.
Actually I don't meet such people now, but twenty years ago in
graduate school, I bumped into boatloads of them. "We need the

bomb," an Indian student on a large fellowship shouted in the graduate dining room at Princeton one night. "We need the bomb to protect ourselves against people like you. Look around," he said to his companion, "nothing but fascist pigs." When the speaker himself looked around, he saw me, a black and white Hampshire hanging above him, rumbling and snorting like a thunder storm. I had been eating across the room with my friend Bill, peacefully speculating on how I could become all things to all women. When the man started shouting, though, and the room became quiet, everyone looking silently down at his meal, I hoisted myself up and grunting pushed through the tables and chairs. "Damn straight," I said bristling above the speaker and slamming my fist down so hard on the table that lasagna bounced off his plate and fell to the floor; "Hell, yes, India needs the bomb—from forty thousand feet."

"By God, Sam, good for you," Bill said when I sat back down; "you showed him. Have you ever thought about going into politics?" "No," I answered; "it's too corrupt and to succeed in Tennessee I would have to be some sort of knee-jerk right-winger. Give me quiet retirement." Actually I wasn't entirely truthful. Despite reluctance to become involved in politics, I have always hankered for the spotlight. As a boy I went to baseball games at Sulphur Dell in Nashville. Whenever the "Vols" fell behind, I yelled "Put Pickering in." "Who is Pickering," someone invariably asked. "He's just come over from Fayetteville in the Carolina League, Class B," I answered; "he was hitting three hundred and seventy and knocking so many balls into the brickyard across the railroad tracks that folks nicknamed him 'Brickyard.' " As soon as people around me began shouting "we want Pickering," I crept off to another seat, and by the end of the game, people all over Sulphur Dell were yelling for Pickering, some of them considerably exercised because the manager had not even let him pinch hit.

Although I have not seen a baseball game in thirty years, desire for attention must have been spreading quietly in my unconscious. This past summer when the Bread Loaf Writers' Conference offered me a fellowship, I accepted. Some years ago I turned Bread Loaf down. My writings having recently attracted notice, however, I was ready to talk about them. In the past I avoided flattery; now I went to Bread Loaf, eager for a thick basting of compliment. The person desirous of attention is usually so stuffed with self that all seasoning disappears from his character. Awash in a margarine of praise, the

Griffin in my nature flowed slick and smooth. Of course once or twice I was forced to truss up my tongue, and, for that matter, other parts. One cool evening as the moon broke full and silver, splintering over the hills and down through the trees, I could not sleep. Thinking a walk might exhaust me, I dressed and crossing the street opposite the Bread Loaf Inn started through a pasture. "Do you mind if I join you," a young woman said; "I have read your latest book. It's super, and I would like to talk to you about it." "Sure," I said, suddenly swept far from insomnia and pasture by the melody of compliment. My companion, however, was not so oblivious to place and occasion, and when we reached a depression in the middle of the pasture and night gathered around us like a hand, she stopped and drawing near looked up at the hat I wore. "Does that say 'Sea Island Beach Club,'" she asked; "it's hard to tell at night." "Yes, that's what it says," I answered. "What sweet memories that brings to mind," she said, pushing her hair back off her forehead and her lips wet and gleaming in the moonlight. "Sea Island," she said softly, "that's where I lost my virginity." For a moment desire for flattery almost became desire for something else, but then I mastered heredity. "What an elegant place for such pleasantry," I said, adding as I turned back to the Inn, "what was it you said about my book and the eternal verities?"

Not wanting to offend anyone who might praise me, I was judicious, restrained, and even diplomatic at Bread Loaf. When a woman who liked my writing gave me one of her poems to read, I was complimentary, albeit the poem described curing a yeast infection with yogurt. Instead of criticizing the subject, I suggested that the poem needed more specifics. "What sort of yogurt was used," I asked, "low fat, all natural, blueberry? Under certain circumstances I can imagine an application of peach melba. In a warm climate, frozen yogurt might prove most efficacious. Such details," I concluded, "are the sorts of things which interest readers and make poems live." My response to the poem was temperate not only because the woman flattered me, but also because I had recently agreed to run for the Board of Education in Mansfield, Connecticut. A little restraint in the summer, I hoped might become tact by the fall, tact tan and anonymous like fallen leaves. Success in educational matters, I suspected, rarely went to the outspoken or the colorful. In September when my son Francis entered first grade, my hunch proved correct. For an art project students in his class drew pictures of dinosaurs. After the children finished their drawings, the teacher bound them together as a book and asked the class for suggestions for the title. Francis suggested "Great Big Stompers." The title chosen was "Our Dinosaur Book."

Despite my hankering for attention, running for the Board of Education was not my idea. In April some Democrats approached my wife Vicki and asked her to urge me to run for the board. When Vicki mentioned the idea to me, I hesitated, saying Pickerings were not political animals. Besides, I added, "the limelight is no place for a man who needs a whitewash." "Come off the canned wit," Vicki said; "it's your civic duty. Besides if you are elected you'll be able to pick out good teachers for the children." That evening I called the Democrats and said I would run. A small problem existed, however. Although I had few partisan opinions, I was a bit contrary, I explained, and when I moved to Mansfield and registered to vote, I told the clerk to sign me up with the party which had the smaller number of members. As a result I was a Republican. "I'll go over to town hall tomorrow, though," I said, "and change parties." "No, no," the Democrats said, "Mansfield has a minority rule. That means that some members of the smaller party have to be elected to the town council and various boards, including the school board. You stay a Republican. We will make a few telephone calls and get the Republicans to nominate you. All you have to do is go to a meeting or two and the nomination is yours."

Two days later the chairman of the Republican Town Committee telephoned. "I understand you are willing to stand for the school board," he said; "that's terrific. We are having a pot luck picnic in May for potential candidates. Do you think you could attend?" When I said I would like to attend, he said he would send me a notice in a couple of weeks. Ten days later the notice arrived. On it was printed "Awake the Slumbering Elephant" and "Let the Political Football Game Begin." "I don't know about these metaphors, Vicki," I said, looking at the notice. "Hush," she said, "we will go and take the children. I'll bake chocolate chip cookies, and everybody will think us a sugary American family. If you will just smile and not say much, the nomination is in the bag." Because of rash Bud Griffin, I was nervous about the picnic. I should not have worried. In pursuit of office my talk flattened out, and I sprayed compliments about like air freshener. Exchanging compliments, Josh Billings wrote, is another name for exchanging lies. To anyone who writes, lying comes naturally, and a month later the Republicans put me up for the school board.

Being nominated for office is far different from running for election. I do not like the telephone and despise knocking on strangers' doors. Even though neighbors know Vicki and me and the children well and expect us to come trick or treating, Halloween almost gives me colitis. When the children ring doorbells, I hide in the shadows. In September I went to a Republican meeting and addressed a few envelopes, but after that I lay low. While Democrats and Republicans roamed neighborhoods digging up votes, I planted flowers in the yard: from Hildenbrant's Iris Gardens in Nebraska thirty-two bearded Iris, ten poppies, and four peonies; from Breck's one hundred twenty-eight crocus and fifty-three tulips. My little boy Edward helped with the tulips. Because tulips rarely weather many springs, I don't normally plant them. This year was different, however. Story has it that fairies sometimes use tulip blossoms as cradles for their babies, and Edward and I put the tulips down in hopes of keeping fairies in our neighborhood. In the rush to become "a great research university," the University of Connecticut has razed the small world around us, leveling Fish Pool Hill, cutting down the Old Orchard and Dancing Wood, and turning Cat's Foot Lane into a parking lot. Never again will Edward walk through the Old Orchard on a dark winter day and see an elf crouched under an apple tree, icicles hanging from his pointed cap. No longer will troops of fairies wear great wheels in the moss around oaks in the Dancing Wood. Now if my boys are ever bothered by warts, I will have to buy patent medicine for them at Storrs Drugs instead of telling them to search for snails in the Fish Pool. To get rid of a wart, old lore has it, one should hang a snail on a briar. As the snail dries and withers away, the wart disappears.

Imagination and sensibility have been diminished. At the end of Cat's Foot Lane where a great honey locust towered, sheltering life and story, now stretches a long flat row of cars, metallic and dead. Long ago a devil, so I was told, broke through the iron bars confining him to the underworld and climbing up into the sky stole a jar of pure white honey from the cloud god. As the devil hurried back to the underground, one of the god's sentinels, a falcon, saw him and swooping down tore the jar of honey from his grasp. Before the falcon escaped into the clouds, however, the devil threw a spear at him. The aim was true, and although the falcon pitched over to one side, the spear knocked the honey loose, slicing off one of the falcon's claws as well. The jar of honey fell to the ground, but before the devil could retrieve it, the cloud god transformed the spear into the locust, the honey becoming the tree's long white spikes of sugary blossoms and the falcon's claw, the blossoms' sharp protecting thorns.

From White Flower Farm in Litchfield I ordered seventy-two Dutch Iris, twenty-four squill, and three lilacs, old-fashioned ones, Ludwig Spaeth, Lucie Ballet, and Ellen Willmott. Familiar sights around old foundation holes and tumbledown barns, the lilacs raised visions of dirt roads, lightning rods, and milk wagons. I planted them almost as replacements for the locust and apple trees, to create the illusion of holding asphalt and dark modernity at branch's length. To plant the lilacs I had to dig up forsythia, but we have lots of forsythia in the yard and its roots are shallow. To plant the bearded Iris, I dug up some of my mock orange. In late spring mock orange blooms creamy sweet, clusters of blossoms and dark green leaves pulling branches in heavy curves toward the ground. Later, alas, no matter how I trim them, my plants grow angular and cutting like cheap, painted fingernails. Most of my digging, though, was for daffodils, some three hundred of them. In my part of Connecticut, the topsoil is thin, and the granite below pushes through the surface. For a month I was my own chain gang, levering up and carting stone to a rockpile behind the house, then filling my cart with black mulch from the woods and spreading it thick over the bulbs. Come May, my yard will be bright with daffodils—red, orange, yellow and white: accent, festivity, smiling maestro, spellbinder, cheerfulness, cragford, Jenny, sugar bush, ice follies. "You had better start campaigning," Vicki said when I showed her the Grant Mitsch bulbs, saying they resembled living sculptures, tanned and veined with potential. "No," I answered, "the election is not important. Next spring these bulbs will bring beauty into our lives. The school board will only cause wrangling."

I had lost enthusiasm for the election. When friends discovered I was running, they delighted in telling me that six years on the school board demanded long hours and a thick skin. "I am voting for you, Sam," Joe said, "but you better hope you lose." I was ambivalent. On some days I wanted to win; on others I prayed to lose. What was constant, though, was the dread of humiliation, receiving sixteen votes. The dread, however, was not enough to make me forsake shovel and cart for doorbells. In early October the Willimantic paper reviewed a book I wrote praising it and printing a picture of me. "That's my campaign," I told Vicki; "I am not doing anything more." Alas, four nights later I wrote a flyer. Sometime earlier my picture had been taken for a Republican advertisement; unfortunately the Republican committee had trouble putting the advertisement together and rumor reported it would not appear. When the Democrats who urged me to run heard about the advertisement, they donated a hundred dollars toward my and another Republican's campaign for the school board. My running mate having accepted the money, I had to buckle down and write a flyer. The hundred dollars bought a thousand flyers. Running actually did not cost me much. Laramie Photography in Willimantic charged eight dollars and sixty cents to take my picture for the advertisement. In September the head of the Republican committee urged to me buy an election sweatshirt. The shirt was white with blue lettering. On the chest in front was printed "R" TEAM in bold letters; to the left over the heart was the town seal, an office building in the center and the date of incorporation, October 1702, running around the edge. In capital letters on the back was my last name; under it was 8B, the number of my lever on the voting machine; beneath that was BD OF ED, standing for Board of Education.

The shirt cost seventeen dollars and eighty-three cents. Not wanting to be a spoil sport, I bought it, telling Vicki that the political animal would fit comfortably into my menagerie of other sweatshirts stamped with "Sewanee Tigers," "UCONN Huskies," and "Princeton Tuna Team." The second week in October Vicki and I attended a fund-raising cocktail party. The evening cost thirty-seven dollars and ninety-nine cents, the big expenses being twenty dollars for the party and ten dollars for the babysitter. Since we knew few people at the party itself, we did not stay long. To make the evening worthwhile for the sitter, we killed time, going to Zenny's Restaurant and having coffee and two pieces of chocolate Amaretto pie for six dollars and ninety-nine cents plus a dollar tip. My running mate distributed most of the flyers by hand, sticking them under doors and in newspaper boxes, but I mailed two hundred and fifty-four at bulk rate, twelve and a half cents apiece at a cost of thirty-one dollars and seventy-five cents.

After the election I bought a dozen bottles of wine as a present for the man who donated one hundred dollars to my campaign. My

returning the money directly would have offended him, but I knew
he could not refuse a gift. Burgundy, Beaujolais, Claret, Cabernet
Sauvignon, the names of wines mean little to me, so I bought by the
label. I bought two bottles of Zaca Mesa's California wine. In the
center of the label was a drawing of the desert, mesas sloping and
rising one behind another like knees. Framing the drawing were
gold and blue bands while underneath Zaca Mesa slid stylishly
across the label, the letters twisting around the bottle like a side-
winder over the desert. In contrast the label on Round Hill's bottles
had a quaint, 1950ish look: a little house, warm and comfortable,
snugged down under a tight round hill with vineyards rising regular
and clean above. The label on Tyrrell's Hunter River Long Flat Red
was almost unadorned, conveying a lean, outdoorsy, Australian
simplicity. The labels on Australian wine were particularly appealing, and I bought several bottles. My favorite was on a wine bottled
by Thomas Hardy, a reproduction of a painting called "Summer
Landscape Near Kapunda." On the left side of the label the earth
gathered in great dusty orange swirls; on the bottom and around
the right, a line of trees stretched, green and brown and desolate.
The wine cost seventy-nine dollars and forty cents. The other candidate gave me forty dollars so I paid thirty-nine dollars and forty
cents. I had some few incidental expenses: ingredients for the chocolate chip cookies and the cheese crackers which Vicki cooked for
the picnic and then cocktail party. To attend the meetings and
parties, I drove a few miles and so the expenses for gas and ingredients came, I estimated, to twelve dollars. My final expense occurred
after the election. The Republicans were so badly beaten that the
head of the town committee was forced to resign. He had worked
hard, and I felt sorry for him, so in appreciation of his effort, I gave
him a copy of my latest book, the cost to me being nine dollars and
eighteen cents. For the election then, my expenses, including picture,
sweatshirt, fund-raisers, mailing, and "literature," came to one hundred and fifty-six dollars and seventy-five cents.

The tone of my flyer differed from that written by the Democratic
candidates for school board. Under headings such as "Proven Lead-
ership," "Proven Concern," and "Proven Responsibility," they
stuck serious, studiously businesslike paragraphs filled with phrases
like professional commitment, curricular development, and creative
educational program. While high-calling hung like a gull over the
Democratic flyer, mine, I am afraid, smacked of the Pepperidge

Farm cookies my running mate and I ate while discussing it. On the address side of the Democrats' flyer was a picture of the candidates standing in a classroom next to the American flag. In the same place on our flyer were corny jokes. "Teacher:" one of the jokes began, " 'Who discovered America?'

"Little boy: 'Ohio.'

"Teacher: 'No, America was discovered by Columbus.'

"Little boy: 'Yes, Columbus was his first name.' "

Printed in bold letters at the top of the reverse side of our flyer was "READING, WRITING, ETC.*" At the bottom of the page was "*ETC. is the word you use when you want people to think you know more than you do." In the middle of the flyer appeared our names, pictures, biographies, and "philosophic" statement. In my biography I stated simply that I had three children, taught English at the University of Connecticut, and spent a lot of time writing about myself. The philosophic statement was similarly straightforward, containing no philosophy. We said we were pleased with the schooling our children were receiving, adding "We want to serve a town we like. Neither of us pretends to be an expert, but we are deeply interested in education and our community." And that, I must admit, was all of that. We might have said more if we stood a better chance in the election. In Mansfield, however, there were twenty-nine hundred registered Democrats and fifteen hundred registered Republicans. Because of the rule granting representation to the minority party, either my running mate or I would be elected. A high school teacher, advisor to the Cub Scouts, and head of adult education in the largest church in Mansfield, my running mate was certain to win. Moreover he understood the problems facing the schools and talked brightly and learnedly about them. For my part I had lived almost as an anchorite, unconcerned about local affairs and devoted to self and family. Because I did not know the candidates, I rarely voted in municipal elections. As for schools and their problems, I knew nothing and said so when asked.

Certain that I would be odd man out on voting day, I began to enjoy campaign doings. When the Mansfield Education Association invited candidates for the school board to address them, I accepted. Unlike other candidates I did not prepare a speech and instead spoke spontaneously. I hated talking about myself but, I said, I loved being talked about. "If you want to know anything about me," I added, "read my latest book." Although most of the things I wrote would bore the behind off a hippopotamus, this book, I said, "was wonderful." When someone asked me why I was running for election, I answered that I didn't know. "I was asked," I said, "and like Adam when he saw Eve, naked and munching on an apple, I couldn't say no." "A person ought to try to serve his community once," I said later, but since serving was dangerously addictive a man "ought not let it become a habit." When another questioner asked what actions I would take to promote better dialogue between the teachers and the board, I said I wouldn't do anything. I was not the sort of person to hover about teachers and make them nervous, I explained, adding that if folks wanted to see me they could catch me in the spring. In winter I hibernated in the house, but in spring I could always be found, I said, sitting outside in the middle of my daffodils. At the end of the afternoon, the educational association gave each of the candidates a rose, and I carried it and a piece of coffee cake home to Vicki. The rose was a domestic success, making a much greater impression than the pots of chrysanthemums I usually bring home.

During the week before the election the League of Women Voters sponsored a "Candidates' Night." All the nominees for town office—judge of probate, zoning board of appeals, planning and zoning commission, board of tax review, town council, and school board—were instructed to give two-minute talks outlining positions and detailing qualifications for office. I talked for thirty seconds. After saying my name, I said that I had no particular credentials for office and "that so far as I can tell all the candidates for School Board were good, decent people, all of whom would be much better than I." I then sat down, and ominously, the crowd cheered. "Vicki," I said apprehensively when I got home, "you don't suppose my lax, offhand manner will attract votes." Vicki was too interested in Peter Wimsey and Harriet Vane's doings on "Mystery Theatre" to answer. Whatever the case, my campaign was over, and the next morning when a leader of the Republican party called and asked me to join a "campaign blitz" that Sunday, I declined. Lying, I said that we would be in Stamford celebrating the birthday of Vicki's brother Geoffrey. "He will be thirty-six," I explained, "and has just been made partner in a big law firm in New Jersey." On Sunday, I told Vicki, we would have to keep the shades down, refrain from flushing the toilet, and keep the sound low on the television, lest a blitzing Republican be in the neighborhood and find me out.

I taught the morning of election day. At one o'clock I walked

down Eastwood to the home of the chairman of the Republican
Town Committee. The previous night he called and asked me to
come over and help out. Feeling guilty because I had not cam-
paigned, I agreed. For two hours I did nothing apart from sitting in
the study with another candidate's little girl and watching Walt
Disney cartoons on television, Daffy Duck, Uncle Scrooge, and
Woody Woodpecker. The chairman stayed in the kitchen, eating
fudge cake and checking town lists to see who had not voted. At
three o'clock he handed me five pages of names and telephone
numbers, Republicans who had not voted, and asked me to return
home and call them, urging them to vote. Although I dislike using
the telephone, refusal was impossible. At home Mr. Shinnick was
painting the trim on the house. To get myself into the proper political
mood, I plugged the phone into a jack in the hall. On a ladder
working on the dining room windows, Mr. Shinnick would hear, I
knew, all I said. Leaving the phone down, I pretended to dial a
number, after which I began an imaginary conversation. I started
with the conventional pleasantries, but then I shouted, loudly and
clearly for Mr. Shinnick, "I don't give a damn; just get your big fat
ass down to the fire station and vote." I then picked up the receiver
and slammed it down. "Some people," I yelled to Mr. Shinnick.
"Uh, huh," he answered, and I dialed a second imaginary number.
This conversation, too, began conventionally, but after a moment
or two I said, again loudly, "well when you get off the commode,
try Metamucil, then vote." "That man, Mr. Shinnick, was suffering
from slow movement of the bowels," I said after hanging up;
"shucks, I have that problem myself, but it doesn't keep me from
voting." Later that day before he left, Mr. Shinnick talked to Vicki.
"I am going to vote now," he said; "I'm a Democrat, but I am going
to vote for your husband. He's different."

The imaginary calls raised my spirits, and I went upstairs and
started through my list. I didn't get far. After four rings, I usually
hung up. On the twelfth or so call, Edward distracted me, and I let
the phone ring six or seven times. Just as I was putting my receiver
down, someone grabbed his telephone, then dropped it on the floor.
I waited and then a woman, breathing heavily spoke. "I am calling
for the Republican party," I began, and urged her to vote. "I would
like to," she said, pausing and breathing heavily, "but I am having
a baby. My husband is coming home to take me to the hospital,"
she continued; "the baby's almost here and I don't think I can vote."

"Well, well," I said, "is it going to be a boy or a girl?" A discussion followed ranging from the desirability of knowing the sex of a child before birth to natural childbirth, breast-feeding, and circumcision. Only when the husband rushed in did the conversation end. That was my last phone call. After hanging up, I took the receiver off the hook so that if the chairman called to check on me, he would discover the line was busy and conclude that I was diligently at work. Afterwards I put on old clothes and going into the back yard, began raking leaves.

When the polls closed that evening I was not at town hall, but at Willard's Lumber Yard, attending an adult education course on home repair. The class ended at a quarter past nine, and I left, wanting to think about wallboard, not the school board, gypsum, daffodils, falcons and honey, anything other than politics. Still, I knew that before I returned home I was obligated to drop in at Republican headquarters and congratulate the victors. After that, I would have nothing more to do with politics. "Maybe the presidency," I said to Vicki two hours later when I got home. "What," she said, busy eating popcorn and watching "L.A. Law." "1400 Pennsylvania Avenue. Then I'll put an end to all these parking lots. After today," I said, "who knows what's ahead." "You didn't win," she said. "Of course I did, one thousand and ninety-two votes," I answered; "what did you expect?"

Canned Stuff

Although Quintus Tyler taught Latin, history, and mathematics at the Male and Female Select School in Carthage, religion was his passion, and whenever possible, he steered classes heavenward. Often he described the New Jerusalem, golden domes bright behind walls of jasper, beryl, emerald, topaz, amethyst, and sapphire. "Just beyond the white gates," Quintus began one morning, "grows the Tree of Life. Through its roots runs a crystal stream and in the distance stretch fields flowing with milk and honey." "Mr. Tyler, Mr. Tyler," Billie Dinwidder suddenly interrupted, waving his hand above his head, then asking, "Do cows and bees go to heaven?" "Mercy child," Quintus said, so disconcerted that he forgot his pet description of the fruits on the Tree of Life: figs and olives, pistachios and pomegranates, followed as he always put it, by "Smith County produce, pears, peaches, and persimmons, persimmons sweeter than those growing along Frog Branch near Graveltown, yellow cantaloupes, watermelons bigger and redder than Durrocks, walnuts, blackberries without seeds, bushes hanging high off the ground so rattlesnakes can't crawl under them like they do on Battery Hill, and Osage oranges, no longer bitter and warty but smooth as eggplant and fresh as apricot."

"Gracious Billie, what a question," Quintus started again, "Why do you ask it?" "Well, if cows and bees don't go to heaven," Billie answered, "then all that milk and honey must be canned stuff, and I don't want none of that." Like Billie, I prefer things fresh, brown dirt clinging to roots and dew, even a white worm or two, on leaves. More than canned food, however, I dislike prepared ideas, pasteurized and packaged for bland, thoughtless acceptance. At the end of a long day of little doings, however, one is usually too weary to cook ideas up from scratch. How much easier and simpler to chew through years on ready-mixed thought.

In part children's ignorance is responsible for their appeal to

adults, bored by conventional living. Something a child gets wildly
wrong frequently strikes adults as original, making them dream of
fresher greener days, that time in their own lives before they were
educated into drab conformity and right knowledge. For the adult
Christmas is often a gray season of tension and inconvenience.
Presents must be bought for difficult relatives, and the house cleaned
for sudden visitors: hearty well-wishers and carolers. Cold hours
are spent bent over in the attic hunting for lost decorations, emptying
boxes stuffed with recipes, lead soldiers, and cancelled checks. Back
from the wall, mattresses are pulled on the off chance that the trolls
which always lurk deep within the holly and pine on the Christmas
mantelpiece might, just for the hell of it, have crawled away from
their "spot" by the chimney and dragging themselves up and over
the mattresses, have burrowed into the insulation beyond the floorboards. Making out the list of people who should receive cards
always spoils an evening. "Why send him a card," Vicki said this
year, "He didn't thank you for your last book." "No matter," I
answered addressing the envelope, "He was once my friend, and he
will always be my friend." During Christmas arguments blow up
suddenly like March storms, raining ice over the glittering snow and
freezing soft feeling. For days Vicki and I nagged at each other about
the decoration for the top of the tree: whether the new gold star she
bought for "our" family ought to replace the worn Santa Claus
who hung atop my first Christmas tree, almost fifty years ago in
Tennessee.

In spite of the poinsettias, the pot of blue crocus, Florentines,
Viennese Cresents, fruit cakes, gingerbread men, and wreath tacky
with bulbs, pine cones, apples, and candy canes, this year Christmas
seemed more troubling than joyous, a season, threadbare and conventional, no longer spontaneous and invigorating. At least that was
what I thought until a caroler told me something my little boy
Francis said at kindergarten last year. When the teacher asked the
class if any of them were going away for the holidays, Francis said
he was flying to Tennessee to visit his grandparents. "Well, then,"
the teacher said, "if you look out the window of the plane, what
will you see in the sky?" "Clouds," a girl answered. "Anything
else," the teacher asked. "Yes," said a boy, "birds and angels."
"What are angels," Francis asked. "Angels," a girl spoke up, "are
dead people." "Oh," said Francis, "There are lots of dead Pickerings. Maybe I will see some flying in the clouds." Francis got things

so wrong that he brightened Christmas for me. I laughed, and when the carolers left, I put Vicki's star at the top of the tree, its lowest point hanging down over Santa's cap, glowing golden and making Santa seem young again.

Despite the flying Pickerings spinning through my mind like trapeze artists, light and magically silver high above ordinary life, I want Francis to live down to earth. I want him to get things right, and I press him to study and urge him to please his teachers. For my children I want a safe canned existence. "I can't wait until I get married," Eliza, my two and a half year old, told me last month, "I want lots of babies." "That's wonderful. Nothing would please me more," I said, hugging her and imagining children around her like Christmas tree ornaments: snowflakes frilly and light, toy soldiers, velvet candles, reindeer prancing like Donner and Blitzen, and birds, red with blue eyes, crowns on their heads and long white tails falling through the spruce like water.

Although I know what suits one generation usually does not appeal to another, I hope my children do the things I did. This past summer I took Francis and Edward to the camp in Maine where I spent five summers as a counselor. In two or three years, they will be old enough for camp. Maybe, I thought, they would be put in Eagles, the cabin where I was head counselor. Walking past the shop, the canoe dock, and nature shack, I smelled the tangy air blowing down the lake and through the pines. Suddenly I realized I wanted the boys' experiences to fall through my memory like slow rain, awakening recollection, not of tents and hikes and sunny days by the lake, but of nights, starry and green with the girls I once knew—laughing, loving girls, girls with breasts like peonies and bottoms like buttermilk. On that warm August day, holding my children close, I felt the cold tug of mortality. Through my boys not only would I live again, but I would live always, young and strong, hot hands stretching out for love.

For the next five and a half hours, though, the only thing in my hands was the steering wheel, as I drove down through Maine, New Hampshire, and Massachusetts to Storrs. On that strip of asphalt, pocked by fast food and conformity, all desire for the children to relive my life vanished. Mood changed, and for them I now wanted the unfamiliar and the different. School was about to open, and as I drove the dreary utilitarian highway to get home quickly instead of taking a slower, less conventional route, so I would begin using functional words from which all sustenance had drained away but which pushed a person rapidly through educational matters—words like insightful, professional, crisis, ongoing, committed, creative, certified. Our society, I often think, cares less for substance than for credentials, rewarding the canned rather than the fresh. "Words, words, words," I said to Vicki one evening after returning from a meeting in which a mediocre teacher was praised as "a real professional" and "a team player." "Daddy," Francis then broke in, handing me a sheet of paper on which he had written words, "I have been practicing my spelling." I skimmed the paper. Francis's list began conventionally, and I saw clock, sat, sit, van, open, pumpkin, I, the, and, tan, it, bat, is, at, red. Reading along I dozed, mumbling the right praise until I came to the last word. In big red letters, Francis had written "CRAP." "Look at this, Vicki," I said; "Francis has it right. All this stuff about credentials and professionalism, the whole educational business, is just a bunch of what Francis says it is." I didn't use the word Francis wrote because Vicki claims Francis has learned bad language from me. "Suppose his teacher called you in and told you Francis used terrible words in class," she said last night, "What would you say?" "Well, I would say I was very sorry," I began, "but it couldn't be helped. Francis's mother, I would explain, cussed like a sailor. She's forever calling people turds or saying they are full of camelpiss. Whenever I ask her to control herself, she shakes her backside back and forth like a pendulum and then prances out of the room, whistling 'Yankee Doodle Dandy.' That's what I would say."

I don't want to hurt Francis's chance of doing well in school, and so even though I think such language, I don't use it outside the house. Still I often hanker to say such things, and I suspect that most polite people resemble me and occasionally imagine bashing decorous speech on the head with a bludgeon of heavy, fragrant words. Frustration with conventional life, speech or attitudes, lies behind much of the appeal of folk art. Although my language rarely startles, the contents of my house frequently attract attention. Almost in reaction to the propriety of my public life, I have picked up furnishings in which things are slightly askew. Over the sideboard in the dining room, for example, hangs a two by three and a half foot painting, a view of Naples, looking across the bay toward Vesuvius. Pink smoke from Vesuvius twists upward through an orange sky. Under the mountain stretches the town, box-like white

villas with a few domes scattered between. In the foreground Nea-
politans promenade back and forth: women wearing black sleeveless
vests, white aprons, green skirts with yellow stripes, and white caps
with trains tumbling over their shoulders. The clothes of the men
vary. Strollers wear balloon-like jackets and tapered trousers, blue
or gray with white or green stripes, while officials, probably private
constables, wear top hats and carry pikes. At a glance, the painting
seems an ordinary study, a mechanical view turned out by one of
the hundreds of artists who flocked to Italy in the nineteenth century.
What makes the painting live, however, is not conventional representation, but where, as Francis did with the Flying Pickerings, the
artist got things wrong. In the right foreground is a palm tree, heavy,
not with dates as could be expected around the Mediterranean, but
with coconuts. Hunkered over a coconut at the top of a tree is a
monkey, its arms bushy and its eyes two red dots. Clearly the artist
had never been to Italy; instead he was probably an itinerant painter,
traveling through New England, earning his keep by furnishing
views for well-to-do farmers. The painter worked rapidly, for one
of the women has a long, curling mustache. She must have started
as a man, and when the artist changed her sex, he forgot to shave
her.

The oddities of the painting stimulate curiosity, and the first time
I noticed them, I rubbed my hands across my face, almost as if I
were wiping fog out of my eyes. Real sight almost always drives a
person away from conventional thought with its acceptable standards and predetermined categories. In my pantry hangs a two by
three foot painting of a hog. Again the artist must have been an
itinerant, traveling the countryside painting, I suspect, gardens and
flowers but not animals. Round and creamy, the hog dominates the
canvas, looming like a huge, bloated tick with twigs for legs and a
tree trunk for a snout. With neither teats nor testicles, the animal's
gender is a mystery. Instead of a pig pen, a gazebo stands in the left
foreground. In truth the hog seems loose in a garden, walking on
grass smoother than that found on a bowling green. A church steeple
splinters the horizon while in front of the hog is jimson weed or
mad apple. The plant is well done; its flowers resemble purple and
white trumpets, and the ripe seed pods are prickly and filled with
black kidney-shaped seeds. Most likely the painter traveled about
with his canvasses partly filled in with gazebo and church, and when

asked to paint a prize hog, he simply stuck the animal in, adding jimson weed as a touch of realism.

The idea of a pig in a garden appeals to me in much the same way as does earthy language. Indeed as concerns about my children's futures lock me into appropriate behavior, I have come to value the inappropriate, words lumbering through gardens, splitting box-wood and rooting under magnolias. Not long ago Vicki and I attended a formal dinner. From the food fumes rose aromatic and piquant; the conversation, alas, clung to the table, thick and soggy, until our hostess served Raspberries Romanoff. "You know," she said as we sat looking at the tall thin glasses elegant as debutantes sweeping lightly across a ballroom, "you know Frederick asked me to marry him in the bath tub." For a moment there was silence; then I spoke. "Good Lord," I said, "I hope you didn't drop the soap." For the rest of the evening conversation was as full-bodied and as satisfying as jugged hare, fried hominy, and Brussels sprouts.

Unexpected remarks make dull days memorable. In contrast canned conversation and behavior are deadening. Not long ago, Alma, a cousin of Vicki's, bought a Mercedes. "What do you suppose the car cost?" Vicki asked me when we saw Alma at Thanksgiving. "Ask her," I said. "I can't do that," Vicki said; "it's just not done." "What difference does it make?" I said, adding that if Vicki were really curious she ought to go outside with Alma when she left. Then you should spit on the hood, I suggested, and rub it in as if trying to see your reflection. Next pull open a door and slam it hard as possible. "Do that twice and nod your head appreciatively," I said, "and you'll have Alma's attention. Then turn to her and say, 'I've been thinking about buying two or three of these things myself. What do they cost?' " Occasionally Vicki is more relaxed than I am, and she did not see the need of orchestrating her question with the pounding of doors and spit and polish formality. Later that afternoon when she and Alma were in the kitchen pouring coffee and dropping great dollops of whipped cream on mincemeat pie, she asked the price. Alma paused, coffee pot in hand, looked puzzled for a moment, then replied, "I can't remember." How many women, I later asked Vicki, born and bred in Iowa on a wholesome, domestic diet of turnips and corn, Fords and Chevrolets buy a Mercedes and three months later forget the price? If Alma had been up to a Mercedes, she would have handled the question with style, either greatly inflating the price, giving the impression of rolling in money, or deflating it, making people think she was a shrewd bargainer, a person with whom one never trifled.

Unfairly perhaps, what people remember about a person after his death is usually not the long fabric of a solid life lived responsibly. Instead they recall the odd comment which so startles that it impresses itself upon memory. For forty-eight years Quintus Tyler was the good servant of Carthage, shaping two generations of students. Yet today he is remembered primarily for a chance remark having little to do with his life's work. Toward the end of his days, Quintus became preoccupied with death. His concern, though, was not with trying to shore up failing strength but with finding the right place to be buried. Born on a farm, he wanted to return, he said, to his origins and be buried in a country graveyard, not the big Carthage cemetery. To this end he hired Rodfer Crabill, who drove the ice wagon, to drive him around on Saturdays to all the country graveyards in Smith County. Quintus was thorough; after going through the small towns—Goshen, Reform, Fickling, Suggs, Sammons Grove—he and Rodfer wandered the backlands, searching out old, forgotten graveyards, through Poorhouse Hollow, up Nickajack Branch, down Turkey Creek, around Devil's Elbow to Tater Knob, where Quintus uttered the statement for which he is remembered. On the south slope of Tater Knob was the old Muldrake and Cardamon graveyard. Most of the stones had tumbled over, and those which remained standing had slipped sideways and were worn almost beyond reading. The location, though, was pretty. Turkey Creek wound its way below the graveyard while cedars grew above, and periwinkle ran over the graves, green and waxy. "Well, Mr. Quintus, what do you think," Rodfer said, thinking that he had found an ideal spot. "It's very nice," Quintus began, than paused and pulled his jacket across his chest, "very nice, but unhealthy."

Age frequently transforms the ordinary into the unique. When continued into the present and out of its time, the common chore, accomplished without thought, becomes almost original, something to mull, consciously running it through the mind, searching out spice and succulence. In Nova Scotia each summer, Vicki cooks on a wood stove, a white, enamelled Findley Condor with six burners. Above the burners is a bread box, below an oven, to the right the water tank, and to the left the woodbin. Each morning before the family gets up, I bring the day's supply of wood in from the barn and build a fire in the stove. Starting the fire doesn't take long, but often I linger in the kitchen, sometimes looking down into the water tank, its sides coppery and flaking like bark on a hickory. For a moment I escape the present and see myself in an earlier time, sitting in the barn braiding next year's seed corn into traces or standing beside a gundalow filled with salt hay, waiting for the tide to sweep me up Salmon River. Occasionally I imagine myself back in Mansfield, back, however, when farming, not developing was the way of life. Sometimes I appear striding across a field, stopping to run my hands over pumpkins growing between rows of corn. Other times I dig potatoes: Pennsylvania Blues, English Whites, Biscuits, rough and mealy, and long red La Platas.

Only in summer do I escape the present by imagining the past. Like camelias summer dreams are too fragile for chill autumn. Aside from the kitchen with the wood stove, the house in Nova Scotia is unheated, and by October Vicki and I are back in Connecticut, arguing over how high to set the thermostat. Of course my vision of the past is sentimental. Blight never strikes my potatoes, and the Colorado beetle hasn't hoisted itself out of primordial slime. Still, the stuff of ordinary existence, its potatoes and pumpkins, are not only a means to but also the furnishings of originality. When looked at closely the conventional often appears exotic. Because furnishings of the moment seem all too present, however, one usually accepts them unthinkingly. Even if one does examine them, the examination is, more often than not, cursory and dismissive. In general I avoid the kind of store loosely known as a boutique, seeing them much like mayflies, swarming in dreary undistinguished clouds, their long tails like fashion swinging them about then dragging them down to disappear into some inert black pond.

Only from a distance, though, does a pond seem dead. Under a microscope its very drops burst with life. The same can be true of a boutique. When peered at closely its contents can defy dismissal and race startling before the eye like strange protozoans darting through water. This past November I spoke at Middlebury College in Vermont. After the talk I roamed the town, searching for a present for Vicki. Shopping wears me out, and I went into a small boutique when I saw a sign in its window, saying "Chocolate Croissant— Fresh Daily." Eating alone makes one an observer, providing opportunity to savour food and surroundings. In company a person is more attuned to a companion's mood and conversation than to place or food.

The boutique was named the Blue Toast. In the front window so that one could look at people passing on the sidewalk were two small, round tables. Around each table were three plastic chairs with spoon backs, resembling if they had been metal, the sort of chairs set under large oaks in formal gardens. Both the chairs and the tables were white; in the center of one table was a blue plastic imitation Tiffany dogwood lamp. In the center of my table was a clear glass bud vase filled with bottle gentian and purple Joe-pye weed. Until my croissant and coffee appeared I looked out the window and paid almost no attention to the boutique. The croissant was served in a square, blue, porcelain plate, shaped like a slice of toast, complete with crust and yellow pat of butter slightly off center. Someone had gone to the trouble of designing the plates, and thinking that the Blue Toast might be interesting, I examined the items for sale. A glance revealed that they were the conventional stuff of the small artsy store. Still, because I looked closely, they suddenly seemed intriguing and almost unconventional. Ordering a second cup of coffee, I walked slowly about the store. Among the specialties of the Blue Toast was coffee. Along a side wall shelves were stocked with coffee and its paraphernalia: a crisp, black "Krupps Expresso Mini" capable of brewing four two ounce cups of coffee at a time and on sale for ninety-nine dollars. Next to it for sixty dollars was a "Melior Filter Pot," made out of heavy heat proof glass set in a dark blue enamelled holder. While over twenty varieties of coffee were displayed, there was a "special" on Jamaican Blue Mountain Coffee, a twelve ounce bag of beans selling for $19.95. On a circular rack in a corner were coffee cups, all decorated with cats. Instead of ranging through alley and fairy tale like Sylvester and Puss in Boots, the cats were gallery felines: Miss Ann White's Kitten by George Stubbs, Renoir's Woman with a Cat, and Gwen John's Sketch of a Seated Cat. My favorite was a late nineteenth-century Indian drawing simply called Cat with a Fish. The cat was yellow with a black tail and black spots along its back. Around its neck was a red collar, the color matching the inside of its ears, themselves bigger than tobacco leaves. The cat's eyes were blue while hanging in its mouth was a gray fish with a doleful expression on its face, its fins spiny and flowing like mustaches combed and carefully oiled.

Canned goods were next to the coffee cups, and as I read the labels I traveled back through time to my Europe. The Flower of Pelion Green Olives carried me to Rhodes and the rocky road beyond Lindos, lizards jerking out of my way and olive trees, leaves silver in the quiet air. Corcellet's Apricot Spoon Jam brought to mind Carcasonne and a summer night of spooning and sweet, innocent affection. If I had not noticed a wicker basket full of Swiss vegetable peelers, I might not have escaped sugary nostalgia. One night years ago I walked along the shores of Lake Lucerne with two girls. While conversation shot into the intellectual ether far above earth, my companions' hands toyed below. In the dark while neither could see what the other was doing, I could feel. While one girl ran her fingers along my right side, the other stroked my left, peeling back my shirt. Not knowing how to stop them without causing embarrassment, I fidgeted and prayed their hands would not stray beyond my sides to meet at my middle.

The Blue Toast sold small gifts for children: plastic slinkies, and a selection of Crabtree and Evelyn's Beatrix Potter Soap: Jeremy Fisher, Peter Rabbit, Mrs. Tiggy-Winkle, and Squirrel Nutkin. Ours is the real age of the dinosaur, there now being more dinosaurs of sundry varieties than ever before in history. In the Blue Toast, dinosaur hand puppets were for sale, ten dollars for one or eighteen dollars and fifty cents for two. More expensive at thirty-four dollars was a hand-painted synthetic stone sculpture of a protoceratops hatching. Similarly, a Zuni Indian carving of a frog, made from natural serpentine, cost twenty-eight dollars. All kinds of creatures lurked about the store. Suspended on the wall above the coffee cups was a papier-maché mask of an African antelope, from the horns of which dropped braids of garlic. Throughout the store bunches of dried wildflowers hung from the ceiling: lavender, everlasting, Rodanthe, blue salvia, and pink larkspur. With gentian and Joe-pye weed in the bud vase, someone in the store was interested in flowers. Stacked in a corner of the window were four-ounce cans of Native Wildflower Seeds, the eastern mixture raising visions of meadows brighter than poetry: gayfeather, obedience, bergamot, yarrow, Drummond phlox, sundial lupine, standing cypress, coreopsis, cardinal flower, and wild red columbine.

The goods of the Blue Toast were of a piece but it was a piece which appealed to me when I looked closely. Nothing seemed out of place until I paid, and then on the floor behind the counter I saw three lamps, made, a small sign explained, "by a local artist." The lamps were twenty inches tall and consisted of ceramic alligators, rising straight up over their curled tails, mouths wide and ready for bulbs. The eyes of the alligators were an incandescent orange while their scales were chartreuse in the middle, becoming violet or mauve at the edges. Here was my present for Vicki; we could put it, I thought, in the pantry under the pig. "Who made the alligators?" I asked the boy at the register, envisioning a crusty mountaineer who had never been closer to an alligator than Rutland. "A man who teaches at the college makes them," the boy said; "they are a rip-off; he does lots of things like this for tourists from New York; they think they are buying folk art. These alligators cost ninety dollars," he went on; "nobody but a fool would buy one." "That's right," I said, turning away, "nobody but a fool." "Have a nice day," the boy said as I walked out the door.

Originality may simply result from minding one's own business. Of course it is often difficult deciding just what that business is. The natural tendency is to expand one's business. As nations expand theirs, poking about in faraway places and imagining interests, so individuals expand their concerns. The expansion usually starts in a comparatively harmless way by subscribing to a local newspaper. As sure as "have a nice day" followed me out of the Blue Toast, so behind the local paper trail national magazines, television news, and opinions concerning places one knows almost nothing about and about which one shouldn't think. People soon look so far into the distance that they don't see anything for themselves. As a result they rely on and even become advocates of canned opinion. Rather than pondering the distant, one ought to study the immediate. Examination of one's back yard does not lead to exotic lands or obscure ideas. Instead such observation shows how close at hand are things conventional wisdom says are distant. Moreover it teaches that the immediate is wonderfully interesting and thought-provoking. I don't pull the mouse-ear or hawkweed that grows next to my house in the front yard because I know the plant was once thought medicinal. According to Nicholas Culpeper in the seventeenth century, it alleviated "the difficulty of making water, the biting of venimous serpents, and the stinging of the scorpion." Perhaps even more useful, in a decoction of wild succory and wine, hawkweed hindered, Culpeper wrote, "venery and venerous dreams." I, alas, have reached that age in which venery confines itself to waking not sleeping dreams. Occasionally, though, I am bothered by, as Culpeper put it, "the Incubus," not, however, a monstrous, wild incubus galloping out of cloud, its mane redder than coals and alive with snakes writhing in the wind. No, my nightmare is more terrifying. I dream that I am in high school, walking toward math class with the day's assignment not done. According to Culpeper, I need not be troubled by such a horror. To rid myself of the incubus, Culpeper instructed, all I need do is collect seeds from the sixteen peonies I planted in the yard and chew a couple every morning before breakfast and every evening before bed.

Not only has study of the immediate made the ordinary, even the weedy, satisfying, but it has freed me from the prison of contemporary notion. Slipping the shackles of conventional perception, I range through time, the past often becoming the present. Even my concept of time has changed. No longer do I confine history to self-contained units; instead I see the possibility of a continuous present and the kinship, not simply of all times but all creatures. In my yard instead of closing, death opens; instead of breaking, it binds. The bodies of dead horses, old tale has it, generated wasps while from the carcasses of bulls came bees. Cattle and horses rarely graze along my street, but down the road is the university farm, its fields white with sheep. If horses spawned wasps, then, I think, sheep must have spawned the pillbugs who gather in timid flocks under my woodpile and who roll panic-stricken into balls then scurry from sudden light like sheep startled by noise.

Nothing in the yard exists in isolation. Stories, the roots of which tap deep into history, link plants and animals. The shrews and voles, all the little folk of the earth, owe their existence to the oak, several of which grow in the yard. At the time of the flood, no small animal boarded the ark. Frightened of being crushed under the feet of big-footed animals—the elephants and hippopotamuses—the little creatures decided to take their chances with the rising water. For a while as the rains continued week after week, it looked as if they had erred. But then the Lord heard them in their trouble and caused the acorns to fall from the trees, their caps popping off and bobbing light and free in the water like coracles. Each little animal clambered into a cap and floated out the flood, occasionally seasick but always safe and dry.

Just beyond my front porch stands a weeping cherry. Because of story, the cherry is more than just an ornamental tree bought from Wayside Gardens in Hodges, South Carolina. In spring when its blossoms tumble pink and white, I think of Galilee and Nazareth and man's dream of everlasting spring. When Jesus was eight years old, he played tag with a group of friends. Running away from the boy who was "it," Jesus, old story says, did not watch where he was going and ran into a bush of Palestine nightshade or Apple of Sodom, scratching his arm on the plant's long briars. At first the nightshade's fruit is a berry, yellow, an inch or so in diameter, and pulpy inside. Later, however, as the fruit ripens, the pulp dries, and when pressed, explodes in a cloud of seed, giving rise to the "smoke and ashes" of Josepheus and allusions to the fate of Sodom and Gomorrah. When Jesus scratched himself, however, the life of this particular plant changed. The briars fell away, and the dry center of the berry hardened into a fertile stone around which drops of Jesus' blood formed red flesh. The plant's spiny branches reached upward toward heaven as if begging forgiveness for hurting Jesus, then seeming to receive its boon, they bent down toward the ground, some say to pay homage to the young Christ, others say because the plant wept for the pain it caused. Whatever the truth, however, this nightshade was forever after the weeping cherry.

For much of the greenery in my yard, I know tales, most so long forgotten they make my conventional planting seem original. Although usually chosen from catalogues, Spring Hill, Wayside Gardens, White Flower Farm, my plants don't seem products of commercial nurseries. Instead they are seedlings of history and seem to arrive not from Peoria or Litchfield but from places both closer and farther. Of course, I don't say this sort of thing to the children when we look at flower catalogues together. Talk about weeping cherries and salvation, history and the presence of the past might make them nutty, although I don't think that's liable to happen, at least not in the case of Edward who is four and a half. We spent last New Year's with Vicki's parents in New Jersey. Above the fireplace in our bedroom is a large oil painting. Beside a bathing pool frolic a herd of chunky nymphs, their withers broad and deep and their rumps more like clabber than buttermilk. Often I found

Edward staring at the painting. "Daddy," he explained one afternoon, "I just love to look at naked women. But don't tell Mommy." Of course I did the right, conventional thing. I promised him I would not tell his mother, and as soon as he was outside in the yard, safely beyond hearing, I told her. "It's your fault," she said pushing my hands away, "all your fault. He's following in your footsteps." "Yes, thank God," I answered; "now if I can only save enough money to send him to Camp Timanous, he'll be set for life."

Winter Writing

Winter is hard on marriage. Monday night I slept on the living room sofa. I wore yellow pajamas with little bears on them, a blue ski sweater, and a gray dickey. I wrapped myself in two down parkas from L. L. Bean, sticking my legs down the arms of the larger parka. For a pillow I used a cushion, on top of which was a bald eagle done in needlepoint by Vicki's father. Even so I was damn uncomfortable and halfway through the night wished like hell I was in the bed upstairs. I stayed downstairs, however, and by morning the first winter temperature storm had blown itself out, and at breakfast both Vicki and I felt foolish.

I left the bedroom because Vicki unplugged my humidifier, saying "I am tired of you and your sinuses." Only during winter do Vicki and I quarrel, and temperature is usually the cause. Having lived for almost half a century, I am not certain about much in life. Of one thing, though, I am positive: in bed women's feet are always cold. On summer nights Vicki opens the windows, wears socks, and her feet stay almost warm. In winter she shuts the windows, turns up the heat, and piles blankets to the ceiling. My sinuses strangle then rise in revolt, and I roll about, coughing and snorting and pitching blankets on the floor. In hopes of pacifying my sinuses I bought a humidifier this winter. For the sinuses it did wonders; unfortunately Vicki blamed it for the chill in the room and almost every night the humidifier was the subject of bedtime discussion. Despite Vicki's objections, though, the humidifier has helped our marriage. When the inevitable January temperature storm arose, it was milder than in the past and blew me no farther than the living room. Last year I was so angry that I stalked out of the house at midnight. Almost as soon as I left the driveway, however, my anger weakened considerably. A heavy, wet snow was falling; the roads were slippery, and I knew I ought to turn tail and head back to the garage. How could I reappear after six and a half minutes, I thought, after looking at my watch. If I returned after such a dramatic exit, I would look like a complete jackass, so I drove to Vernon, slipping and sliding down back roads until I found an open truck stop. Filled with loud teen-agers who ought to have been home and with lonely, disreputable-looking men, the truck stop was not my kind of place. Still, I ordered breakfast: toast, sausage, two eggs sunny-side up, and coffee. For forty-eight minutes at the cost of four dollars and sixty-two cents plus seventy-five cents tip, I pushed toast about, sopped up egg, and drank coffee. When I returned home, two hours and fifty-four minutes after I left, I made a lot of noise. The next morning Vicki said she did not hear me come in, but I didn't believe her.

Of course it could be that our domestic temperature storms are caused more by my inner thermostat than by that in the hall. Because husbands and wives are confined inside and are forever bumping into each other winter is the season of lust and tension. In the summer the eye roams, in the process carrying thought beyond familiar wayside and over far hills into distant, puzzling valleys. In winter the eye stays home, and like coals glowing in the fireplace, thoughts burn. Unfortunately, as adults are confined, so are children, and by the time children are asleep, parents are exhausted and the coals of romance have cooled, leaving behind dusty frustration, piled and waiting to be blown about by air from a humidifier.

Whatever the case, though, winter affects more than domesticity. It influences my writing. I want to write about nature, but I don't know how to look at winter. As my house is tightly shut, so my vision seems confined. To be sure I recognize a few sights, the tracks of mice, squirrels, and rabbits, though, in truth I usually confuse these last two. When the snow is wet enough, the children and I make snow families, using weeds for faces: goldenrod and astilbe for hair, milkweed pods for ears, stalks of mullein for noses, the centers of coneflowers for eyes, lines of burdock for mouths, and bittersweet for beauty spots. In winter the tunnels of bark beetles are more prominent on dead trees than in summer, and I wander the woods, searching for them, seeing them as butterflies, snakes, even snowflakes, some appearing as stars, others as ornate dinner plates. Once in the side yard, I discovered the place where an owl caught a mouse. For five or six feet markings extended across the snow. At one end the owl's tail feathers dragged the ground; at the other the owl lifted off the ground, wings extended and feathers beating through the snow like long fingers.

I recognized what happened in the snow because recently I had seen a program on public television which showed an owl capturing a mouse in winter. After finding the tracks, I urged my family to come outside and look. Saying the snow was too deep and the day too cold, they refused. In summer a cabbage butterfly brings them out fluttering and observant. Winter, though, is not the time for communal activities outside, and the person intent upon seeing must endure chilly loneliness. After discovering the tracks, I began reading and learned many things. Deciduous trees, for example, absorb radiation from the sun, raising the temperature of bark thus causing the trees to emit energy. In turn this energy is absorbed by the surrounding snow, melting the snow immediately around the trees, often down to the ground. The facts I learned, however, were not easily shared with small children or Vicki, always busy with scarves and snowpants, boots and mittens, so eventually I put books aside and began taking walks. On the walks I thought I would see things I could tell the children about. I walked through the university farm, watching the Morgan horses on Horsebarn Hill, their coats thick and bristly and their breath like clouds. In the sheep barn I looked at the newborn lambs, shivering under hot, red lights. On snowy nights I walked up and down the street, sucking in the cold air and waiting for Mr. Hall to turn up Eastwood, the plough grinding over the pavement and lights blowing in ribbons through the falling snow. On Thursday nights I walked through the woods to school board meetings at town hall. In my pocket was a bag of figs, and on the way home, I always stopped and sitting on a rockpile, ate figs and looked through the trees toward the nearby dormitories. Light from the windows turned the snow pale yellow, and at times I imagined myself part of an impressionistic painting, shadows of trees slipping through the yellow then gliding off toward a dark, blue distance.

More and more I saw winter, not as itself, but as something else, a mood or a painting. As afternoons grew longer and spring approached, I began looking beyond the immediate to the future, and winter slipped out of sight. Garden catalogues arrived in the mail, and I ordered a golden chaintree. I called Mr. Hall and asked him to haul away my woodpile in the spring and then dump two loads of topsoil in its place. In the dell on the other side of the yard there were already too many flowers. With the woodpile gone, though, I could plant a new garden: in the sun hollyhock and aster, behind in the shadows gayfeather and foxglove and deep in the shade sweet violet and lily of the valley. In thinking about gardening, I forced the seasons, much like plants in the house had been forced: the paperwhites with a heavy fragrance too rich for winter, the blue crocus, dark and Victorian, and the Amaryllis, its blossoms pink and green, ornate horns suited more for the fat hands of some pasty-bottomed putto than for the clean white mystery of a New England February.

Eventually I stopped walking the woods. Instead I stayed inside and read magazines about antiques, spending days furnishing the rooms of my imagination. Along one wall of the living room I set a mahogany Canterbury, filling it with magazines not china. Into the study I moved a Boston bonnet-top secretary with claw feet; on the desk top I set a wooden tea caddy shaped like a pear and then three volumes of *The Works of the Rev. Sydney Smith*, bound in deep orange leather. In the hall by the front door I put a Connecticut River Valley lowboy, carved from cherry. On top I set knickknacks, toward the back an eighteenth-century Worcester butter tub, seven inches long and decorated with exotic fowl, reddish crosses between a tom turkey and a bird of paradise. To one side standing in a silver Victorian frame with scallop-shell decorations at the corners was a small, two by three inch sketch of a hedgehog, drawn by a follower of Thomas Bewick. Toward the left front of the lowboy I put an enamelled box. Actually I often changed the box, sometimes displaying a garish turn of the century Russian box, other times one of my eighteenth-century Bilston boxes, my favorites being a round box with a robin in the center, around which was written "Remember him who Gives this Trifle" and then a square box with a heart in the middle and verse around the edges reading, "May Charms like Thine / Be still my Lot, / And Love like mine / Be ne'er forgot."

Because days were still short and the house dark, I brightened the walls with paintings, usually impressionistic scenes of winter. Over the sideboard in the dining room I hung a Childe Hassam. Although the particular painting changed, its colors were always light blue, tinged with yellow, vaguely resembling Hassam's *Late Afternoon, New York: Winter, 1900*. In the study I hung an Ernest

Lawson, something with more yellow and green than the Hassam, usually a painting resembling *Spring Thaw*, in which winter slipped away like ice down a spotted, warming stream. As I moved from room to room, I was, I suppose, changing the seasons. Over the mantelpiece in the living room, I hung a specific painting, George Inness's *Sunshine and Clouds* or, as it was once known, *Scenes on the Pennsylvania Railroad*. Flowing with yellows and whites, blues and greens, the painting seemed almost spring itself, a garden of color, melting snow from the mind.

Not capable of recording winter, I played, and instead of using language to capture actuality, I used words to define and even make reality. Sound reflected sense, no matter the distortion of truth, and after decorating my imagination, I associated the language of antiques with the seasons. Light on the tongue, dappled, perhaps even flakey like fine pie crust, Hepplewhite sounded like early spring, while late spring and Chippendale began with the short, nervous cry of a small animal peering out of a burrow, then fell suddenly away into hardening strength, finally ending by running smooth like water through a green wood. Early summer was Campeachy, soft and golden; late summer, Georgian, firm and red. Fall broke into three seasons, Satinwood, followed by Pembroke then Sheraton. Finally winter arrived, the first deep snow falling during Windsor then hardening into ice and the dark, heavy days of Mahogany.

Because writing did not come naturally, odd things rooted in my mind and I forced them, hoping they would blossom into the stuff of bright prose. I have a bad back and every morning I swim three-quarters of a mile in the university pool. Swimming bores me, but what strikes me as infinitely more tedious is the undressing then dressing, before and after swimming. One day I decided to see how much time I spent wrestling with my trousers and shirts in the locker room. An essay, I thought, could be written about putting on and taking off clothes. The essay would not, of course, be restricted to the locker room but would also include doings domestic. In the spring of life, I decided, I took my clothes off more often, alas, than I did now. Spurred on by things lusciously Campeachy, I undressed quickly. Nowadays I undress slowly, and although I undress less frequently than I did in those Hepplewhite days of prancing about in the Spode, I probably spend as much time at it as I ever did. "It all," a friend of mine said when I discussed the matter with him, "it all comes out in the wash." In any case on February 3, I timed myself in the locker room. Undressing took four minutes and nine seconds; dressing after the swim took six minutes and eleven seconds. The day was moderately cold, and I wore boxer shorts; Sears Perma-Prest trousers, admittedly tight around a layer of winter fat; tube athletic socks with two red stripes at the tops; a blue shirt with a button-down collar which I didn't button; L. L. Bean Maine Hunting Shoes, laced only to the third eye; a baggy pullover sweater; a long scarf, claret and pink, the colors of my college at Cambridge; a light-weight zip-up parka; and a loose red acrylic stocking cap made in the Philippines and bought by Vicki at a tag sale for fifteen cents.

Although I left the gymnasium certain I had made a good start on an essay, I thought little more about the subject. My inability to see winter seemed to have undermined all concentration, and I began then stopped a bundle of essays. Instead of digging under the snow and discovering the ways of spiders and the runs of small animals, I raised plans for writing on the surface, plans which tumbled away at the first thaw or change of mood. When a friend described a beauty parlor at Brighton Beach called Hello Gorgeous, I thought about building a story about it. I am, however, an old-fashioned, all-male, barber shop sort of guy and know even less about how women talk to each other, particularly women in beauty parlors in Brooklyn, than I do about winter. Crammed full of lowboys and highboys, my imagination simply did not have room for curlers, permanents, hair dryers, and manicures, and after a little thought I washed the beauty parlor out of mind.

Inability to settle on a subject frustrated me, and unable to create, I became critical. When I read in *Education Week* that the American Association of School Administrators was holding its convention in Las Vegas, I wrote a letter to the editor. "In scheduling their convention for Las Vegas," I began, "the American Association of School Administrators appears to have no more sense of decorum than a cucumber on an empty stomach." Within *Education Week* was a supplement called "Conventions in Print." Containing a program and information about Las Vegas, the supplement was to be used, *Education Week* explained, "as a planning resource for education." On pages fifteen and sixteen, I pointed out, the planning resource contained "Gambling Tips." "Some Resource," I wrote, getting into the sharp spirit of criticism, "local school boards ought to be advised whether they should bolt their cash boxes before or after the convention. Since," I continued, " 'Conventions in Print' is determined to be helpful and responsible, why does it not include instructions 'on the proper use of a condom,' written for those administrators who arrive in Las Vegas intent on being educationally active."

As could be expected *Education Week* did not print my letter. I was not disappointed, however, because I was busy reading my mail. In winter letters are more important than at any other time of the year. Unable to write I read what people wrote me. Letters which I skimmed four months earlier I read carefully. Having lost confidence in my writing ability, I sought reassurance from letters. When the Dickens Society of Knoxville, Tennessee, recommended one of my books to its members, I was pleased. "Listen to this," I said to Vicki when a newspaper man wrote, saying "you may be accustomed to getting this kind of mail, but I am not accustomed to writing it. I did write one before, about twelve years ago, to John McPhee. I had to: his writing was so compelling. And I have to now." I sought praise like a bee pollen, no matter that the prose from which it came was a thistle. "Your simplistic style," a woman wrote, "and dry humor encompass the heart of anyone who reads your essays."

Odd letters appealed to me almost as much as flattering ones. Much as a broken limb lying atop a smooth expanse of snow draws the eye, so oddity, bent and stumpy and always out of season, attracted me. Having read a review of a book of mine about growing up in the south, a man wrote, sending a list of questions for which he wanted answers. "Would like very much," he asked, "to have the name of the person given the contract to widen the Wilderness trail—for wagons; and/or the age (year, date of birth) of Frederick I's son that went on to the Crusades, I believe with the same name as father (i.e., Frederick). But can not pay anything for help." Obscure knowledge interested my correspondent. "For a long time," he explained, he had "the mistaken notion" that Khwarizm and Khorasan might have been the same place, adding that it came as a surprise to him to learn that from a Chinese trader's point of view Khwarizm and Ferghana might have been the same. A school teacher in West Tennessee wrote asking me to donate to her class's reading auction. For reading books students received points which they used to bid on donated items. In the last auction, the teacher recounted, the most highly sought after items were a Starman television script, "a Snowbird sweatshirt from Nashville news anchor Jeff McAtee, an autographed photograph of Bruce Willis and Cybill Shepherd, a tie from U.S. Representative Ed Jones, and a book *The White House* from President Reagan."

Despite the opportunity of being on the block with such a high falutin crowd, I didn't contribute to the auction. In truth the letters I most enjoyed were those which drew pictures of the authors or their worlds, things I seemed unable to accomplish during winter. From Iowa a woman wrote and after remarking on one of my essays described a horse sale. The horses were all draft horses—Percherons, Belgians, and Clydesdales. Of a good workhorse, the woman recounted, the auctioneer remarked, "hauled a lot of manure with that one, and still will." "She's got what you call a little Iowa brand," the auctioneer said of a mare with an injury, "got into a little wire there in the stem—but it's just in the stem, not lame." After noting that she had a good time at the sale but didn't buy a horse, the woman ended, saying "I am to the point now that I can eat lemon meringue pie regardless how strong the smell of manure. Horses are not bad. It's a real test of character if it's pig shit."

In response to a piece I wrote about Cambridge, I received a different kind but just as interesting a letter. Both the writer and I attended St. Catharine's and had Tom Henn for tutorials, the great difference being that my correspondent entered Cambridge in 1928 and I entered in 1963. Among his "many stray recollections of Tom," the man wrote, was "a supervision where I had to read out my inevitable essay on 'Keats the sensualist.' Being 19, I was very proud of my Carlyle–Thomas Browne prose and I had worked up to an immortal last paragraph. I stopped reading and there was a two-minute silence. Dixit Tom, 'that ending is either as far as thought can reach, (pause)—or it's plain bloody nonsense. I incline to the second opinion.' I abandoned purple prose for ever and my volumes of Pater remained unread for nearly 60 years."

Oddly, the inability to write about winter has never undermined my confidence. If anything it frees me to swell ambitious. Unable to roam across the yard and observe, I range through the atlas, dream, and then apply for jobs. Every winter I apply for big academic posts, always, I am afraid, disconcerting Vicki and the children. Two years ago after I made the short list for a college presidency, I asked Francis, then four years old, if he didn't want his daddy "to be a big man, the head of a college." When Francis answered no, I asked him why not. "I want you," he said simply, "to be my daddy." That, clearly, was that, and I withdrew my candidacy. Now that I think about it, though, the season might have had as much to do with my withdrawal as Francis's answer. Winter was on the wing; a robin or two had appeared, and I was preening myself to write. This year I have applied for a couple of posts. Just today I mailed an application. March is starting to hop about in the blood, though, and my heart wasn't in the application. At the end of the letter I added a postscript, one which I hoped would prevent my being taken seriously. Recently, I wrote, I read a review of my latest book of essays in which the reviewer stated that my essays "reveal a restless, cantankerous personality in love with ordinary family life." "That's probably accurate," I added, "except I'm not cantankerous. What kind of SOB would say that!"

Not long ago I bought the *Children's Bible*, and every Sunday I read thirty or thirty-five pages to the children. After I finished the accounts of the Creation, the Garden of Eden, and Noah and the Ark, Edward, who is almost five, asked "How did God get that magic?" Edward then paused. Happily, though, before I stumbled through a rocky response, he answered his own question. "The only person who knows that is No One," he said adding "right, Dad" when I looked puzzled. Like Tom Henn after hearing his student's final paragraph on Keats, I can't decide whether Edward's response was foolish or profound. Fathers, though, are usually more generous to little listeners than teachers are to students, and I incline toward thinking Edward profound. Whatever the case, No One is a good, reassuring character to have in mind. If I can't describe winter, then, to draw upon Edward, No One can.

Selecting a Past

My right arm has become weak, and recently I have spent many hours in Boston undergoing tests at Massachusetts General Hospital. As I sat in waiting rooms, the names of diseases spinning through my mind, I realized that I had little control over my future. What choices I might once have made would now be made for me by luck or illness. The realization depressed me, but not for long. If I couldn't control the future I decided, riding the bus back to Willimantic one afternoon, so be it; I would select a past. Besides I was middle-aged, and behind me lay almost fifty years of experiences—experiences like a mountain of marble, not Carrara or Pentelic, but marble seamed by veins of lively imperfection, green, pink, and yellow. From Providence to Danielson I imagined myself a master stonecutter, and the landscape which rolled past my window was not that of Rhode Island and eastern Connecticut but that of Attica and the Apuan Alps.

No man, alas, with a bad arm could ever be a stonecutter, and after arriving in Willimantic and eating a pizza, I stopped considering my past as raw material for a St. Peter's or a Parthenon. I did not, however, stop thinking about selecting a past. In fact I pushed ahead. The sense of a past, I decided, banished insignificance from life, creating the fiction that one was more than just a minute part of long biological and geological processes. A past provided identity and I began to shape mine, not in Greece or Italy but at home in Storrs. The past one left behind, I soon realized, was more often than not a matter of chance. In the attic, I knew, were boxes stuffed with old clothes, toys, papers, the detritus first of childhood and then more recently, of happy married life. Initially I considered pruning the attic, stripping away branches I did not want to be part of my past and then grafting something green into a trunk to be discovered in the future. Unfortunately I got no closer to the attic than my study. Opening boxes in the attic, I suspected, would upset

Vicki and so I kept putting off the chore. Then on the day I finally decided to climb to the attic, the children asked me to help them explore the woods behind Horsebarn Hill.

In walking through the lowlands toward the Fenton River, I recognized flowers: purple trillium, marsh marigold, bluets, wood anemone, Solomon's seal. Later that night I realized that for me the landscape was a flower garden. Because I have never been able to associate names with leaves and barks, I hardly noticed the trees, the most conspicuous part of the woods. Another person would have recognized trees and not flowers. Going to the attic, I suddenly concluded, would probably resemble the day's walk. I would see a few flowers, but no trees, and what pruning I did would be arbitrary. Far better was it to concentrate my energies on things more limited and less strenuous.

Because I knew biographers usually described what their subjects read, I decided people curious about my past would examine my reading. Moreover if the attic were beyond my energies and control, bookshelves in the study were not. By the quick and simple process of shifting books, I could influence how people would read my reading, thereby sketching in part of a past. Most books in my study were ordinary: paperbacks of the happier Victorian novelists Dickens and Trollope and then leatherbound sets of Charles Lever and Bulwer-Lytton, gifts from friends. Two shelves contained studies of natural history, mostly beginner's guides to birds, flowers, insects, and rocks. Books by essayists filled other shelves: Montaigne, then from the nineteenth century Charles Lamb and William Hazlitt, and from the twentieth century E. B. White, A. J. Liebling, John McPhee, Joseph Epstein, and Edwin Way Teale. Books so conventional would, I decided, have little effect upon a past, and I couldn't imagine drawing conclusions from them. Perhaps someone bent upon interpretation might note the essayists and then searching for frustration speculate about the difference in quality between my reading and writing. But that I decided was pushing conclusion too far. What would influence a past would not be the ordinary books I owned, stretching long in lines around the room, but the few oddities, scattered and dusty at the ends of shelves. So that a past would be convenient I gathered the oddities together.

Given to me as a birthday present twenty years ago by a lively spinster who knew I was interested in eighteenth-century things, the first book I picked up was ONANIA; or the Heinous Sin of Self-

Pollution, And all its frightful Consequences in both SEXES, Considered. With Spiritual and Physical Advise for those, who have already injur'd themselves by this Abominable Practice. Printed by John Phillips in Boston in 1724 and "Sold at his Shop on the South side of the Town House," *Onania* had enjoyed great popularity in Britain, over fifteen thousand copies of earlier editions, Phillips claimed, having been sold. "SELF-POLLUTION" is, the author explained, "that unnatural Practice, by which Persons of either Sex, may defile their own Bodies, without the Assistance of others, whilst yielding to filthy Imaginations, they endeavour to imitate and procure to themselves that Sensation, which God has order'd to attend the carnal Commerce of the two Sexes, for the Continuance of our Species."

Although he warned "all Masters of Schools" to keep a "strict Eye" over their boys to prevent "the Commission of this vile Sin," the author emphasized that self-pollution was not limited to adolescent males but ran the gauntlet of sexes and ages. The governess of "one of the most eminent Boarding-Schools," he recounted, had surprised one of her scholars "in the very Fact; and who upon Examination confess'd, that they very frequently practis'd it, cum Digitis & Aliis Instrumentis." Although noting that both married and single men practiced "this abominable Sin," the author was particularly hard on females, not simply, as he put it, widows and "Married Women that are Lascivious" but upon pious, proper ladies. Unlike other kinds of "uncleanness" which needed a "Witness," self-pollution could be undertaken alone. "Some lustful Women of Sense," he elaborated, made outward shows of virtue and morality. "In the midst of strong Desires," not only did they reject "disadvantageous Matches" but they also refused to betray "a Weakness to any Man living," preferring instead to abandon themselves to self-pollution.

Onania, the author argued, was the unacknowledged source of many common ailments. In men it brought on Phymesis, Paraphymosis, Stranguries, Priapisms, "Gonorrhaa's," fainting fits, epilepsies, and consumptions. For men who desired heirs it had sad consequences, causing both the "Spermatick Parts" to "become barren as land becomes poor by being over-till'd" and "a Weakness in the *Penis,* and loss of Erection, as if they had been Castrated." Not only did it affect women's complexions, making some pale and others "swarthy and hagged," but it caused "Hysterick Fits," consumption, and barrenness, or if not actual barrenness "a total ineptitute to the Act of Generation it self." Even if people who had recklessly indulged in self-pollution managed to conceive children, such children would not live long, being puny and lingering, "more brought up by Physick than Kitchen diet."

Even more terrible than the physical were the moral consequences of self-pollution. While one could lead only to the grave the other led to Hell, and the author urged readers to discipline the imagination and resist temptation, writing "when Man grows stout and courageous, Satan grows cowardly." Once the barrier that fenced chastity was broken, however, "the enemy to Purity and Holiness makes daily Inroads, and ranges through every Passage of the Conquered Soul."

Besides being a hearty moral tract, *Onania* was a self-help manual, and the author suggested many ways to keep self-pollution beyond arm's length. The best antidote was early marriage, but if marriage were not practical, he urged sufferers to eat sparingly. Particularly to be avoided were beans, peas, and artichokes because, the author wrote, they make "those Parts more turgid." Also banished from the diet was salt meat. "A learned Physician of our own observes," the author explained, "that in Ships which are laden with Salt from Rochel, the Mice breed thrice as fast as in those Ships laden with Merchandize." In bed, men, in particular, were urged to sleep on their sides, not backs "for that heats the Reins, and causes irritations to Lust." Additionally, the author noted, neither men nor women should "handle those Parts at any Time, but when Necessity of Nature requires, for handling of them puffs up, irritates and raises Fleshly Inclinations." If after following all the suggestions regarding diet and domestic habit, a man committed "involuntary POLLUTIONS" in his sleep, the author proposed a fail-safe remedy. "I would advise you," he declared, "whenever you are apprehensive, or in fear of them, to do what Forestus, a noted Physician in his time, lays down, as certain when every thing else has fail'd, which is, to tie a string, when you go to Bed, about your Neck, and the other End of it about the Neck of your *Penis,* which when an Erection happens, will timely awaken you, and put an effectual end to the seminal Emission."

I realized *Onania* could almost single-handedly distort my library and me. In truth I am not the kind of person who for medicinal reasons must sleep on his side and avoid peas and artichokes. My library is a cool place. I think people ought to behave themselves, and I own almost no books in which people misbehave. Long ago I jerked Emma Bovary off the shelf because I didn't want her around radiating heat. The only book I keep which contains warmish parts was written by a friend, and since he visits occasionally I cannot throw it away. I have, however, buried it deep on a damp lower shelf and only dig it up and plant it in the sunshine just before his arrival. One scene in the book does, as the author of *Onania* put it, raise fleshly inclinations, and when my friend's mother-in-law read it, she immediately dropped the book to the floor and kicked it out of the living room, down the hall and out the front door into the snow, after which she called her daughter, shouting into the telephone, "you have married a pervert. Come home."

Lest *Onania* make me seem a pervert or literary peeper, I surrounded it by other, more respectable oddities, cooling it down with leatherbound copies of the *Arminian Magazine,* on the left by the volume for 1787 and on the right by the volume for 1788. I bought the volumes fourteen years ago in London because they contained the autobiography of one of my favorite characters, Silas Told, a friend of John Wesley and an eighteenth-century good Samaritan. Born at the limekilns near the hot wells in Bristol in 1711, Told was the son of a wealthy physician, who, unfortunately being a "great schemer" lost thirty-three hundred pounds in building a wet-dock at Bristol after which he was forced to work as ship's doctor on "a Guinea-man" where in the course of his first voyage he died. At fourteen Told himself was bound apprentice on a ship sailing from Bristol to Jamaica. On the trip the ship was becalmed, and the sailors ran out of food and were forced to drink water alive with maggots. In nine years at sea Told endured worse than maggots, however, suffering through beatings, shipwrecks, pestilential fevers, and service on a slaver captained by a sadist. At twenty-three he escaped the sea becoming first a bricklayer, then a servant, and finally in Wesley's service, head of a charity school. Ultimately, after a second marriage which brought modest means, he devoted his last years to visiting "malefactors in the several prisons in and about" London. He nursed the sick, prayed with debtors in Newgate, and converted the condemned, often riding with them in the cart to the place of execution. Told's charity did not stop with deathbed conversions, and he aided the families of those executed, finding jobs for widows and children. Unlike many spiritual autobiographies, Told's is filled with both the grit of hard living, nights during which forty-one out of eighty slaves suffocated in a "loathsome den," and the grainy surface of cruel justice which condemned one Anderson for stealing cloth worth sixpence to feed his starving family. After talking to Told, however, Anderson embraced the gallows declaring, "This is the happiest day I ever saw in my life! Oh! who could express the joy and peace I now feel! If I could have all the world, I would not wish to live another day!"

The quiet assurance which enabled Told to endure the scorn of turnkeys and persist in helping his fellows did not come easily. Even after meeting Wesley and taking up schoolmastering, he doubted himself. Despondent, he went for a walk early one morning after preaching. Near Ratcliff Row he met a cow. So troubled was he that he wished to be transformed beyond thought into the cow. A little later he noticed a disreputable man some yards away and thought "that man would afford me the greatest happiness I ever before experienced, if he would put an end to so wretched a life." In part because he was depressed Told wandered into a lonesome corner of a field. Once there, a hand struck him on the head whereupon he cried, "Praise God! Praise God!" Looking up he saw the "air and sky, full of the glory of God," after which all became black for a moment. Before opening his eyes again, Told beseeched God to let him know if the event signalled the remission of his sins. Feeling "an unspeakable peace," he dared to look up. Before him the heavens opened into a seam, tapering "away to a point at each end." The center of "this sacred avenue," Told recounted, was "about twelve feet wide, wherein I thought I saw the Lord Jesus, holding up both his hands, from the palms of which the blood seemed to stream down. On this, the flood of tears gushing from my eyes, trickled down my cheeks and I said, 'Lord, it is enough!' From that hour I have not once doubted of my being freely justified."

Our age seems to focus on matters sexual almost to the exclusion of all else, and so I drew a line down the margin beside this part of Told's autobiography and in bold letters wrote "N.B." Still, I wasn't sure it was enough to mortify *Onania's* fleshiness. Consequently, beside the first volume of the *Arminian Magazine* I put *Lois Dudley Finds Peace*, a tract published in 1923 by the Bible Institute Colportage Association of Chicago and telling the story of an orphan girl's accepting the Lord as her "personal Saviour." Beside the other volume of the *Arminian Magazine* I put T. A. Faulkner's *From the Ball Room to Hell and the Lure of the Dance* (1922). "Tell me, you dancing Christians," Faulkner asked, "how many lost souls have you led to Jesus?" According to Faulkner dance polluted more souls than any other activity, and in chapters typically entitled "Christ at the Ball" and "The Dance and White Slaves," he cited statistical and anecdotal proof. "*Eighty per cent* of the thousands of the denizens of the underworld," he noted, "have been members of some church where dancing was permitted." From California a Catholic priest wrote, saying he had interviewed two hundred girls who were "inmates of the Brothel." "Dancing schools and ball-rooms" directly caused the downfall of one hundred and sixty-three of the girls, the priest reported, while "Drink given by parents" ruined twenty, "Willful choice, caused by low wages," ten, and "Abuse and poverty," seven.

Today the lure of interpretation is greater than that of the dance, and I realized someone could conceivably bind the carnal to the spiritual on my bookshelf and thereby reach a conclusion about my past, a conclusion which, like Lois Dudley's peace, would pass "all understanding." In selecting a past, however, one cannot forestall perverse interpretation. After having made "the Outward Shew of Virtue," all I could hope for was that whoever examined my library would do so with an eye less rancorous than that with which the author of *Onania* oogled "lustful Women of Sense." In any case the library constituted but a chapter of my past, and after finishing it I picked up the bigger signature of memory, not initially, though, my own but family memories. On Mother's side of the family, the Ratcliffe side, many people do not marry. Single and singular, they only occasionally approve of each other and almost never approve of outsiders. Just recently, I learned that my great aunt Betty almost married. When youngish, she fell in love with a man from Pennsylvania, and fleeing family and spinsterhood left Richmond on the evening train, rolling toward Philadelphia and matrimony. She got as far, I was told, as King William or Caroline County, where the train was shunted onto a siding and she was pulled off by relatives armed with virtue and pistols. For his part her lover was encouraged to continue to Philadelphia and advised not to return to Richmond. Finding Virginia courtships a little too passionate, he remained in Philadelphia and married there, not before, however, suing the

Ratcliffes for alienation of affection, a suit settled out of court by my grandfather, who, despite not being involved in the railway incident, was the only member of the family at that time with means.

Although the story of Aunt Betty's elopement appeals to me, I wish I knew if it were true. Even if it were, I'm not sure I should include it in my past. One of the problems with selecting a past is that the past is always vital. Not only can it shape perceptions of the moment but it can influence futures. Grandfather Ratcliffe died when I was small, and after his death, Mother often described the things he and I did together. I was, she said, a source of amusement to him. Once while he lay napping in the back parlor, I burst into the room, having tried unsuccessfully to build a toy box. "Big Ga," I shouted, waking him and holding out my hands, "get the axe and chop these arms off. They are no damn good!" Even thinking that such an anecdote could influence a child's development seems perverse, yet I have never been good with my hands. The workings of a hammer, a nail, and a wall are just as mysterious to me as those of a microprocessor. And once or twice over the years, I have thought that if Mother had not told me the story about my hands and the axe I might have tried harder to learn about tools.

What bothers me in the account of Aunt Betty's elopement is the violence. Although family tale has it that my great-great-grandfather Pickering gave up schoolmastering to fight in the Mexican War, eventually becoming a lieutenant colonel, rarely have either the Pickerings or the Ratcliffes been violent. In general we labor to avoid being drawn into conflicts. During the Viet-Nam War when I stopped teaching in order to attend graduate school, my draft classification changed to 1-A. If drafted, I don't know what I would have done. Leaving the country was not something my friends did, and I suspect I would have enlisted in the navy. In any case I didn't face the dilemma. Various universities had awarded me scholarships, including a couple of National Defense Act Fellowships. Gathering the fellowship offers together, I made an appointment to see the clerk of the local draft board. For the appointment I put on my best suit and smoothest manner. After reading through my materials, the clerk turned to me and said, "Mr. Pickering, I cannot tell you what an honor it is to have you registered here."

In thinking about it now, I suppose I should not include this account in my past. It makes me appear smug and cunning when the truth of the matter was that at twenty-five the possibility of my being called up, manners and fellowships aside, was almost nonexistent. Of course by taking word or event out of context, selecting distorts. Years ago when I asked Vicki to marry me, she hesitated, explaining that she did not know whether to marry me or become an ornithologist. To find out she volunteered to work for the Wildfowl Trust at Slimbridge in Gloucestershire. After she flew off to Britain, I thought there was little chance of her roosting quietly in my domestic nest. Three months later Vicki called me. She was in Princeton. "I'm back," she said, "and I'll marry you." "That's great," I answered, "but what brought you home." "Ducks," she said, "ducks shit a lot"—with the inference being, I suppose, that my performance in such matters was somewhat more satisfactory. A decade of affectionate family life and three fledglings later, all inferences seem beside the point, and smacking of a flightier, migrant time, the story has little to do with the woman who moves through my days softer than birdsong. What the story does, however, is underscore the problem raised by time when one selects a past. Mentioning the Viet-Nam War makes the 1960s seem important in my past when actually the sixties like the war did not touch me, not the music, the drugs, the social protests, not even the sexual revolution. I think I read through the sixties, but I am not sure, for never have I had a clear sense of time.

Not just in January but throughout the year I date checks incorrectly. Connecticut Bank and Trust is so used to my mistakes that instead of returning the checks they correct them silently. Of course selecting a past may decrease the importance of time, forcing one to view time not as a series of discrete historical units but as a continuum, a line on which date is less significant than mood. A person finding the initial notes I took for this essay could conclude that I lacked any sense of ordered, historical time. Instead of jotting down ideas as I normally do in a hundred page, eleven by nine inch yellow spiral notebook printed for the "UConn Co-op," I wrote ideas down in a small, four by six and a half inch "Vanderbilt Notebook Student Series," taken by my father to lectures in the 1920s. On the cover Father wrote his name several times in blue ink and then drew scores of whirling attached circles, shaped like slinkies. Inside he jotted down remarks about Thoreau, Emerson, Whitman, Melville, Twain, Lanier, and Poe. His teacher spent much time discussing Puritanism and things southern, and Father's notes referred again and again to H. L. Mencken and Stuart Sherman. For my part I started my notes on a page at the top of which Father had written "For Saturday—a paper" and "Thursday week—a quiz." Underneath he drew an anvil, on the side of which he wrote the first ten letters of the alphabet in capital letters.

I don't mean to imply that time or, better, the times are unimportant in selecting a past. The spirit of the present may actually influence selection more than conditions of time past. I spent childhood summers on my grandfather's farm in Hanover, Virginia. Hanover was rich in country things and country people, both black and white. As the dirt roads wound about between farms, so people's lives twisted together, endlessly supplying matter for stories, some poignant, some gentle, and a good many racist—or perhaps not racist so much as racially aware for the tales often revealed intimacy and affection. In the late 1940s William the oldest son of Molly, grandfather's cook, left Virginia for New York where he became a successful undertaker. "Oh, Miss Katharine, William is doing just fine," Molly answered when Mother asked about him; "he's so light people think he's a spaniel." Mother and Molly were good friends, loving, if not each other, then the world in which they grew up. For years after the farm was sold and we stopped visiting Hanover, they talked on the telephone. I must have heard the story of William's success a score of times, for Mother told it to me after each conversation with Molly. Yet if William were to become part of my past, he would have to be even lighter—whitewashed out of time and beyond offense.

In the class notes he took on Mark Twain, Father wrote "Dangerous to carry humor too far in dealing with great subjects." Not only does the present force one to shun particular subjects but it also distorts the past by compelling avoidance of certain types of anecdotes. Importance is often equated with solemnity, and the light treatment of any subject, great or small, is dangerous. No matter the selection, if I write humorously, chances are I will have no past, at least not one judged worthy of thought. Consequently, I was tempted to select mostly cosmetic, serious anecdotes for my past, in the process distorting daily life. This weekend I talked on the telephone to Aunt Elizabeth in Richmond. She asked if I remembered going to Uncle Wilbur's office one day when I was eleven or twelve. After learning from the receptionist Mrs. Lane that Uncle Wilbur was busy removing wisdom teeth, I burst into his office and turning to him looked him up and down before saying, "Well, Dr. Ratcliffe, it's good to see you almost sober for a change."

Although I would not want such knowledge to become part of a past, the truth is that for as long as I can remember I have been outspoken. Recently the University of Connecticut condemned four hundred acres of farmland and established a research park, and yesterday in the campus mail I received a letter inviting me to become an associate of the Science and Technology Institute of New England, a consortium of faculty members interested, as a friend put it, in "enhancing earning potentials." Although ostensibly written to the entire university, the letter was really addressed to the science faculty. For some reason that lodged awkwardly in my sensibility, and I telephoned the secretary of the institute. I appreciated his letter, I said, adding that I wanted to become an associate of the institute. The institute, I continued, when he paused on learning that I taught English, would need people to write propaganda and reports. In fact, I stated, I had considerable experience with the legal side of business writing. "Let me give you an example of how I would write a contract for you," I said; "the party of the first part, hereinafter known as greedy sons of bitches, contracts with the party of the second part, hereinafter known as sell your birthright for a dime bastards."

The conversation with the secretary did not last much longer, but walking home, I felt good. That evening I realized my remarks sounded remarkably like something Mother might have said, and I wondered if thinking a person could select a past was only delusion. Maybe a past, even the very words I used, had already been selected for me by heredity. Instead of being free to speak my mind, perhaps I was hung in a groove which had rolled round through generations of minds. Two weeks ago in class I tried to explain how the birth of children changes romance. After the appearance of children, I said, romance lost its dreamy appeal, quickly becoming a practical matter of schedules and consequences. My students were, alas, too young even to want to understand. "Just because of a moment of pleasure," I finally broke out; "just because of a passing thing like chewing Teaberry or Juicy Fruit gum, I haven't slept a night in seven years." What I said was, of course, almost true. Since Francis's birth seven years ago, I haven't spent an undisturbed night. At least once, and more often than not two or three times a night, a child awakens me or I wake on my own and go look at the children to be sure they are still breathing. What was also true was that what I said in class Mother had said to me years earlier in a slightly different way. "Great God!" she exclaimed in exasperation, "because of you I haven't slept a single night in twelve years."

Despite the possibility of heredity's selecting one's past, I want to believe that a person has at least some freedom of choice, in my case freedom enough to distort the past consciously. I do not want my past to have a great influence upon my children's futures, forcing them to live contrary to their inclinations, endlessly measuring themselves against steep, high standards. I don't want my life to weigh them down. Instead I want them to feel superior to me. Superiority brings the freedom to dismiss. And although I hope the children will occasionally remember me lovingly, I nevertheless want them to forget me and live natural, self-assured lives, unburdened by my past. To this end I have distorted my life, selecting a past which reflects a me, often silly and always odd. No person is ever consistent for very long, though, and while selecting a modest dismissible past for myself, I have tried to shape the children's futures.

If my lack of mechanical ability stems from Mother's recounting my desire to have my arms lopped off, then perhaps the tales I tell about the children will influence their lives for the better. To some extent I guess I am selecting pasts for them, pasts, I hope though, of mood not abilities, pasts soft and gentle and smiling. Edward who is five admires "G. I. Joe" and everything military, and although Vicki and I refuse to buy him toy guns, he fashions them out of sticks and Legos. In contrast Eliza who is three likes dolls and is forever having tea parties or staging ballets with them. One afternoon last week Eliza and Edward were playing quietly upstairs until Eliza suddenly appeared crying. "What's wrong, peanut," I said when Eliza came into the study. "Crystal Star and I were having a party in my room," she sobbed, "and then in came the army." Lest this story someday give Edward a wrong impression of himself, I ought to add that Edward's army is usually composed of peace-keepers. Rarely does he invade tea parties because he generally walks about the house with my pillow on his head, sucking his left thumb and rubbing the edge of the pillow case between the thumb and index finger of his right hand. Four nights ago while I read him a story in my bed, I asked him to massage my weak arm. "I will Daddy," he said, putting the pillow on his head and beginning to

rub the case, "but first I have to fill up with gas at the pillow station."
After rubbing the pillow case for ten or fifteen seconds, he started
massaging my arm. Because his hand is small, it, evidently, could
not hold much gas, having to return to the pillow case and be filled
several times.

Under the heading "Things associated with the South by People"
Father listed six items in his notebook. The first was Sentiment,
about which Father wrote, "Passes too often into Sentimentalism."
Part of the southern past sixty years ago, sentimentalism is part of
my past today, and I can not help being sentimental about the
children. In fact if I examined the present closely I would probably
discover that sentimentalism pervades my days. In contrast to time,
particular place matters to me, and when I thought about selecting
a place for my past, sentiment influenced me, pushing me toward
childhood and the South and away from maturity and Connecticut,
a stage of life and a place in which I have been wondrously happy.
For a while I thought my place would be Carthage, Tennessee,
Father's hometown. I even did research, learning that Grandma
Pickering bought her home on November 5, 1909, paying four
thousand dollars. She sold it in 1952 for fifteen thousand, five
hundred dollars. This past Easter, though, Mother died and was
buried in Carthage, and suddenly Carthage seemed a place of losses,
both homes and joy. In Connecticut I own almost no land, and
after Mother's death I suddenly wanted a place rich with acres and
possibilities. Recently I read Teale's *A Naturalist Buys an Old Farm,*
and after following him across the hills and streams of Hampton,
Connecticut, I returned to Hanover and the Virginia farms of childhood, farms I had roamed like Teale's Trail Wood, observing and
naming: Sliding Hill, Red Barn Creek, Piney Woods, The Circle,
Bamboo Forest, and Turtle Pond. I remembered the way along old
Route 614 from Cabin Hill to Etna Mills: down a long hill and
around and over Norman's bridge across the Pamunkey River into
King William County. Just on the Hanover side of the bridge was
an old house in which gypsies stayed every summer. One August
Grandfather took me there and I watched them dance, skirts spinning
yellow and red in the green shade. Across the bridge we once stopped
so a mother skunk could escort her kits across the road. On the left
farther into King William was Hornquarter, a farm Grandfather
tried unsuccessfully to buy. At Bleak Hill Fork we turned right,
passing Gravatt's Mill Pond and then reaching Etna Mills.

In turning toward childhood for place, I turned toward the past itself, selfishly neglecting both the present and those about me. On sunny weekends my family and I often walk in the woods, down behind the university's barns or through Schoolhouse Brook Park. On the walks I behave much as I did as a child, overturning rocks, digging out the rotten hearts of fallen trees, and wandering off to climb small bluffs or explore marshy lowlands. "Gosh," I said to Vicki last Sunday, "this is great. I don't envy the Weavers scuba diving in Montego Bay." "That," Vicki said after a pause, "that would be fun, too." Although Grandfather Ratcliffe owned twenty-seven hundred acres, his farms seemed small to me, not so much in size, as I now think about it, but in mood and pace. The city's fast pace probably lay behind my not placing my past in Nashville. The elementary school I attended has been torn down, and so much is new in Nashville, even the old, that the place seems to have no past, or at least little sympathy for a past like mine, not crisp Scalamandré roped off in a museum but frayed kitchen oilcloth.

As I want simplicity to be a great part of my place in the past, so my past itself should be simple. In arranging the books in the study, I may have made interpretation needlessly and confusingly complex. With the chest of drawers upstairs I did better, only putting an eighteenth-century Pennsylvania spice box on top. Eighteen inches tall, fifteen wide and twelve deep, the spice box has thirteen drawers, surrounding a keyhole opening. While ginger, nutmeg, and cloves were kept in the drawers, the mortar and pestle for grinding spices probably sat in the opening. When I found the spice box in Mother's attic, it was almost empty, containing needles and thread and three blue buttons. Since putting the box on the chest, I have filled two drawers. In one I put a small silver locket, seven-eighths of an inch in diameter. The locket was given to Vicki's grandmother when she was a student at Wellesley, and engraved on the back are her initials MFJ and the date 1908. On the front is the orange and black crest of Princeton University. Vicki's father was an undergraduate, and I was a graduate student at Princeton, so the school is part of our family's past, and perhaps like my southern sentimentalism, it will crop up in the future. At least I hope so, and to this end, I put the locket in the spice box as a sort of seed. Someday, maybe the children will find it, and becoming aware of the past, will consider going to Princeton.

On the other hand my family is various, and if attending Princeton is part of my past, so is not attending Princeton or for that matter any college. After applying to and being admitted to several schools, Mother refused to go, choosing instead to spend months hunting and riding in Arizona. "I'd had enough school," she said; "books are only part of life." To balance the austere Princeton locket, I put two pieces of Mother's jewelry into the spice box: a heavy gold ring in the middle of which sat an amethyst as big as a tangerine and then a pin shaped like a salamander, its body greenish-blue malachite, its eyes rubies, and diamonds glistening at the tips of its fingers. I had the jewelry because Father insisted I bring it to Connecticut after Mother's death. I stuffed it into the bottom of a handbag, on top of which I crammed four or five purses which Father also asked me to take. At the airport the bag was certain to be inspected, and I envisioned being arrested as a masher or cat burglar. "Well," the woman opening the purse at the airport said, "you certainly have a lot of purses." "Aren't they divine," I answered inspiration twisting about like a hot salamander; "I never travel without a purse for each outfit. Wait until you get to the bottom of the bag and see my jewelry. It is just scrumptious." "So it is," the woman said looking at me out of the corner of her eye and drawing back. "Just scrumptious," she said, cursorily pushing a purse aside before handing me the bag and adding, "have a nice flight."

I haven't put more family jewelry into the spice box, partly because I'm not sure I can blend the austere and the flamboyant in a way which won't affect my children's futures. Moreover I have almost come to believe in an accidental past, one smacking more of the geological than the rational. The effects of glaciers can be seen all over my part of Connecticut. When the ice melted, glacial drift remained behind. Here in the Eastern Uplands, the drift is till, sediment of all sizes jumbled together: pebbles, stones, clay, and boulders. Whenever I dig in the yard, I hit some kind of rock. Perhaps that, too, is the way of a past. Scraping across then withdrawing from the surface of time, a life leaves till behind, and if someone starts to dig, he's sure to hit something with his shovel. Although I have put nothing more in it than locket, ring, and pin, the spice box has begun to accumulate till: paper clips, pencil nubs, a pearl button, and then mysteriously the buckeye and shark's tooth Mother kept for good luck and which she put in the overnight bag she took with her to the hospital that last time.

At Work

"At work," Vicki exclaimed, raising her hands then turning her palms and spreading her fingers in disbelief, "at work—look at this bed." In truth the bed was a mess. The sheets lay in waves, washing and ebbing whenever I moved. Against a chair a blanket curled awkwardly like a periwinkle stranded high on the sand at low tide while pillows fell across each other and tumbled to the floor. Still, I had been at work, reading notebooks and planning an essay. Around the house, though, my writing is not very important. Once when Vicki was rinsing dishes and I asked her to listen to something I wrote, she looked up from the sudsy water and said, "Can't you see I'm busy. You could read to me but the trees outside would make a better audience."

I had been reading in the bedroom because it is the only room in the house where I can work. During the day my study is the children's playroom; at night it is Vicki's television room. I could, I suppose, work in the living room but the light there is dim. Besides the idea of working in a living room offends my sense of propriety. In my mother's and grandmother's houses the grit of abrasive living never settled in a living room. Pillows and chairs were always fluffed; silver was polished, and china bowls bloomed with fresh flowers. The living room was not for notebooks and pencils and hard, twisting, disruptive thought. Kept apart for the right sort of guests, civility, and ordered elegance, it was a better place, a room barred to brutish living and in which high platitudes about manners and morals and spiritual value rang comforting and true.

Although I plan essays in the bedroom at night, I write only in the morning and not at home but in a study, which the university provides for me on the third floor of the Whetton Graduate Center, a six and a half minute walk from my house. I get up at half-past six but rarely begin writing before nine. First I must wake the children. Edward bounces easily out of bed, and by six Eliza has almost always climbed into bed with me. Francis, though, rises to a different dawn and takes much coaxing. Once Francis is out of bed, I help the children dress, buttoning, pulling on stubborn socks, and untangling willful belts. After breakfast I supervise the brushing of teeth. Then I go outside and wait for the school bus with Francis. We pass the time talking about flowers, this spring pleased that seven of the fifteen peonies bloomed and disappointed that only two of the ten poppies appeared. When the bus stops, I talk with Ralph, the driver, to whom I gave a copy of one of my books in appreciation of his taking good care of Francis. During the week I spend considerable time chatting with people who have read things of mine: Tom who drives the UPS truck or John who reads the gas meter and devotes weekends to helping retarded children play sports.

Once Francis's bus disappears around Hillside Circle, I leave for the study if I have no more chores. Often, though, I have something else to do. This June, for example, I watered laurel which I planted behind rocks in the back yard. This past spring the university erected a Facilities Building at the edge of a field not far from my house. Low and prefabricated with square gray heat pumps churning on the roof, the building resembles a back-street warehouse, the sort of warehouse in which shady characters host weekly sales for damaged goods. Behind the building grew small laurel bushes; these I dug and replanted in the back yard. To a neighbor who afterwards informed me that digging laurel was illegal, I explained that constructing such a building was a worse crime, offending sight and good taste, the kind of thing which people who used living rooms as studies or worse yet, turned them into "family rooms" were forever doing.

In the study in the graduate center I keep a cup, hot plate, tea kettle, and pot. Each morning I take a small thermos of milk with me to the study, and as soon as I arrive brew tea, usually Earl Grey or English Breakfast. Once tea is under way, I go next door and visit with Raymond, a friend from the English department. Like me Raymond is an early riser, but since his child is older than mine he beats me to the Graduate Center six days out of seven. After we chat about the state of the world and the university, in the process making ourselves comfortably gloomy, I return to the study, pour a cup of tea, and begin writing about what I mulled over in bed the night before. I leave the door open and my desk faces out into the hall. My study is next to the bathrooms and as a result I see practically everybody on the third floor sometime during the morning. Coming or going, most stop outside my door and visit. Almost never does a deadline tug at my writing and after jotting down a phrase which will pull me back into writing, I lay my pencil aside and chat. And so I pass the morning, writing, talking, drinking tea, and visiting the bathroom once or twice myself. At noon I usually stop writing and start the day's chores: teaching, attending committee meetings, raking leaves, mowing grass, planting laurel. My days, I like to think, resemble the essays I write: slow, relaxed, punctuated by fits of pique and occasionally lust, but all in all meandering and gently contemplative.

Not long ago a critic dubbed me "the last Agrarian gone East." "What does that mean?" Vicki asked when I read her the comment. "Damned if I know," I said, "but whatever it is, it's pretty doggone big." Since talking to Vicki I have thought about the critic's words. Some truth adheres to the label, not all of it of my mixing however. I have lived in New Hampshire and Connecticut because no southern school has ever offered me a job, this despite my having applied for posts at most of the bigger state schools at least two or three times each during the past twenty years. As the absence of job offers has forced me east, so the matter of my essays is also determined by a negative, the lack of money. This past year I earned $1,507. Two hundred dollars came from reading manuscripts for university presses; two literary quarterlies paid $465 for articles while a New York publisher paid me $100 to reprint a piece. The rest, $742, consisted of royalties for five books, two of which were recently published, one last November and the other this May.

Since my writing does not earn much money, money, oddly enough, influences what I write. With three small children and a healthy wife with a hearty appetite, leg-of-lamb nights in craggy Scottish castles and purple treks through long ferny borderlands are not for my pocketbook. With no sponsor, no advance, no *New Yorker* paying expenses, I stay at home—at peace, certainly, far from the lash of deadline and the hounding bay of publishers—but still at home, seeing and writing about the familial and the personal. The junkets I take are those which arise naturally out of ordinary life, trips to Tennessee to see my father and to Nova Scotia where Vicki and her brothers own an old farm. In the absence of advances from publishers, teachers often obtain grants to support travel and writing. Although I am not well connected enough to have won any big fellowships, I have received some money. Over the past three years, the University of Connecticut has given me $1,900 to help pay for summer trips to Nova Scotia. Taking the family to Nova Scotia is costly; six weeks there this summer cost just under $3,200, and without aid from the university I might not have been able to go there and write about the farm.

I began writing about the farm because when I married Vicki it, like babies, soon became part of my life. I make use of all my travel, no matter how unpromising. My mother died last Easter, and this June after school ended, Vicki and I and the children flew to Nashville to visit Father and help him clean out Mother's desk and chests. Although we flew on a family rate, the trip was expensive, my ticket costing $642 and the other four $118 each for a total of $1,114. To help defray expenses and in truth to give my ego a boost, I arranged to autograph my latest book at Davis-Kidd Booksellers at the Green Hills Mall in Nashville on Sunday, June 26, from two to four in the afternoon. Davis-Kidd advertised the book signing in the local evening newspaper, the *Nashville Banner,* and to several hundred customers on their mailing list sent an announcement inviting them to the store. Davis-Kidd is big and sells lots of books, particularly on Sundays, and as I drove there I imagined signing eighty or maybe even a hundred books. "After all," I thought, I was from Nashville and still knew hordes of people. To get into an expansive mood for the signing, I ate eggs Benedict at the Belle Meade Country Club. I wore my best clothes, an H. Freeman suit which Mother bought me many years ago at Davitt's. Much as Davitt's had vanished, I mused, so I could no longer afford H. Freeman suits. In fact the newest piece of clothing in my possession was a Rumanian-made corduroy sport coat which Vicki bought at Caldor for thirty-eight dollars. "Oh, well," I dreamed, "this signing will give a fillip to my career and be the start of flush times."

Unfortunately dreams are rarely the stuff of high living. During the two hours I signed nine books for a royalty of approximately nine dollars, or looked at another way, a wage of four dollars and fifty cents an hour. I sat inside the store on a tall stool, placed twelve or so feet away from the front door. On a desk in front of me towering, it seemed, like great industrial chimneys were copies of my three volumes of essays. Everyone who entered the store saw me. Most looked away quickly and striding to either side of the desk rushed past like water flowing downhill around a rock. Some people with small children were forced to pause when the children stopped and looked up at me quizzically. "That man wrote all those books; he's really smart," a woman with a toddler said, beaming benevolently at me before she jerked her little boy along, practically bowling him back into the store. Oblivious to my books and the sign on the post behind my head explaining my presence, many people mistook me for an information desk and asked the locations of particular books. Because I had arrived at the signing early and had explored the store, I provided accurate information. Rushing through the door his face red with anger, one man demanded to know why *Barron's* was no longer for sale on Saturday. "We" labored to satisfy our customers, I said, always displaying papers and periodicals as soon as they arrived. The fault lay not with Davis-Kidd, I explained but with *Barron's* publisher. Four women from Augusta, Arkansas, heard me talking to someone and pausing looked carefully through my books. "You write wonderfully," they said almost in chorus, then asked me to recommend books for them to read. I suggested four volumes, all of which they bought, and leaving the store, they thanked me profusely and wished me "great success." They did not, however, buy any of my books. Neither did the old friend who quizzed me for twenty minutes on the mechanics of getting published. At four o'clock the store manager came over and seeing books still looming over me said, "things aren't so bad as they look. During this past week we have sold almost twenty-five of your books." The manager was right. Things were not so bad. If the signing didn't inflate my ego, it did provide matter for an essay, and that evening I filled a page in a notebook describing the afternoon at Davis-Kidd. Since editors don't assign subjects to me, practically anything can become part of an essay, and accounts of little experiences like that of the signing fill my notebooks. On returning to Father's apartment from Belle Meade Drugs the next morning, for example, Father and I met Norvell Skipwith and his wife unloading their car after a vacation at Sea Island, Georgia. "Good morning, Norvell," Father said. Neither Norvell nor his wife was young, and after handing the key to the trunk of his car to the doorman, Norvell turned to Father and said, "Sam, good morning. This is a surprise, and how was your trip?" Norvell then paused and looked puzzled for a moment before shaking his head in mild exasperation and adding, "Aw shucks, I've got that wrong. *I* went on the trip."

I enjoy such remarks, and the world of my essays is made small probably as much by inclination as by economics, although, of course, after a time distinguishing inclination from habit of thought is practically impossible. William Blake the English poet and mystic claimed that he could see the universe in a grain of sand. Unlike Blake I'm no visionary; I have never kicked sand up into the air on a beach and suddenly enjoyed sublime moments of understanding. The few places which make up the world of my essays are small and particular, not universal or abstract. I write about Hanover Courthouse, Virginia, where I spent summers as a child; Middle Tennessee, primarily Nashville but with an occasional excursion fifty-five miles east to my father's hometown, Carthage; the southwestern tip of Nova Scotia, fifteen miles along the coast northeast from Yarmouth to Port Maitland and Beaver River; and then Connecticut from Storrs in the Eastern Uplands down to Willimantic in the Windham Basin, a distance of seven miles. Last Sunday when I wanted to furnish a shed in an essay, I drove to the Mansfield Drive-In. Each Sunday the Eastern Connecticut Flea Market is held there from nine in the morning until three in the afternoon. For fifty cents admission, I filled a cardboard box in my mind and carried it back to my study in the Graduate Center. Wrapped in tissue paper in a Peter Schuyler cigar box were four ceramic ashtrays. At the bottom of the box was a blue souvenir ashtray from Walt Disney World; atop it, hung with American flags at half-mast and banded by black banners, was a Reverend Martin Luther King, Jr. ashtray; above it was an ashtray with the pictures of John and Robert Kennedy in the center; lastly, filling the box and pushing the lid slightly open was an ashtray from Newport, Rhode Island. In the center was a drawing of a man standing in a rain slicker behind a ship's wheel. Engraved on a stone beneath him was "They That Go Down to the Sea in Ships, 1623–1923." So that it landed upside down I tossed a rat trap into a corner of the shelf, a "Four Way Better Rat Trap" manufactured by McGill Metal Products in Marengo, Illinois. Under the shelf and leaning against the back wall of the shed was a copper bug sprayer, patent number 2,014,616. The pump of the sprayer was nineteen inches long; at the end just above the quart well was an adjustable nozzle, enabling one to spray insecticide in either a fine mist or a thick stream.

The flea market was four and a half miles from my house; normally things closer to home clutter the sheds of my imagination and the pages of my essays. Until I bought my house five years ago I had never owned a home. Moving in eager to be self-sufficient and economical, I ordered three cords of wood and had them dumped and stacked in the side yard. Wood fires, though, are smoky and inconvenient, especially on cold, rainy winter days, and aside from the occasional log, none the last two years, the wood has remained untouched. Slowly the shoulders of the pile have slumped, making it, if not an eyesore, at least an inelegance. In winter I decided to have the wood carted off and in its place plant flowers. One bright June morning, though, I saw a chipmunk dart past the garage and disappear into the woodpile. What creatures, I suddenly wondered, lived in the wood, and I decided to look closely at the woodpile before it vanished. After Francis left on the school bus, I went to the garage and bringing out a round plastic table and a folding lawn chair, both bought at Caldor, I set up an observation stand next to the woodpile. After brewing tea and placing it and a pile of natural history handbooks on the table, I sat down and began examining the woodpile. I studied the woodpile for an hour, not without breaks, however. Edward insisted I visit the sandpile to see some curious red ants he discovered, and Eliza asked me to read Maurice Sendak's *Outside Over There* to her. During the short time I studied the woodpile, though, I found an ark of small creatures: black ground beetles, bagworms, slugs, an orange and white crab spider, a long-necked seed bug, sow bugs, daddy longlegs, a gypsy moth caterpillar, aphids, two ladybug larvae eating skippers, little black ants, gray millipedes, velvet mites, earthworms, and scarlet plant bugs.

What I found interested not me alone but also the chipmunk, and he scampered to the top of the woodpile and watched me watch. At times I must have resembled a stick of wood, immobile and seemingly unthinking. Paradoxically, close observation often leads to distant thought, and as my body bent before the woodpile my mind hiked over Cape Milianos across the harbor from the acropolis at Lindos on Rhodes. Under a small log I found a pale orange centipede, two and a half inches long. Unaccountably another centipede suddenly twisted out of the past and flamed through memory. One May seventeen years ago I walked out Cape Milianos toward the tomb of Kleoboulus, one of the seven wise men of the ancient world, remembered today for saying "Nothing in excess." The path was both hard and soft; sheep had overgrazed the land, and rain had run over the limestone washing the soil down into pockets and creating little canyons, hedged about by knife-like rocks. The day was heavy with heat; I wore a great loose white hat, with a rim which hung bohemian-like down over my forehead. All along the path flowers bloomed: yellow chamomile, holy thistle, poppies luminously red with centers black and shining, and daisies, blue, yellow, and white. Near the end of the cape, just before the climb up to the tomb, was a ruined windmill, which in all the romanticism of spring and flagging youth I conjured into a tower, "a stony reminder," or so I put it quoting poetry as then I sometimes did, "of the glory that was Greece." I entered the windmill, thinking I would climb to the second story and, leaning out, stare wordlessly across the sea into the blue distance. The poetic, however, is rarely able to hold me in her elevated grasp for very long; with a shrug the fit usually passes and in a moment I have slipped back to the solid earth. On the floor of the windmill were broken wooden boxes; the printing on them was German; and assuming they were remnants of the Second World War, I turned over a pile of slats, expecting to find treasure, casings from spent cartridges or maybe even a rusty Iron Cross. What I found was the centipede, fiery and longer, it seemed, than my forearm. For a second I froze; then I laid the boxes down gently and left the windmill.

Much as close observation can transport thought far from the present and home, so writing essays occasionally forces me to wander through other times and places. More often than not I do the wandering in the library, in the Map Room, for example, studying geological surveys or the Microfilm Room where recently I read reels seven hundred and eight and seven hundred and nine of the *Early English Periodicals,* searching the *Arminian Magazine* for the autobiography of a good Samaritan. Sometimes I travel by telephone; this fall when I wanted to know the names of cities sponsoring teams in the Carolina League in the late 1950s, I called the headquarters of the National League in New York. Frequently, though, I roam without leaving the house. In November when I wanted to stock a boutique in an essay, I looked through the catalogues which swim through our mail in shoals and which, much to my disapproval, Vicki beaches and stacks in a corner of the dining room, catalogues like those of Chadwick's of Boston; Voice of the Mountains; J. Jill, Ltd; Horchow; and Smith & Hawken.

Research to patch a small pothole in one essay sometimes paves an entire drive in another. For a time I took a goodly number of names for characters in my essays from the *Register of Members of St. Catharine's College,* my old Cambridge college. While searching for books which explained the rituals of Freemasonry, however, I came across *The Universal Masonic Record and Directory,* published in Philadelphia in 1860 and purporting to list "all Masonic Lodges in the World." In addition to the lodges themselves, the directory listed the locations of American chapters and whenever possible entire memberships. As a result characters named Mulno, Neefus, Mosgrove, Vowinkle, Higby, Gammage, Tunny, and Conkey people my essays and live in places like Duck Springs, Enon, Green Pond, Oquawks, Posey, Mattoon, Thurmond, Perseverance, and Faithful Friend.

My essays don't start taking firm shape until I have a title. Although for some time I had wanted to describe how I wrote essays and had gone so far as to fill two pages of a notebook with ideas, this essay was practically an abstraction until Vicki came into the bedroom and said "At work." As soon as she spoke, the essay became concrete, and the next morning I began reading through my notebooks to see what I could use in "At Work." Not only do the notebooks contain notes for my earlier essays but they are repositories for all sorts of jottings. I am fond, for example, of puns and they are sown throughout the notebooks. Bringing green laughter puns please and astonish me. Miss Olmstead, a teacher in Bottsville, a little town in Smith County, Tennessee, a typical pun begins, asked her students to construct a sentence containing the word *amphibious.* Initially the class was puzzled but then Chaffer Inks, son of the local butcher, raised his hand and said, "Most fish stories am fibious."

Of late I have become interested in flowers, and plant lore has spread through the notebooks of the past three years like forsythia, shallow rooted but everywhere. Although there are no adders in Connecticut, I find it comforting to know that an adder's bite can be cured by binding a cross made out of hazel wood to the wound. Crushing yarrow in a cut stops the flow of blood, something handy to know in Nova Scotia where black flies draw blood like nurses. Occasionally I run across an old tale which needs revision. According to legend when Satan fled Eden after the fall, onions sprang up from the spots on the ground where he put his right foot and garlic from those where he put his left. Now, garlic and onions strike me as gifts to man, not plants likely to be left behind by the arch-deceiver. How much better for his footsteps to be filled by a noisome, inedible plant like skunk cabbage or by poisonous mushrooms, Leaden Entoloma or, more fittingly, Devil's Boletus. Maybe it would be even more appropriate if an alluring flower like the wrinkled rose grew in his footprints. On the breeze the rose smacks of Victorian gentility—paperweights, a maiden aunt's dresser, Staffordshire dogs, and lemonade cups. Like sin, though, the rose deceives. Behind the fragrance vines curl hairy with spines and hips dangle fleshy and wantonly red.

Many of the entries in my notebooks reflect domestic life. Instead of the quarrels of nations, I record differences between Vicki and me. The borders we argue over have to do with flowers, not desert mounds or frozen plains. Vicki does not care for ornate flowers, preferring what she calls "wholesome, straightforward, serenely elegant flowers," daisies, primroses, sweet William, marigolds, and old-fashioned bleeding heart. I, too, like these flowers, but I also like Iris, and last fall planted a border of tall bearded Iris in the side yard. Vicki objected, saying the blossoms reminded her of the fuzzy "coverlets" which people crocheted and wrapped around toilet paper rolls. In truth I have gone a little beyond the plain blue Iris which my grandmother grew in Carthage and have planted flowers with gilded, even crocheted names: tangerine dream, Spanish leather, marmalade, prancing pony, casbah, strawberry sensation, cozy calico, and designer gown. When the border bloomed this spring, it was bright, and Vicki asked why I didn't call Sussman & Perry, the plumbers, and instruct them to put the john in the side yard. Even better, she suggested, I should donate Iris to the university. Outside the Facilities Building they would look "swank," she said, her voice piercing and wintry, not soft and spring-like as befitted the season. Before going to Nova Scotia, I did order more Iris, not for the university, though, but for the yard. In hopes of forestalling a late cold snap next spring, I also bought two flats of pink asters from Andre Viette in Fishersville, Virginia, and planted them as a surprise for Vicki. Running deeper than forsythia, Vicki's and my difference over the flowers cuts right down the wall to the foundation of our marriage, and the asters can only paper over the quarrel, not repair it. This May when I asked her to come with Francis and me while we searched for lady's slippers along Schoolhouse Brook, she refused, declaring lady's slippers reminded her of scrotums. "With two boys and you, I see enough of those things in the house. Now," she exclaimed, "you expect me to look for them outdoors. My God, what a life!"

What a life, indeed, what a wonderful writing life I enjoy. Because no editor threatens to blight my career if I don't prune weedy air-blown growth from my essays, I am free to hoe waywardly through the rich soil of married life. I can plant or dig whatever I wish. If horse balm pushes the phlox aside and jewelweed suddenly appears in the drainage ditch, so be it. As I plant flowers for the pleasure of my family, so I write, not to convey truth or principle, but to give my children memories, be they fictitious or not. To this end I write down the doings and the sayings of the children in my notebooks in hopes of fitting them into essays. Just last week Edward said to me, "Abraham Lincoln doesn't need a birthday because he is dead, right Daddy?" Edward is, of course, right and more profound than he realizes. As a nation changes so does its calendar and like Militia Day and Whitsuntide, Lincoln's birthday will eventually pale into cultural history.

I suppose my notebooks resemble an attic. In them I have stored incidents from my past which someday I hope to bring downstairs and polish and then display in essays. Before writing I always rum-mage through the notebooks and pull out events, much like a person searching an attic for ornaments for the tree and mantel at Christmas. Sometimes I consider an incident for six or seven essays before I use it. For some time, I have tried unsuccessfully to write about a trip I made fifteen years ago to Samarkand. What stuck in memory was not blue domes and golden caskets, Tamerlane and Mongul horsemen, but an incident provoked by careless driving. One night as I roamed Samarkand, I noticed a motorbike dart out of a side street into the path of a car. To avoid hitting the cyclist, the driver of the car swerved, pulling out of his lane and almost crashing head-on into another car. Despite the close call, the cyclist didn't pause. Turning his motorbike toward the sidewalk where I stood at the bottom of a hill, he raced toward me as fast as his bike would go. After jumping the curb, he grabbed the motorbike and carrying it, ran past me up and over the top of the hill into the dark. His behavior puzzled me until I saw the car in front of which he had pulled turn sharply around and rush toward me. The driver stopped at the curb near me; five men jumped out and without saying a word chased over the hill after the cyclist. Eight minutes later they returned, without the cyclist but with his motorbike. This they set about destroying, smashing what they could against the curb then putting it into the gutter and driving back and forth over it, shifting it about so not a single piece was salvageable. The men ignored me, and standing almost among them I watched fascinated, part of me disapproving the destruction of property, yet another part of me, probably the major part, silently applauding the rough justice.

Besides incidents out of my past the notebooks contain stories which I have heard or read. I am fond of the little towns which I describe and often people them with character and tale. This summer I spent an afternoon looking at houses in Port Maitland, trying to decide which one Bertha Shifney bought after she became a widow for the second time. Bertha appeared in my last book when the owner of a carriage shop, Perry Weebe, married her. Bertha was not easy to live with, and when Weebe died suddenly, his death was, as habitués of Gawdry's store put it, "a blessed release." Not long afterwards Bertha surprised Port Maitland by marrying Worby Thursh, one of her late husband's assistants. Thursh was a ne'er-do-well who had recently arrived in Port Maitland, supposedly from Maine. From the perspective of people in Port Maitland Worby didn't seem sound marriage material. He drank and after having spent a convivial evening was given to urinating in back yards. When upbraided about his behavior, he always said, "he that's afraid of grass shouldn't piss in the meadow." The statement did little to explain his actions to anyone other than Worby himself, but in one of those strange twists that mark a man's passage through life, it somehow stuck to recollection, and the coastal lowland just east of the Port Maitland beach is today known as Worby's Meadow.

Bertha was beyond the age of passionate excess, and her marriage provoked much gossip. Raisin Nubbin, tannery owner and general entrepreneur, probably got things right, however, in asserting that Bertha married Worby for social not fleshly reasons. Having heard that Worby belonged to a lodge in Maine, Bertha, Raisin speculated, assumed he was a Shriner and married him so she could become a Daughter of the Nile. "Imagine the shock when she discovered that instead of the Masons, Worby belonged to the Odd Fellows," Raisin said; "instead of dreaming of being The Grand Crocodile or a Golden Scarab or White Ibis, she had to be content as a Rebekah Sister." Refusing even to acknowledge the Shifneys in her birthplace, Hectanooga, Bertha was not about to become anyone's sister, and the marriage to Worby was not a success. Happily for Bertha, though, it only lasted four months. One cold fall afternoon Worby went out with Otis Blankinchip in Otis's lobster boat. Instead of sailing along the coast pulling up traps, they dropped anchor offshore, "appropriately enough," Raisin noted, over Garsed's sandbar, and sitting in the cabin spent the evening tossing down rum. At about ten o'clock Worby went up top to relieve himself where, so it was said, mistaking the deck of the boat for a meadow he stumbled overboard and drowned. The next day he washed ashore, and Demmick the undertaker did such a good job of filling in the holes where crabs had gotten to him that Bertha was able to have the coffin open at the funeral. Long years of drink had served Worby well, "pickling" him, to use Raisin's words, so that despite his immersion he looked red in the face and almost alive. "Poor Worby," Otis said as he passed the corpse and then stopped by the grieving widow in the first pew, "poor Worby, he still looks warm." "Warm or cold," Bertha said, flicking a fly off her veil, "warm or cold, he goes this afternoon."

Vicki does not allow me to call the children to dinner, saying I bray and hurt her ears. I'm not musical and my attempts to control tone and volume have failed. After but a few pages even melodious prose can irritate. To vary the sound of an essay, I not only create fictional characters but I also include other voices. Often I quote letters. In July an acquaintance wrote, informing me that he had returned home after many years of living abroad. "Most of the surface of the planet," he wrote, "was subjugated by the enemy during the four hundred and fifty years preceding my birth. I was born into a world already under enemy occupation." Despite having gone to great lengths to escape oppression and complicity in it, he had failed and was "compelled," he explained, "to return to the heartland of the enemy by two ineluctable forces—children and taxes." Occasionally I include an excerpt from something written by one of my students. "As soon as I entered the university and certainly at the first day of it, my father died," a Syrian girl wrote in an autobiographical paragraph ten years ago; "After that I became a girl hesitance in every thing. My mother becomes crazy, because we haven't money to live after death my father. Just then my uncle took the house which we lived in. After some days later he comes to our shelter to take the furniture. Meanwhile I can't prevent him because he is a strong man. One evening he comes to and said to me he doesn't want me to study at the univercity, because I am a girl. He said, You should marry and, you should let the studying. After that I said with crying I didn't marry, and I didn't leave the univercity. Just then he threw me with chair and went. And when my mother heard me crying she comes and asked me why I was crying, but I didn't say anything. After some months ago my mother died with ill in her heart. After that I decided to let the shelter in the village and go away from the people. In the evening I threw my self in the river, but my friend saw me from his room's window and save me. At last I decided to work in a factory and to continou the studying at unevercity. And now I am living with sorrow and pain."

Writing essays both pleases and upsets. Binding word and tale one to another like brick and mortar satisfies me. As I grow old, though, I encounter greater losses. Reading through my past now does not delight so much as it saddens. In creating fictional characters like Bertha and Worby, perhaps I am unconsciously preparing for the inevitable time when facing reality will be impossible. In cleaning Mother's desk this past June, I found a letter which she started but never completed. "My dear children," she began, "All I am working for is to get well so we can come up and see you all when it warms up. Daddy is in the process of selling his car. One car is enough. When I realize how far away we are I nearly die—no one here. I wish we hadn't bought this place. We paid 187,000 for it and 500 a month to live here. So if we leave here, you get what you can for it."

When nothing—thinking, observing, looking through letters and notebooks—gives me an idea for an essay, I read, usually books for review. Sometimes reading or the act of writing a review will start me on an essay. Usually, however, after I have lain fallow for two or so weeks, an idea will suddenly and inexplicably sprout, green and growing. Before I wrote regularly I assumed I would find ideas for my essays in books which I read. I was wrong. Reading can help swell an essay, but usually it leads only to enthusiasms, most of which prove unusable. In April I read an account of an anthropologist's travels in Indonesia. On one island when men want to insure peace and good will, they greet one another by sucking various portions of each other's bodies. Starting at the nose, they work across the face to the earlobes, then over to the chin, down to the nipples, out to the ends of the fingers, after which they descend to lower, less appetizing, to my taste at least, appendages. "Gosh," I said aloud. Then after marking the passage to read to Vicki, I began sketching an essay on the ritualistic greetings of American males. Although American males often rub one another's hands, their greetings are, certainly in the circle in which I move, more verbal than physical, generally consisting of formulas like "Hey, sport" or "How's it going?" With the exception of what is politely known as a "Christmas gift" or "oil pressure check," greetings rarely descend below the waist. When they do, they generally remain verbal, taking the form of rhyme thus being formulaic and relatively impersonal. A typical example being: "How is your mother?/ How is your brother?/ How is your sister Sue?/ And speaking of your family,/ How is your old Wazoo?" I must confess that at this point I fell asleep, waking only to read my excerpt to Vicki when she came to bed. Vicki didn't think much of the subject, and the next morning I abandoned it, although a page of jottings remains in one of my notebooks.

The notebooks in which I record ideas and enthusiasms and plan essays are ordinary spiral notebooks, nine inches wide and eleven long, containing one hundred pages, each with a margin and thirty-eight narrow lines. The notebooks cost two dollars and nineteen cents apiece, up forty cents this past April. I could buy comparable, cheaper notebooks, but these notebooks are yellow, my favorite color, and have a handsome drawing of the Wilbur Cross Library on the front. In buying things I do not pamper myself except in the matter of notebooks and pencils. I take all my notes and write my essays in pencil, Faber-Castell Velvets, medium soft number twos. The pencils are not cheap; sometimes I pay two dollars for a dozen, but their wood is hard and they sharpen easily. Almost never does a side split or a long finger of lead snap off in the sharpener. Moreover they are manufactured in my home state, Tennessee, and using a Tennessee pencil makes me feel good. As I think about what should be in an essay and then read through my notebooks looking for suitable material, I keep one notebook open to a group of blank pages. On these I write down appropriate idea and incident. I always start on the right-hand page, writing the title of the essay at the top and never crossing the red line marking the margin on the left. Oddly, when I fill the right-hand page, I cross over to the left and write straight across, paying no attention to the margin. Although my notes are often messy, with arrows running down a page from one item to another, I don't doodle in the notebooks. Occasionally, however, one of the children will draw pictures in the notebook, a square man with marshmallow-like feet and baseball glove hands. Because my essays are in part a record of the children's doings, I don't erase the pictures but instead write around them. Normally while I write one essay, I make notes for a second essay. Occasionally I will make notes for an essay for three or four months. Sometimes I stop taking notes and try to forget the essay for weeks at a time. Usually when I return to it, I harvest pages of ripe ideas. Although my essays often appear spontaneous, I plan meticulously, and behind each hour of writing lies another four of thought. Even when I am not consciously thinking about essays, they seem to percolate in the unconscious. In April while I was walking through the intensive care unit of a hospital, an idea suddenly came to me. Not having a pencil and paper with me, I rushed to the nurse's station. "Quick," I said; "quick; I have to have a pencil and paper." The nurses assumed I was a doctor, and two jumped up and handed me a pencil and paper.

When I have taken six or seven pages of notes and the essay seems clear to me, I outline it. I do this on eight and a half inch by fourteen inch yellow lined paper, sold in ninety-nine cent pads at the university bookstore. I turn the paper sideways and print my outline, the writing being smaller and much finer than that in the notebooks. The outlines are extensive, the one for this essay filling three pages. I try to complete the outline in a sitting so I don't lose train of theme. After taking a day off, I begin writing. I write essays on the same yellow pads used for the outline. Each page has thirty-eight lines and a margin which I ignore. I write on only one side, using the back for an occasional addition. At the top of the first page I print the title in capital letters and underline it twice. The writing itself is mechanical, something perfected by practice like driving a straight nail.

To the study each morning I carry a dozen sharp pencils, a rubber band around them, three or four notebooks—always the one containing the notes for the essay which I am writing—and of course my outline. If ideas come to me while I write, I add them to the outline. When I have covered the ideas detailed on a part of the outline, I mark through them. That night I mark out the same material in the notebook or notebooks, giving me a sense of progress and making the notebooks easier to read when I look through them searching for material to use in the next essay. Also at dinner I keep

Vicki posted on my progress albeit she isn't really interested. She has only read two of my essays, and I mention my progress to her for reasons which I can't articulate. It may be that I mention it because the subject—three pages today, four yesterday—is boring, and I think boredom, unlike excitement, is sane, even healthy.

I write only one draft, and I don't erase. Erasures are messy, so instead of erasing I mark out, usually with the shortened nub of a pencil. I put the pencil almost under my hand, thumb on what in effect becomes the pencil's left side, index finger on top, middle finger on the right side, and using short, strong strokes, I blacken passages. Although I sometimes write more on weekends, I ordinarily write between two and five pages daily, with between a third and a half of each page marked out. For the past three and a half years I have written an essay a month, excluding summer months in Nova Scotia. If I contributed regularly to a magazine or newspaper, I might write more, although that is by no means certain. Physically, writing is hard on me. After a morning of writing my eyes are dry and tired. My legs are weak, and I stagger when I walk. Worse yet, writing irritates the bulging disk in my neck, making neck and back ache and making my right hand and arm tremble and feel useless. In bed when I go over an outline and notes after a hard day of writing, I lie flat on my back, a cervical pillow under my neck and notebooks propped up against a mound of pillows on my stomach. Pain probably affects each writer differently, but for my part I suspect pain has contributed to my being an essayist. I am unable to sit for long hours at a time; as a result writing a lengthy work, a novel for example, which would bind me to a desk for several months or years is not something I can bear even to consider. Although my essays can collectively be compared to the chapters of a novel, beginning an essay is very different from beginning a novel. When I start an essay, the end is always near at hand. I know the pain will not last longer than three weeks at the outside.

After completing the hand-written copy of the essay, I bring it home, and after resting for a day, I type it. I type at the kitchen table, an inexpensive piece imported from Yugoslavia and made from pressed wood. Or, if Vicki is busy in the kitchen, I, and I am ashamed to admit it, put the card table up in the living room and type there. In the past I typed many of my essays on a portable Underwood which Father gave me in 1968 when I was in graduate school. The typewriter has a congenital weakness, however, and after Francis broke the carriage arm for the fourth time, the eighth time it has broken, I began using an old Smith-Corona, which Mr. Toomey at Ferris Business Machines in Willimantic gave me. Although the nine has now broken off as have the opening parenthesis and the lower half of the letter *p,* the typewriter has stood up well. I never use parentheses, and I simply write in nines and fill in the *p's.* Because I type poorly and must concentrate on the typing itself, I revise little. What revisions I make are almost all stylistic, not substantive. These I pencil in before giving the essay to a professional typist at the university.

By the time I receive the essay back from the typist, I have usually begun another essay, and I have to force myself to read through it for errors and then submit it for publication. Sometimes an essay will sit on my desk for six weeks before I mail it out, and even then my accompanying letter is carelessly spontaneous, nothing like the essay itself. Often I type the letter at my desk in the afternoon while the children watch "Sesame Street" or "Mr. Rogers' Neighborhood." The resulting correspondence sometimes leads to matter for other essays. Last year a quarterly sent back an essay unread, an editorial assistant having marked grammatical errors in my letter after which he graded it, giving it a C+. Accompanying a rejection from another journal was a very pleasant note. After writing that she enjoyed the essay, although noting it wasn't suitable for her magazine, the editor suggested that in the future when I submitted essays for publication "perhaps it would be to your advantage if you did not include the rejection slip from the magazine to which you previously offered your article." Of course if my essays were never published, I would not enjoy such notes. Happily, though, most of my essays get published, and tonight despite the pain, I will be in bed, reading through my notebooks, and planning an essay about the quaking bog on the farm in Nova Scotia.

Faith of the Father

O n weekdays Campbell's store was the center of life in the
little Virginia town in which I spent summers and then Christmas and occasionally Easter vacations. The post office was in a
corner of the store, and the train station was across the road. In the
morning men gathered on Campbell's porch and drank coffee while
they waited for the train to Richmond. Late in the afternoon, families
appeared. While waiting for their husbands, women bought groceries, mailed letters, and visited with one another. Children ate cups
of ice cream and played in the woods behind the store. Sometimes
a work train was on the siding, and the engineer filled his cab with
children and took them for short trips down the track. On weekends
life shifted from the store to St. Paul's Church. Built in a grove of
pine trees in the nineteenth century, St. Paul's was a small, white
clapboard building. A Sunday School wing added to the church in
the 1920s jutted out into the graveyard. Beyond the graveyard was
a field in which picnics were held and on the Fourth of July, the
yearly Donkey Softball Game was played.

St. Paul's was familial and comfortable. Only a hundred people
attended regularly, and everyone knew everyone else and his business. What was private became public after the service as people
gathered outside and talked for half an hour before going home to
lunch. Behind the altar inside the church was a stained glass window
showing Christ's ascension to heaven. A red carpet ran down the
middle aisle, and worn, gold cushions covered the pews. On the
walls were plaques in memory of parishioners killed in foreign wars
or who had made large donations to the building fund. In summer
the minister put fans out on the pews. Donated by a local undertaker,
the fans were shaped like spades. On them, besides the undertaker's
name and telephone number, were pictures of Christ performing
miracles: walking on water, healing the lame, and raising Lazarus
from the dead.

Holidays and funerals were special at St. Paul's. Funerals were occasions for reminiscing and telling stories. When an irascible old lady died and her daughter had "Gone to Jesus" inscribed on her tombstone, her son-in-law was heard to say "poor Jesus"—or so the tale went at the funeral. Christmas Eve was always cold and snow usually fell. Inside the church at midnight, though, all was cheery and warm as the congregation sang the great Christmas hymns: "O Come, All Ye Faithful," "The First Noel," "O Little Town of Bethlehem," and "Hark! The Herald Angels Sing." The last hymn was "Silent Night." The service did not follow the prayer book; inspired by Christmas and eggnog, the congregation came to sing, not to pray. Bourbon was in the air, and when the altar boy lit the candles, it seemed a miracle that the first spark didn't send us all to heaven in a blue flame.

Easter was almost more joyous than Christmas. Men stuck greenery into their lapels and women blossomed in bright bonnets, some ordering hats not simply from Richmond but from Baltimore and Philadelphia. On a farm outside town lived Miss Emma and Miss Ida Catlin. Miss Emma was the practical sister, running the farm and bringing order wherever she went. Unlike Miss Emma, Miss Ida was shy. She read poetry and raised guinea fowl and at parties sat silently in a corner. Only on Easter was she outgoing; then like a day lily she bloomed triumphantly. No one else's Easter bonnet ever matched hers, and the congregation eagerly awaited her entrance which she always made just before the first hymn.

One year Miss Ida found a catalogue from a New York store which advertised hats and their accessories. For ten to twenty-five cents ladies could buy artificial flowers to stick into their bonnets. Miss Ida bought a counter full, and that Easter her head resembled a summer garden in bloom. Daffodils, zinnias, and black-eyed Susans hung yellow and red around the brim of her hat while in the middle stood a magnificent pink peony.

In all his glory Solomon could not have matched Miss Ida's bonnet. The congregation could not take its eyes off it; even the minister had trouble concentrating on his sermon. After the last hymn, everyone hurried out of the church, eager to get a better look at Miss Ida's hat. As she came out, the altar boy began ringing the bell. Alas, the noise frightened pigeons who had recently begun to nest and they shot out of the steeple. The congregation scattered, but the flowers on Miss Ida's hat hung over her eyes, and she did not see the pigeons until it was too late and the peony had been ruined.

Miss Ida acted like nothing had happened. She greeted everyone and asked about their health and the health of absent family members. People tried not to look at her hat but were not very successful. For two Sundays Miss Ida's "accident" was the main subject of after-church conversation; then it was forgotten for almost a year. But, as Easter approached again, people remembered the hat. They wondered what Miss Ida would wear to church. Some people speculated that since she was a shy, poetic person, she wouldn't come. Even the minister had doubts. To reassure Miss Ida, he and his sons borrowed ladders two weeks before Easter, and climbing to the top of the steeple, chased the pigeons away and sealed off their nesting place with chicken wire.

Easter Sunday seemed to confirm the fears of those who doubted Miss Ida would appear. The choir assembled in the rear of the church without her. Half-heartedly the congregation sang the processional hymn, "Hail Thee, Festival Day." Miss Ida's absence had taken something bright from our lives, and as we sat down after singing, Easter seemed sadly ordinary. We were people of little faith. Just as the minister reached the altar and turned to face us, there was a stir at the back of the church. Silently the minister raised his right hand and pointed toward the door. Miss Ida had arrived. She was wearing the same hat she wore the year before; only the peony was missing. In its place was a wonderful sunflower; from one side hung a black and yellow garden spider building a web, while fluttering above was a mourning cloak, black wings, dotted with blue and a yellow border running around the edges. Our hearts leaped up, and at the end of the service people in Richmond must have heard us singing "Christ The Lord Is Risen Today."

St. Paul's was the church of my childhood, that storied time when I thought little about religion but knew that Jesus loved me, yes, because the Bible told me so. In the Morning Prayer of life I mixed faith and fairy tale, thinking God a kindly giant, holding in his hands, as the song put it, the corners of the earth and the strength of the hills. Thirty years have passed since I last saw St. Paul's, and I have come down from the cool upland pastures and the safe fold of childhood to the hot lowlands. Instead of being neatly tucked away in a huge hand, the world now seems to bound erratically, smooth and slippery, forever beyond the grasp of even the most magical deity. Would that it were not so, and my imagination could find a way through his gates, as the psalm says, with thanksgiving. Often I wonder what happened to the "faith of our fathers." Why if it endured dungeon, fire, and sword in others, did it weaken so within me?

For me religion is a matter of story and community, a congregation rising together to look at an Easter bonnet, unconsciously seeing it an emblem of hope and vitality, indeed of the Resurrection itself. For me religion ought to be more concerned with people than ideas, creating soft feeling rather than sharp thought. Often I associate religion with small, backwater towns in which tale binds folk one to another. Here in a university in which people are separated by idea rather than linked by story, religion doesn't have a natural place. In the absence of community, ceremony becomes important. Changeable and always controversial, subject to dispassionate analysis, ceremony doesn't tie people together like accounts of pigeons and peonies and thus doesn't promote good feeling and finally love for this world and hope for the next. Often when I am discouraged I turn for sustenance, not to formal faith with articled ceremony but to memory, a chalice winey with story.

Not long ago I thought about Beagon Hackett, a Baptist minister in Carthage, Tennessee. Born in Bagdad in Jackson County, Beagon answered the call early in life. Before he was sixteen, he had preached in all the little towns in Jackson County: Antioch, Nameless, Mc-Coinsville, Liberty, and Gum Springs. Although he was popular in country churches, Beagon's specialty was the all-day revival, picnic, and baptizing, usually held back in the woods near places like Seven Knobs, Booger Hill, Backbone Ridge, Chigger Hollow, and Twelve Corners. Beagon made such a name that the big Baptist church in Carthage selected him as minister. In Carthage, Beagon tempered his faith to suit the mood of the county seat. Only once a year did he hold a meeting out-of-doors. For his first four or five years in Carthage, he led a revival near Dripping Rock Bluff across Hell Bend on the Caney Fork River, the spot being selected for name not location.

The narrows of the river were swift and deep, and crossing Hell Bend was dangerous, a danger Beagon celebrated, first reminding the faithful that Jesus was a fisher of men and then buoying their spirits up on a raft of watery Christian song: "Shall We Gather at the River," "The Rock that is Higher than I," and "Sweet By and

By." Beagon's meetings across the Caney Fork were a success, with people traveling from as far as Macon and Trousdale counties to be baptized. But then one spring Gummert Capron or Doodlebug Healy, depending on whose memory is accurate, became frightened in mid-river and tipping over a rowboat changed "Throw Out the Life-Line" from word to deed. If Hosmer Nye had not grabbed Clara Jakeways by the hair, the dark waters, as the hymn puts it, would have swept her to eternity's shore. As it turned out Clara's salvation turned into romance, and three months later she and Hosmer were married, much to the disappointment of Silas Jakeways who owned a sawmill and the Eagle Iron Works and who disapproved of Hosmer, until that time an itinerant bricklayer. Clara, Silas was reported to have said, would "have been better off if love hadn't lifted her from the deep to become the wife of a no-account." Whatever the case, however, Beagon never led another revival across Hell Bend; instead, he stayed dry on the Carthage side of the Caney Fork, once a year holding a temperate affair, more Sunday outing than revival, on Myers Bottom.

After Beagon had been in Carthage for twenty years, he grew heavy and dignified. No longer would he preside at river baptizings. In his church he erected, as Silas Jakeways said, "a marble birdbath," a baptismal font, copied from one he had seen in an Episcopal church at Monteagle. In Carthage, though, pretension was always liable to be tipped òver, if not by simple-minded folk like Gummert Capron or Doodlebug Healy, then by daily life. Addicted to drink, Horace Armitage, the disreputable brother of Benbow Armitage, occasionally cut hair at King's Barber Shop. One morning after a long night of carousing at Enos Mayfield's in South Carthage, Horace was a bit shaky, and while shaving Beagon cut him slightly on the chin. "That's what comes of taking too much to drink," said Beagon, holding a towel to his chin. "Yes, sir, Reverend," Horace replied, "Alcohol does make the skin tender."

The account of Beagon and Horace is itself tender, making me feel good about religion. When religion is a matter of people and story, it attracts me. In contrast regulation has often repulsed me. In grammar school I was the only one of my Episcopal friends who did not become an acolyte. Years later at Sewanee I disapproved of compulsory chapel and each fall semester attended church for seventy days in a row to rid myself of the year's requirement. I approved when students read the *Daily Worker* in church to protest compulsory chapel. They went too far, however, when taking scotch, soda, an ice bucket, and silver mint julep cups to Evensong, they sat in the back of the church and mixed drinks. No longer does Sewanee require church attendance, and the Episcopal church itself has changed, too much, I'm afraid, for my liking. No one's character is consistent, however, and despite my disapproval of hard rule and line, some structure, particularly that which increases familiarity and makes a person comfortable, seems good. Before the latest revision of the Prayer Book, I could enter almost any Episcopal church in the country and feel at home. Now as I stumble through the prayers, resisting change and breaking prose on every line, I feel out of place, a stranger apart from community, resentful and eager to criticize. For my children I approve structure and send them to Sunday school. He was satisfied, Josh Billings wrote, that every man who lied for fun would eventually lie for wages. Some discipline and a few lessons early in life will help the children. Although they probably won't become acolytes, maybe habit will be stamped upon them, and they won't lie or do worse for wages.

Sometimes I think the Episcopal church like the landscape of our country is in the hands of developers. Wetlands are drained, and crisp, functional buildings rise where cattails once bent in the breeze, dragonflies clinging to them like ancient liturgies, awkward but somehow rich and alluring. In part, I suppose, my disenchantment with religion resembles that of the dreamer, disappointed to discover that his beloved is mere flesh. I wanted more than religion could accomplish. I wanted religion to make man better than he is capable of being. Even worse, commitment to a faith, I saw in the Holy Land, more often than not does not elevate but lowers. Crushed between the ideals of stony doctrine, people bleed. "We saw the buildings pulled down," wrote a Syrian student who fled the Golan Heights in 1973; "we saw the people killed. We saw our house pulled down. We left the city. We left everything there. Our city was occupied. I was so sad. I left my dolls. I left my small room. I was afread. I could not forget this picture. It left a bitter wound in my heart. I could not recognize it at the time. I was too young. It is afread me a long time later."

Not simply religion's inability to patch up pitiful, flawed human-ity, but its tendency to destroy community, crushing dolls under the mechanical tread of doctrine, has long been lamented. In almost tacit recognition of such weakness, divines have preached otherworldliness, urging the downtrodden and the suffering to look to heaven for justice and decency. Too often whatever is is wrong, and when doing research for a study of early children's books, most of which were religious, time and again I was bothered by tales preaching stolid acceptance of misfortune. In Samuel Pratt's *The Paternal Present* (1795) appeared the story of Nahamir, an account which taught children to be satisfied with their lots in life because they were ordained by God. "Old, hunch-backed, lame, crippled" and "half-starved," Nahamir, Pratt wrote, begged alms before the gates of Bagdad. Nahamir had once been handsome and had a wife and six children, but suddenly his family died and a "hideous bunch of superfluous flesh" appeared on his shoulders. Then in an accident he lost an eye; following this misfortune, he tumbled down a stairwell and broke a leg while going to aid a small boy who was being beaten. Later feeling compassion for an old man slumped over by the side of the road, he stopped to offer assistance. When Nahamir bent down to help him, the old man drew a sabre and sliced off Nahamir's right arm. Finally Nahamir's business failed and his friends forsook him.

Somewhat understandably, at least from my point of view, Nahamir thought himself unfortunate. One day as he lamented his fate, an angel appeared and rebuked him, telling him his torments were blessings. When Nahamir asked for an explanation, the angel observed that Nahamir survived when his family died. In truth, the angel said, the deaths of Nahamir's wife and children were examples of "the benevolence of heaven." If they had lived, the children would have been disobedient and Nahamir's wife would have betrayed him. Moreover, the loss of his good looks had preserved Nahamir's life; if he had remained handsome, the angel said, he would have been involved in "a scandalous intrigue" and on its discovery would have been impaled. Even the loss of his eye was fortunate; unknown to Nahamir, the Cailiff wanted to make him a harem guard. "Certain ceremonies would have been necessary" but the Cailiff rejected the idea when Nahamir lost an eye. In falling down the staircase, the angel next recounted, Nahamir had been fortunate to break only one leg. The loss of his right arm was also a blessing; at a feast sometime later, the angel reminded Nahamir, he had been insulted. If he had not lost his arm, he would have drawn a sabre and committed a mortal sin. Even the bankruptcy was fortunate, for Nahamir would have used wealth in a detestable manner and be-

come "an horror to thyself, and a disgrace to human nature."
"Suffer patiently," the angel told Nahamir, "after death, thou shalt
commence a new career, where every happiness shall be complete
and uninterrupted." The angel convinced Nahamir that he was
fortunate, and, satisfied with his lot, Nahamir returned to begging,
thanking "heaven with all his heart that he was old, deformed,
blind, and crippled, and limping, without fortune, without a wife,
and without children."

Strangely although the tale bothers me, it has some appeal, particularly as I look about and see a society rushing madly to lay up
treasures where moth and rust corrupt. Blessed, I want to believe,
are the poor in spirit, if the phrase refers to those who seem dull
and unambitious because the simple satisfies them and glitter does
not attract them. Vicki and I and the children spent New Year's
with her parents in Princeton, a town in which everything seems for
sale. Between Washington Road and the home of Vicki's parents on
Linden Lane, a matter of three or four short blocks, I counted the
offices of eight realtors. Like bees about a hive, Mercedes cluster
around Palmer Square, its cell-like shops fragrant and dripping with
expensive honey. With imported tea kettles marked at eighty-five
dollars, prices in Kitchen Capers are too highly seasoned for the
Bible's "salt of the earth." Thoughts focused only on raiment, white
hunter impersonators wander through Banana Republic, planning
expeditions to Bucks County, Pennsylvania, for dinner. Across Nas-
sau Street even the university, its buildings stony and heavy, seems
insubstantial. Faculty appointments are "media events," and instead
of a community of teachers, some of whom are scholars, the university promotes itself as a galaxy of stars, the stuff of publicity not
people. The sweets of Princeton are ever-alluring, however, and
resisting them is almost impossible. Munching on a chocolate muffin, I told Vicki that I wanted the children to attend Princeton,
although the school is priced far beyond our means. "Princeton will
give them tone," I said, "and make them aware of possibilities."
And in truth not all Princeton is show. Apart from the bustle of
the shops, the chapel stands, empty, but nevertheless dignified and
substantial.

Of course a community of people and tales still exists in Princeton.
Unfortunately it resembles St. Paul's, a part of my childhood rarely
touching everyday life. Almost as tender as Beagon's chin are memories of the classes I took, taught, to be sure, by learned but still

ordinary folk: the man from Texas who pushed Dr. Johnson aside one day and said that when he was young he found it difficult to choose between books and baseball. Both, he said, offered ways out of his small town, and he was a good baseball player, potentially, he thought, a better second baseman than scholar. Then there was the Miltonist who once a semester would turn from Eden to Oklahoma and tell tales of his schooling, inevitably describing how friends in medical school circumcised each other and then suffered painful inconvenience when they got erections and their stitches popped loose. In the telling, Oklahoma seemed a richer garden than Milton's Eden, a place of broken stitches and bursting with hope, a place which one left, not solitary like Adam and Eve with "wandering steps and slow," but jauntily, apple in hand and stories on the tongue.

Perhaps behind vital education and religion lies not idea, a trumpet sounding before it, but modest, humanizing tale. Particularly appealing to me are creation stories. In one of my favorites the apple wasn't forbidden but was instead the loveliest tree in Eden, its branches moving in the breeze sweeter than harps. Drawn by the music on the wind and fragrance like beds of spices, Adam tried to pluck an apple from the tree. The stem of the apple was thick, however, and Adam had to slice through it using a sharp stone he found on the ground. After cutting off an apple, Adam wiped the stone on his thigh, in the process scratching himself and letting a drop of apple juice seep under his skin. Almost immediately the stone became a garnet, and Adam's thigh began to swell. Nine days later his thigh split open, giving birth to Eve, her breasts full, the ends red like apples and the nipples thick as stems.

In contrast to that of the serpent and Eve, this story is one of healthy appetite and love, not fear and temptation. The heaven it leads me to is not that of Revelation, a New Jerusalem surrounded by shining, bejeweled walls, smacking of exclusion and chilled affluence, a Palmer Square of the clouds in which kings of commerce tread narrow, golden paths. Not for me a Fabergé heaven with gates of pearl, walls of jasper, and glassy domes spun from gold. My heaven is as large as breath and, like an affectionate bride awaiting her husband, is adorned with goodly weeds—literally weeds, plants of wayside and gully, abandoned pasture and hilly slope, the common, often over-looked plants of my New England: pigweed, scoke, bull rattle, sleepy catchfly, fleabane, steeplebush, wild carrot, cranesbill, winter sweet, butter-and-eggs, Indian tobacco, and even beggar ticks and burdock. The heaven of my dream is a simple place, hospitable to plants and people of little cultivation. Absent is doctrine. The product of harrowing and ploughing, fertilizing and pruning, doctrine disrupts peaceable kingdoms. Without roots in people and stories, it draws sustenance from abstraction and like a pale horse tramples the meek and the merciful. Fifteen years ago in Jordan, a Moslem fundamentalist told me that only a conflagration in which forty million people were killed could cleanse "the Arab nation." From its ashes, he said, Islam would rise, purified and glorious.

The mind is weak and doctrinal certainty enticing. In the hot embrace of doctrine, gentle people often become zealots, ready to level the towers of Cairo or fight over the Trinity, Predestination and Election, and Salvation by Faith or Works. In trying to become saints they forget humanity and become beasts. My fear of the seductive wiles of doctrine has driven me from formal faith and indeed from any kind of advocacy sustained by an abstraction. Partly as a consequence I am a conscious trifler. The man down to trifles is rarely up to no good, and passing days toying with matters of little concern, I let other people and the world spin peacefully along.

Most recently slogans on license plates have caught my attention, and I have written letters to governors about them. "Dear Mr. Casey," my letter to the governor of Pennsylvania begins, "*You've Got a Friend in Pennsylvania* made me feel wonderful when I first saw it. I was on my way back from having my piles chopped out at the hospital. Dr. Jurgen here in Willimantic did it. He chops out most of the piles in this part of Connecticut. He is old, and some folks say he ought to stick to sinuses and leave behinds alone. But he did a fine job on me and my bottom is just as rosy as a baby's cheek. Before, it was wrinkled up like a nest of tent caterpillars. Anyway, I have never been to Pennsylvania, and I didn't think anyone down there even knew me, much less was my friend, and all the way down the road I thought about the get-well card my friend must have sent and which would be waiting for me at home on the commode. That's where I keep all my cards because I just don't look at them once and then throw them away. No, I look at them again and again, each morning, don't you know, between eight and eight twenty-five, though I ought to say that since this operation I haven't kept so close to my schedule. I'm sure you can understand. Anyway, governor, you can imagine my disappointment when I got home, and there was no card from my friend. What sort of friend is that, governor, that don't write when a person gets her butthole damn near tore off. I call that friend, governor, a shitass, and I'm writing to you to find me a new friend."

To Governor Hunt of Alabama I wrote a shorter letter. "Dear Mr. Hunt," it begins, "I'm Professor of Internal Medicine here in New Haven at the Yale Medical School and, as you might guess, am just a little bit interested in things anatomical. Recently I saw the Alabama license plate with *Heart of Dixie* written on it and that started me to thinking. Governor, why the heart of Dixie? Why not the liver or the spleen or maybe even the fundament? I talked to one of the big shots at the university around here and he said that as far as he was concerned Alabama was the 'Prick of Dixie.' He votes Republican and is a man whose opinion I respect. He is always dispassionate, and I ought to say right now that he can't be accused of prejudice. He wasn't, I am prepared to testify, born in Alabama, but Arkansas, Fort Smith, I believe."

Before mailing the letters I showed them to my friend Grahame. "Great God Almighty, Sam," he said; "you can't mail these. Write all you want about Beagon Hackett and religion. Nobody gives a hoot in hell about that sort of stuff. But if you mail these letters and somebody finds out you wrote them, you'll be fired. The Governor of Alabama will call the Governor of Connecticut and say you wrote him that the state was full of pricks. What would you do then?" "Well," I said, "I'd apologize and apologize publicly, saying I was wrong to insinuate that the fine citizens of Alabama were pricks. Recently, I'd say, I had met a splendid woman from Gasden who told me there wasn't a prick worth a damn in the whole state and that's why she moved to New England."

I haven't mailed the letters yet. It's not that I am frightened of losing my job, but that something important came up. Since birth my little girl Eliza has been sickly. She coughs terribly; her lungs get congested, and twice she has been in the hospital, once under an oxygen tent. Even when she looks well, her nose runs like a river. When she got sick again this past December, the doctor decided to run tests on her. Scheduled last, three weeks after the others, was the sweat test for cystic fibrosis. My love for Eliza knows no bounds, and as I thought about the possibility of her having a fatal illness, the world seemed to collapse like Jericho around me, my fine wordy constructs crashing silently into dusty nothingness. And so like many another father, frightened for a child and scared of life, I prayed. Living still in spite of all my ponderings, the old faith supported me. Then after three weeks Eliza took the test, and my heaviness turned to joy. What a privilege it was, though, once again to carry everything to God in prayer.

These Essays, My Life

"How are they fixed for dogcatchers up there," Father asked after I told him I resigned from the school board. "I am sure," Vicki began after I told her, "there have been shorter political careers, but . . . ." I had been on the board for one hundred days from my election on the third of November until my resignation on the eleventh of February. It was long enough; the essay in politics was over and I was ready for something else. Later when I thought about things, I realized that if I wrote novels or lyric poems, almost anything other than essays, I might not have resigned. Unlike the essayist for whom life is a patchwork affair, the novelist sees continuity of event. Instead of laboring for the essayist's simplicity and momentary sense of things, the novelist spins cause into effect, turning the low comedy of daily life into complexity. If the virtue of the novel was commitment, I thought, that of the lyric poem was enthusiasm. Of course imagining myself a poet was ridiculous. There is nothing lyrical in my nature. My language is plain, and my clothes are unadorned and musty at best. As for my love calls, I am afraid they are not poetic. I'm the sort of fellow who gargles once or twice a week before bed, then a bit later puts his book down, raises himself on his elbows and turning to his mate says, "How about it, old girl?"

The character of the essayist differs from that of the novelist. Essayists don't believe in anything except, perhaps, the inevitability of change. As life is fragile so is truth, and the essayist writes essays in part because the form like happiness itself is brief. Believing in the mortality of everything, essayists are pessimistic and melancholy. Often they are sad people, and although they try to stop time with pencils, they know that words like leaves can be blown away by a single dark day. Seeing change as the primary condition of life, essayists are not ambitious and rarely commit themselves to causes. Consequently they are not zealous or cunning. Knowing that today will soon be yesterday and a different tomorrow forever hurries forward, they are not revengeful. They are curious but impractical, incapable of devoting long hours to mastering a skill. Since truth changes rapidly, they are sentimentalists, not realists. Dreaming of different and better worlds, they judge the hard objectivity of the realist as false and suspect grandiose plans puffed high on piles of survey and study. For that matter, they suspect education itself, thinking most of its claims pishposh, self-serving boosterism, not fact.

Because they believe in little they are playful, treating words as toys. Incapable of being overly serious or solemn, they are poor lovers. Often, however, they are conversationalists, outspoken where others are conventionally pious. From words reputations flow and more often than not they become known as eccentric. Although they frequently pride themselves on their individualism, they respect ceremony, hoping always that form and order can hold wild change off until tomorrow. Not experimental, they are conservative socially and though they think moral pronouncements silly, they live conventional lives and make good, if slightly dull and occasionally embarrassing, mates. More quick-witted and curious than thoughtful, they are interested in links between things, rather than the structures upon which things are raised. And lastly, if my little Eliza is right, and on such matters she generally is right, they are good-looking. "Daddy," she said just the other morning, throwing her arms around my neck, "you are so handsome; you are my sweetheart."

If the virtues of the novel and the lyric poem are commitment and enthusiasm respectively, that of the essay is temperance, leading to liberty. Holding moderation to be an eminent virtue, the essayist controls his enthusiasms and rarely devotes much of himself to a particular subject. When interest wears thin or the subject calls for substantial commitment, the essayist simply packs his pencils and shifts his eye to something else. Three years ago I began planting flowers, explaining to friends that although I was beyond blooming my yard was not. Flowers in a garden, though, last longer than those in the mind. This spring rust has infected my interest, and thrips have gnawed at my energy. I began gardening eagerly, reading books and catalogues and joining both the American Iris and American Daffodil societies. Without much effort I learned a lot about flowers, in the process transforming my yard from a still gray to currents of colors: pinks, yellows, oranges, purples splashing over and through each other, bright in the day like rain falling in the sunlight. Unfortunately I have gone about as far as simple reading and planting can carry me. What lies ahead is hard study of landscape gardening and the real culture of flowers, that stage beyond sticking rhizomes and bulbs into the ground, the stage in which one begins to hybridize, learning the differences between anthers and stigmas, perianth tubes and spathes.

This past December I received a questionnaire from the Connecticut chapter of the American Iris Society. In filling it out I explained that I had lost interest in Iris. "I, the devoted husband and father," had a philandering span of attention. Now that I had bedded fifty or so rhizomes, my eye, I wrote, was drawn beyond the privet hedge toward softer, greener pastures. Literally green pastures—while my interest in particular flowers had waned, concern for the environment of my plot of Connecticut had grown. Ponds are being filled, trees felled, hills leveled, and where corn once grew yellow and mockingbirds darted, alive with song and promise, condominiums rise, heavy and dead. Sight and heart are being diminished almost everywhere, it seems, in this country. "Tennessee," a minister who reviewed one of my books wrote me, "has fallen victim to tribes of developers. They ravage our land so that it is not fit to nourish people or jonquils. How they hate life and the Creator of it!" "Look," my friend David said to me recently, "there is nothing you can do about 'progress.' Stick to Iris. The only thing that can stop the destruction of the world is a nuclear war, and we are bound to have one before long. With luck man will be eradicated, and the earth will have a chance."

David is a realist and is probably right. As an essayist, I'm a sentimentalist and have gotten myself appointed by local Republicans to their environmental watch committee. Would that my participation will be long and vigorous. In truth, however, I know my involvement will soon fall away like the roots of Iris infected with scorch. Essayists are private, contemplative people. Occasionally, though, they become curious about the ways of the world and wandering beyond their gardens turn over stones, momentarily disturbing all sorts of strange doings. After a short time, however, they inevitably withdraw into domesticity. Instead of the hard labor of making ways through the rocky landscape of buying and selling they prefer the gentler pleasure of ranging through the recesses of their own minds.

For an older writer, not willing to devote time or perhaps unable to stick to a subject, the essay is a congenial form. If I had started writing earlier, I might have tried my hand at the novel. Thirty years ago I was persistent and practically unaware of time. Sewanee, my college, required students to wear coats to class and to attend compulsory chapel. Before classes began my first year, I visited a coat factory in Decherd, Tennessee, and for seventeen dollars and forty-one cents bought a "Flambeau," a brown checkered jacket which I later renamed "the Decherd Special." For my three years at Sewanee, I wore the coat everyday, including Saturdays and Sundays. On the rare occasion when it was cleaned, I made certain to get one-hour cleaning. Despite friends who urged me to vary my dress, I stuck to the Decherd Special, only putting it aside for graduation. Not only do I now lack the persistence to continue any activity for a longish time, although the activity is more serious than slipping into a jacket, but my memory is so poor that I can barely remember clothes from one night to the next morning, much less thoughts. This past Sunday Bill, an old friend from Nashville, telephoned to thank me for sending him my last book. In part the book was about growing up in Nashville, and Bill recognized many of the stories. Why, though, he wondered, had I not included an account of "the rock." When I asked what rock, he said, "the one you used to lift in the front yard to build up your muscles—you know before you got barbells." I remembered the barbells and muscles vaguely, but the rock had turned to gravel and washed out of memory.

My memory, alas, is as great a philanderer as my attention. Instead, though, of memory's remaining faithful to event, events forsake it, forcing memory to whore after false recollection. Last summer I attended the Bread Loaf Writers' Conference in Vermont. Late one afternoon I joined a group of acquaintances on the porch of the Bread Loaf Inn. "Sam," one of them said as I pulled up a chair, "we were just talking about you. I want you to tell everybody what you did with the two telescopes at Dartmouth that time you had drinks at the home of the chairman of the English department. It's an astonishing, hilarious story." Funny the story may have been, but I was the one astonished; I remembered nothing about it. To be sure the head of the English department owned a couple of telescopes. But what the hell, I wondered, could I have done with them? What could anyone do with two telescopes except look at stars? In purpler Dartmouth days, I was inventive but not with telescopes. I have hazy recollections of fruit and feather evenings, so hazy that I am not certain they actually occurred, and if they did occur, the fruits, as I now think about them, might just as well have been vegetables, turnips instead of grapes, eggplant rather than peaches. Still, despite a good record as a teacher and writer, Dartmouth fired me a couple of years later. Perhaps, I thought as I sat down on the porch, telescopes had something to do with it. "No, Wyatt," I said, shaking my head solemnly, "you know I can't tell that story." "Well," he said, "I guess you are right, but it's a shame."

Getting bounced out of Dartmouth wasn't a shame, but a blessing. Still, that, if I remember much about it, is the stuff of another essay. For the writer who has occasional flashes of recollection and whose mind works by association, the essay is an ideal literary form. In an essay association runs freely, not snagging on plot, its eddies and swirls mirroring the currents of the essayist's mind, or on another plane, the odd ebb and flow of life itself. As he examined his birthday presents last month, Edward, who is five, suddenly became thoughtful. Putting down Lion-O, a hero of the Thundercats, a heavily muscled body builder with light orange skin and dark orange windswept hair, wearing blue boots, an undershirt with the front cut away, a blue jockey strap, and a weightlifter's belt with a panther on the buckle—and I ought to add, putting Lion-O down carefully, a good distance from the evil Skeletor, a blue chap with bandy legs, bat wings on his battle garb and a greenish skull for a head—Edward turned to me and said, "Daddy, did you play with Masters of the Universe toys when you were a child?" After I said no, he asked what I played with, and for a moment I saw myself at five, a little boy in short pants, clutching a battered stuffed animal, a muskrat, Nurse Jane Fuzzy Wuzzy from the Uncle Wiggily stories. I loved stuffed animals, and Mother told me that once while I was in the elevator in the old Jefferson Hotel in Richmond the singer Lily Pons entered. She wore a long fur coat, and on seeing it a beatific expression broke across my face and reaching out I stroked the coat, saying "dog, oh dog—dog, oh dog." Like so much, though, that clings in memory I don't remember Lily Pons or the elevator. What I remember is Mother's story and, then, the alligators in the lobby of the Jefferson. For three months each winter my grandfather moved from the country into the Jefferson Hotel. When Mother and I visited, I spent much time in the lobby. There in tiled pools surrounded by green ferns in tubs were two or three small alligators.

Besides Nurse Jane, I remember toy soldiers. One of Father's friends who had two daughters gave me his collection of artillery and toy soldiers. Camouflaged, their barrels grayish and their carriages splotched with red, yellow, and green, some of the cannons resembled French 75s. Others, manufactured by Marklin in Germany, were siege guns with heavy treads on their wheels and long, thick barrels. From Britain came whippet tanks. Summer blue and top-heavy, they looked gawky and silly, a bit like newly hatched puffins. Most of my soldiers also came from Britain: Bengal Lancers astride black horses, yellow pendants streaming from their lances; swordsmen in red and black riding ponderous white horses; bagpipers, in fact Highlanders of all sorts in kilts of various colors, the favorite combination being green and yellow; Beefeaters, on their heads black hats like hornets' nests; the French poilu wearing his ridged helmet and kneeling behind a machine gun; Legionnaires, no longer sandy or scruffy, but painted silver and red by me; and then Arabs and Confederates, all manufactured in Britain. On ridges and in trenches and craters in the back yard, my soldiers fought across the western front, along the Marne, then at Ypres, Verdun, the Somme, Passchendaele. The names of battles, I suppose, must have come later, albeit they now seem to have been with me as long as the soldiers. Much as I thrust Confederate sharpshooters into trenches to stem the German advances at Lys without regard to history, so I am no longer capable of making fine distinctions about time.

Essayists rarely concern themselves with fine distinctions. Smacking of the artificial, careful distinctions seem imposed. In the mind the significant and the insignificant jumble roughly together. Unlike more formal writing which forces tale and recollection into highly wrought forms, the essay is comparatively unstructured. In its reliance upon association, that higgledy-piggledy rush of the significant and the insignificant, the essay may reflect the reality of thought more accurately than other kinds of writing. When, for example, anyone mentions Gilbert and Sullivan in my presence, I invariably recall an incident which occurred during a performance of *Iolanthe* at Sadler's Wells in London. While the fairies pranced about on the stage "tripping hither, tripping thither," a woman suddenly rose out of her seat in the sixth row. Turning to her companion, she drew in a deep breath and then yelled "Sucks to you," whereupon she strode out of the theater and, I presume, into the night, with, as the fairies put it in the next line, no one knowing why or whither. Always, however, after this recollection, memorable only because hot anger was out of place in an evening devoted to peers, peris, and After Eight mints, I remember something which has made a great difference to my life, my courtship of Vicki. Years ago Vicki's father and I were both in London working on books. One afternoon he told me his daughter was lonely and asked me to take her out. I did not know what to do with a quiet twenty-one-year-old girl until I thought of Gilbert and Sullivan. The next week we saw *The Yeoman of the Guard*, the week after *The Mikado* and then *Ruddigore*. Until the intermission following the first act of *Ruddigore*, Vicki and I were just friends, but then as I turned from the bar, glasses of wine in my hands, and saw Vicki pushing through the lobby toward me looking like Rose Maybud, softer than "the warm west wind" and sweeter than "the new-mown hay," everything changed—"sing hey, Lackaday."

Of course age and failing memory may not be responsible for the essay's appeal to me. I may simply be the essay type. If, as many folktales recount, not even a good fairy can completely change a character, the essay would, I suppose, have attracted me, no matter what books I bedded down with in school. One of my favorite fairy tales stresses the impossibility of changing personality. In the story, a kindly rat snake saves a toad from a cruel rat. Although the rat does not like to eat toad, he plans to torture it to death, out of meanness. When the toad begs for mercy, the rat laughs loudly and harshly, waking the snake who pities the toad and saves his life. On being set free from the rat, the toad tells the snake he will never forget her and then disappears under a rock. Unknown to the snake, the toad is an enchanted prince, and after some narrative hopping about and kindness to mosquitos, the toad is changed back into a human by a good fairy. On his reappearance the prince's father orders him to marry. Although all the maidens in the kingdom are presented to him, some with "eyes like stars" and others with "hair silver over their shoulders like a waterfall," the prince does not fall in love. Instead he dreams about the snake who saved his life and wasting away seems destined for an early grave until, happily, the good fairy reappears, riding in a golden chariot. With her is the most beautiful girl ever seen in the kingdom. She is, of course, the snake transformed, her outward beauty simply a visible sign of her inner virtue. The prince recognizes his love and the couple marry, after which a great wedding feast is served. All goes well until dessert. Then just after the candles are snuffed out and a huge baked Alaska is rolled flaming into the hall, a mouse runs down the table. As the mouse passes in front of the princess, she twists about on her throne, runs her tongue over her upper lip, and hisses. Because the room is dark and the dessert sizzling, no one except the prince notices. The next day he goes to the market and, buying a cartload of cats, returns home and turns them loose. Shortly thereafter all rodents disappear from the castle. Never again does the princess hiss in public, and she and the prince live happily ever after.

In truth I may have been born an essayist. Although vision is short, pride or presumption makes us declare it long. Its length reflecting brevity of vision, the essay does not make large intellectual claims. For my part I enjoy writing about the moment. Although sometimes revealing, moments are never so grand as truths. I like describing, for example, the way a parent goes into a child's room late at night and looking down suddenly becomes frightened, wondering if the child is still alive. How many times during the first three or four years of a child's life will a parent slip a finger under a nose to see if his baby is still breathing? During that moment when the parent bends over the bed supported by a hand on a railing or mattress, love and fear block out the rest of life. In this moment is the stuff of the essay, not the great world's posturing and declaiming, but a child's bedroom: wallpaper lined with buttercups and bouquets of pink roses and bachelor's-buttons; a tea set scattered across the floor, on the plates a freckled little girl wearing a straw hat and standing in front of an apple tree red with fruit; hanging in the window a merry-go-round of fat, smiling bears made by a great-aunt; under a dressing table a jigsaw puzzle of Lady LovelyLocks and the Pixietails, these last being pudgy squirrels with ribbons on their heads and long, colorful tails; atop the puzzle a gift from the local fire department, a plastic helmet with a shield on the front reading "1 Fire Chief"; and then all over the room stuffed animals: ponies, pandas, rabbits, Miss Piggy given to a sick girl in the hospital, and on a pillow in the bed a small worn yellow kitten, this child's Nurse Jane, a little girl's best friend for two years and to the father bent over the bed somehow the most valuable possession in the house. "I don't think," the mother says, "that I could bear it if Kitty were lost." But then, of course, kitties like childhood itself and crisp, clear memories of little boys and girls are always lost.

The small things of life satisfy me, and I find the essay infinitely congenial. Not every one, though appreciates the form. Vicki rarely reads my essays. "Look," she said the other day; "they are boring. All you write about is life and death and lust." Although I can be gloomy, my constitution can heat up slightly, particularly in the spring, and if Vicki read more of my essays, she would discover that I write about many different things. I am forever beginning small projects and then writing about them. Just yesterday I mailed a letter to the mayor of Carthage, Tennessee. My father grew up in Carthage, and last summer we spent a day there. Outside the courthouse was a monument listing the local citizenry who fought in various wars. Missing from a long list of combatants in the Civil War was my great-grandfather. Born in Athens, Ohio, he joined Company C, Third Regiment, Ohio Volunteer Infantry when the war broke out. In 1863 he was stationed in Carthage as adjutant of the Fifth Tennessee Cavalry. After the war he settled in Carthage, married, and remained there for almost sixty years. "Few men in Smith County or in the Fourth Congressional District," the *Carthage Courier* wrote on his death in 1919, "were better or more favorably known." He was active in local affairs, holding several political offices and running for Congress. For over thirty years he was superintendent of the Methodist Sunday school. "He was," the paper stated, "a well-read, useful, substantial citizen, broad-minded, charitable, thoughtful and considerate of the feelings of others; he was a faithful and devoted companion, a tender and loving father; and hundreds of warm personal friends and admirers will be touched by the death of this grand and noble man of God." In my letter to the mayor, I stated that if the monument listed only the names of people born in Smith County then I understood Great-grandfather's absence. But, I said, if outlanders born in such distant spots as Trousdale, Macon, Putnam, and Jackson counties were listed, then I thought Great-grandfather, only from Ohio, ought to be present.

I hope that the mayor sees to it that Great-grandfather's name is engraved on the monument. If he does, then the next time I visit Tennessee, I will drive the family to Carthage and take pictures of the monument. We will also walk about the town. I set many of the tallish tales in my essays in Carthage, and if I know more about the town maybe the tales will be better. According to Father, Great-grandfather was a fine storyteller. In one of his favorite tales Luther Bugbee was arrested for shooting craps at Enos Mayfield's "Inn" in South Carthage, or Russia as it was known across the river. Sweep

Tyree was the county prosecutor, but since the Tyrees and the Bugbees both came from Mutton Bluff and had long been associated in some of the low doings of the local Democratic party, Judge Russell relieved Tyree of the case and requested a temporary prosecutor from Nashville. Gambling in Smith County was not a big concern of the state attorney general's office, and although the office honored Judge Russell's request, they did so only barely, sending their newest recruit to Carthage, Grover Thackston, a young graduate of the Y.M.C.A. law school. Thackston was a sweet boy and an ardent Methodist, but he knew nothing about gambling or any other sin for that matter. "I want you," Thackston said, addressing Bugbee at the beginning of the trial; "I want you to tell the jury just exactly how you deal craps." "What's that," Bugbee said, grinding his fists into his ears, "What did you say?" "I want you," Thackston repeated slowly and carefully, "to tell the jury how you deal craps." "Great God Almighty," Bugbee roared, rolling his eyes and looking heavenward toward Judge Russell; "let me out of here. The next thing he will ask me is how to drink a sandwich."

Although I don't gamble, I have a bit of Bugbee in me. If the mayor doesn't answer my letter about the monument, I won't pursue the matter. I like moving on to new projects and going to different locations, leaving familiar ideas and places behind, be they courtrooms or living rooms. Recently I applied for a teaching post in Mississippi. Vicki was not pleased. "You were homogenized when I married you," she said, "and if you go down there, you might separate." Vicki is probably right, and if I am offered the job, I don't know what I will do. Keeping one from becoming too smooth, an occasional separation, though, isn't bad for an essayist. Separations don't do much for the reputation of a school board member, however. In any case essayists don't make good politicians or public servants. Impatient and easily exasperated, essayists suspect abstractions, large aims, and solemn platitudes. Outspoken, they are often misunderstood because they play with words. Of course, they are not always misunderstood. When I said that the emphasis on guidance counseling in the schools struck me as bogus, a bunch of people heard clearly. What they did not realize because they hadn't read enough essayists was that my statement like my interest in the war monument was not something I had thought much about or would think much about in the future. That aside, though, the chairman of the school board got upset, and without informing me wrote a letter of apology to the guidance counselors in the school system. The time was ripe to move on to something more ceremonious, I decided, when I learned about the apology and so I wrote a letter myself. I preferred, I wrote, to do my own apologizing and would gladly have done so if asked. I then resigned, noting that serving on the board had given me characters for essays and concluded signing my name "Samuel 'Bogus' Pickering."

After delivering the letter, I felt relieved. I would no longer spend afternoons negotiating with unions. Instead of attending meetings on Thursday nights and drinking gallons of coffee to keep awake, I could stay home with Vicki and watch "Mystery Theatre," maybe even warble a melodious lovecall or two. Certainly, I thought, I could complete a couple of neglected essays. I was wrong. That night pressure began building, initially from Vicki who I suspect wanted to keep me and thus the family firmly tied to Mansfield and away from Mississippi, then from friends and strangers. Instead of retiring into quiet private life, the quiet of my privacy was broken as the telephone rang throughout the day, and night. Repeatedly I was told that I had a moral duty to serve on the board. Although they live conservative lives, essayists rarely respond to appeals to duty, generally thinking them felonious. What startled me, however, was the number of people who despite having read my books still called. "Damn it," one woman exclaimed, "we need someone on the board who shoots from the hip and gallops through all this educational crap." "Well," Vicki remarked when I told her about the call; "If I were you I would canter. Galloping could be a trifle messy." At the end of a week I was beaten. Every time the phone rang I ran for the bathroom and tried to hide. "It's clear," Vicki said, "that you have to withdraw your resignation. Look," she added, "why not write an essay about it. Remember that woman's call and pretend you are a cowboy. Instead of 'Back in the Saddle Again,' call the essay 'Back on the Board Again.' " And so here I am, once more attending school board meetings on Thursday nights and worrying about the nurses' contract. Since returning I haven't said much, but my pencils are oiled and loaded with number two lead.

Still Life

A still life has always hung over the sideboard in my parents' dining room. When I was small the painting frightened me, and I wouldn't look at it. The varnish over the oils had aged and turning dark hid the fruits in a pall of shadows. Like creatures from a troubling, half-remembered dream, forms hovered circular and indistinct on the edge of vision. In the painting fruits were piled on a table, covered with a white cloth. On the lower left side of the painting were pineapples, one cut open, its color pale and tubercular, like some entrail sliced in half, first wet and glistening then browning as it dried. Next to the pineapples were three pomegranates, one torn apart, seeds spilling across the tablecloth like drops of old blood, cracking and flaking. Behind and above the fruit was a greenish flagon, its spout hooked like the beak of a vulture and light preening from its sides like feathers iridescent in a broken shade. Along the lower right side of the painting were more pomegranates, translucent grapes, their leaves waxy in decay, and then a peach, broken open, the pit still in place and bulging like a tumour. In the shadows behind was a fluted bowl, rolling with what seemed to be apples, grapes, and peaches.

Until this year I wasn't sure what lurked in the background because I had never examined the painting closely. Then during a visit to Nashville in March, I took the painting from the wall and placing it in the sunlight looked at it carefully. Under the varnish brightness flowed like spring. Instead of white the pineapple was yellow, and the texture of the fruit was delicately, lovingly drawn. For their part the pomegranate seeds resembled red violets, not splintering, but glowing with promise and fertility. Instead of a vulture, craw swollen with carrion, the flagon smacked of newly turned earth and vines heavy with blossoms. Colors ran across the painting like a rainbow, down through the apples and across the grapes to the peach pit, pink and breathing, then over the pomegranates up through the pineapple to a stalk of firm, green leaves, tapering to sharp golden quills.

For a moment I was elated. If the painting were cleaned and hung over the mantel in our living room in Connecticut, it would glow throughout the year, I thought, like a warm welcoming fire, lifting expectations and pushing sadness out of sight into corners. That moment, though, passed quickly; something there was in me that preferred dark to light. Youth and the time of extravagant expectation were over, and instead of attracting, bright color, more often than not, repulses me. Rather than promising a future shining with lively possibility, colors remind me of joy left behind, all those things I once did and can never do again, all the things I imagined doing and now know I will never do. No longer did the painting frighten me, and as I hung it back above the sideboard, I realized I would not have it cleaned. Although part of me wanted light promise and bright hope to whistle through life, I could not help being drawn toward melancholy. There in the gloom about the fluted bowl and flagon lay my future, bleak reality, not now the easy intangible fluff of a child's dream.

Of course in contemplating the shadows of my still life, I occasionally see fruits clearly, apples red and orange, and peaches, pink and fuzzy. Not only that, I am not always melancholy; in fact I frequently behave in ways more fruity than funereal. I have a bad back and three mornings a week I swim a half or two-thirds of a mile in the university pool. Swimming is boring; all one does is splash back and forth from one end of the pool to the other. Talking is impossible. The person who tries to talk is sure to swallow a mouthful of water, if not drown. After the swim the silence of the pool continues into the shower. Nakedness inhibits conversation and bathers turn their backs on words and each other, singlemindedly gripping soap and scrubbing. Like a grape unnoticed in the background of the still life, most mornings I pass unobtrusively through the shower, washing quickly and silently. Occasionally, however, words like fruit will ferment and last Wednesday when I walked into the shower and saw eight silent strangers, words burst out. "Well, girls," I said, ambling over to the wall, "this growing old sure isn't much fun. Damn it," I exclaimed to get people's attention while turning on the shower; "I've gotten so I can only eat one meal a day. No matter how many vitamins I take I can only manage a single meal and even then I can't eat dessert. Strangely enough," I went on, pausing to soap up my front side, "my sex life has also changed. Instead of four, I have to do it five, sometimes six, times a day. What a nuisance! Still," I said, vigorously rubbing the soap in, "that's not what's bothering me. It's this eating. I just don't know what to do. I'm too young to limit myself to one meal a day, so I have been thinking about taking monkey gland shots. You fellows have any suggestions?" I said, working the soap in and through a neglected cranny or two, before glancing about and adding, "you guys look pretty normal. One of you must have had this problem." The group, I am afraid, must all have been stalwart trenchermen with hardy three-meal-a-day appetites. No one spoke; the sound of lathering grew intense, and soon I had the shower room to myself.

Despite an occasional locker room outburst, however, my life is quiet and lean. Recently a student wrote a paper for me in which she described the rich sweets of German coffeehouses: strudel, apples dark with raisin or hazelnuts, all smothered with whipped cream; Sacher torte; Black Forest cake, cream and cherries, white and red, folded between layers of chocolate; pastry leaves bulging with mocha or hazelnut buttercream; and tarts, their fruits crisp and glazed atop mounds of vanilla cream, the whole sitting in scalloped shells, sparkling and resembling little, dumpy boats hung with jewels. The description freshened my appetite, bringing to mind younger, wandering days, days of morning coffee at Demel's in Vienna and afternoon tea at Louis's in Hampstead. Now I rarely travel, thinking the drive to Willimantic seven miles away a trip.

When I go to Willimantic, I usually take the children and stop at Frank's Bakery for milk and doughnuts. Frank's is sugary and functional, a lifetime away from my youth and dream sweets on silver carts. By the door is a cigarette machine; on one side is a yellow poster advertising the New England Tractor Trailer Training School, "Training People Today," the poster states, "for a Better Tomorrow." Along one wall is a series of shiny ektachrome pictures of a man fishing, probably for rainbow trout,somewhere in the Canadian Rockies. In the distance above him jagged blue mountains reach toward the sky, while at his feet a stream runs through a long *S*, tumbling over rocks before pitching past a clump of green spruce trees. At one end of Frank's counter is a pile of plastic boxes from Benny's, the ninety-nine cent price tags still glued on. In them are ornaments for cakes: a pink swan for thirty cents, a golf club and ball costing fifty cents, and again at thirty cents a silver heart with "Sweet 16" written in the middle. In boxes behind the counter are statues of brides and grooms for wedding cakes, the most expensive costing fifteen dollars and ninety-five cents and the cheapest eight dollars. On the counter itself are cakes, all covered with white icing and colored flowers, the favorite flower being a dark blue rose, surrounded by green leaves. In the icebox beside the cash register are cream pies costing five dollars: chocolate, banana, strawberry, and pineapple. The last time we went to Frank's Francis ate a "Yellow Bird's Nest," a doughnut-like pastry covered with sprinkles and filled with jelly and white icing. Edward ate a Cream Horn, a longish worm-like tube swollen with artificial cream. Both Horn and Nest cost sixty-five cents while Eliza's brownie cost forty-five cents. For my part I had not started the monkey gland regimen, so I sat quietly and didn't eat anything, although, to be honest, a chocolate doughnut covered with thick, brown icing and blue and yellow sprinkles tempted me.

For moments while the children ate, I drifted away on thought. My days are so calm that I spend much time thinking. Not surprisingly, I suppose, my thoughts reflect the stillness of my life. Almost never do I delve into the quick and the disturbing, and I generally ignore religious or political matters. When my friend Neil asked me whom I fancied for president, I answered that I didn't favor anyone, adding only that I wanted someone who had never been in the military. The best candidate, I explained, would be a coward, a person who connived his way out of the draft when young. A "track record" of avoiding conflicts was important, I said, lathering up the conversation, because such a person would probably do his best to keep himself, his family, the nation, and then what was more important, my family, at peace. The conversation with Neil was out of character. Rarely do I become so enthusiastic about matters governmental. Instead I ponder the immediate: carpenter ants in the attic and furniture in the living room. Recently I stored a Victorian chair in the basement. Manufactured during the rococo revival in the 1850s, the chair was designed by John Henry Belter and is the ornate wooden equivalent of a cluttered still life. Bunches of grapes, entwined not only with leaves and vines but with scrolls and what looks like roses, hang down the legs while vegetables, nuts, and flowers grow up the sides, eventually wrapping around a bowl of fruit at the top of the chair. His haunches rounder than eggplant, a putto crouches in the bowl, a conch shell at his ear. Instead of the busy roar of the sea and fruit spreading like kudzu, I wanted silence in my rooms, and I replaced the Belter chair with a smooth, finely finished Pembroke table. No matter how I try to push the quick and the lively into the basement and out of my living room, however, I am never completely successful. Something as small as exasperation with a dull swim or the legs of a table betrays me, and probably will always betray me. Instead of falling straight and tapering clean and narrow, the legs of my table are cabriole legs, bowed out and then sweeping back and around down to the floor and ball and claw feet.

Although age makes the still life easier to achieve, a still life is never completely natural and always requires forcing. In part custom and its consort propriety impose quiet. Twelve or so years ago in more viny, rococo days, I attended much Italian opera. As the melodies flowed, stopped, and then rushed ahead, stripping restraint from the emotions, much as cleaning removes varnish from a painting, I often pitched forward to the edge of decorum. The closest I ever came to tumbling into misbehavior occurred during the last scene of *La Bohème*. Shortly after a burst of passionately, mournful song, the heroine Mimi dies. Her lover Rodolfo is not immediately aware of her death, realizing it only after noticing the expressions on the faces of Bohemian friends. On first seeing the sadness in his friends' faces, Rodolfo is puzzled and strides about the stage, ignoring Mimi's body and asking what is wrong. At this point during a performance at Covent Garden, I almost rose out of my seat and yelled, "she's dead, you damn fool, she's dead—died of tuberculosis, don't you know." To keep from shouting, I balled my hands into fists and clamped my teeth down on my cheeks, cutting them, the blood pooling then oozing out at the corners of my mouth.

Silence comes easier now. I haven't chewed into my cheeks for years. Occasionally, though, I do have trouble being properly quiet. During my visit to Nashville in March, hearing aids came up in a conversation with a group of father's friends. Rapidly the men ran through the usual topics: expenses, batteries, and the difficulty of hearing in a crowd. Then, though, they discussed losing hearing aids. Everyone present had lost at least one, and most had no idea where they had lost them. "Well, I know what happened to mine," Mr. McGinnis said; "the dog ate it. I saw him do it. Ate it right off the top of a book." When the talk paused, I almost interrupted. "What kind of dog was it," I wanted to ask, "big dog or little dog;

black dog, white dog, spotted dog, or old yellow dog; a dog with a long tail or short tail, or even a curly tail? And what kind of book was it the dog ate from? Hardback or paperback? Was it a cookbook or mystery?" Maybe, I suddenly thought, it was one of mine—after all Mr. McGinnis was father's friend. Although my books weren't very good, I didn't want one to end up as a dog bowl. Eventually, I decided, the book wasn't likely to be mine. My sales were so low that only a handful of people in Nashville had read anything I wrote, and I was pretty sure I had talked to all of them already, and Mr. McGinnis wasn't among them. "Great God," I thought, "what a tale. I have to ask questions." Of course I didn't ask and keeping silent before age let the conversation drift away to another subject.

In saying that today I rarely travel farther from home than Willimantic, I overlooked trips to Nashville. In my mind real travel is associated with sidewalk cafés, dark chocolate, and mounds of whipped cream floating on rich, black coffee, not, I am afraid, with Delta Airlines, afternoon flights from Hartford to Cincinnati, then Cincinnati to Nashville, peanuts in little red or blue bags, and cans of Campbell's orange juice, made from concentrate extracted from fruit grown in Florida and Brazil. Because Mother and Father moved into a condominium last summer, this March Vicki and I and the children stayed in a Holiday Inn near Vanderbilt University. Since our room was near the roof of the hotel on the twelfth floor, Vicki refused to turn on the air conditioning, saying we might get legionnaire's disease. With one exception, nights at the Holiday Inn were still. One day, however, the empty rooms in the hotel were booked by delegates to a convention of Young Baptists. All through the evening our telephone rang and pranksters banged on doors and ran through the halls screaming. At half past eleven I finally called the desk and asked the hotel management to calm the children down. "We are trying," the clerk said, "but we aren't having much luck." "Didn't some preachers accompany the kids?" I asked. "Yes sir," the clerk responded, "but we can't find any of them."

Every morning after breakfast I drove to Mother and Father's apartment. After leaving Vicki and the children with Mother, I took Father to Belle Meade Drugs. A group of young women had converted part of the drugstore into a bakery and sandwich shop called The Picnic. Ferns hung from the ceiling in baskets, and tables, chairs, and plates were blue and white, giving The Picnic the homey feeling of old delftware. Every morning Father and his friends met to talk about politics and hearing aids. The women who ran The Picnic were kindly affectionate, remembering birthdays and asking about ailing wives at home. Mornings at The Picnic were slow, but I didn't want them to end. Nevertheless, I knew, like all picnics, the mornings had to end; knives, forks, plates, cups, and memories would be packed away. The old tablecloth, spotted and stained, would be rolled up; the trash gathered, the hillside left bare, and a day or two later no one would be able to tell that a picnic had occurred. "Daddy," Eliza, my three-year-old, said after we had been in Nashville for five days, "I love Ree-Ree and Baa-Baa, but I'm tired of going back and forth." Like Eliza I was tired of coming and going, but unlike her longings for a still life, I wanted to stem the inevitable falling away of friends and green hillsides, laughter and hampers bulging with fried chicken, potato salad, homemade rolls and devil's-food cake.

At three or four every morning Eliza wakes to go to the potty chair. Almost always I hear her climb out of bed, then pad rapidly through the hall to Vicki's and my room. "Daddy," she says, and I get out of bed, cut the bathroom light on, hand her a cup of apple juice, and then sit with her. After she finishes, I go to her room with her, and as I cover her, she puts her arms around my neck and says, "I love you Daddy; you are the best Daddy in the whole world." When I return to my room, I often sit for a moment on the edge of the bed. Tears well up in my eyes and I long for permanence, a still life in which Eliza is forever small, telling me in the dark night that I am the best daddy in the world.

Although a still life cannot stop change, it can create the illusion of slowing time. In days uncluttered by bustle, hours sag loosely, and sometimes seem great bottomless bags. Duties and appointments rarely weigh me down, and I spend hours simply and quietly, just looking about. Last Saturday at noon I stretched out in the dell in my side yard. The daffodils which I planted last fall had begun to bloom, and I wanted to see what they looked like from the ground. Standing above them I was tempted to count blossoms. I wondered how many of the bulbs I planted came up and if I had gotten "good value." On the ground concerns about money and numbers disappeared. The daffodils seemed to stretch endlessly, lush pinks and reds, pale and bright yellows, golds and oranges, with stalks, firm and green. Instead of passing unnoticed at my feet, colors were in my face, and the world seemed a patchwork of light.

Behind me grew periwinkle, its blossoms, purple and starry, drawing bumblebees like eyes. Nearby were yellowish tufts of sweet William while all about were the dark green, almost metallic, leaves of gill-cover-the-ground. By summer the gill would not be so retiring, runners stretching in all directions and its leaves light green and alight with violet blossoms. As I lay on the ground I thought about ordering more daffodils, "to," as I told Francis my first grader, "bring more beauty into the lives of people passing on the street." In my mind I ordered Audubons, mostly white with pink about the cup, cherry spots, laundry clean petals and a shining orange cup; and Inca gold, a trumpet daffodil almost two feet tall and as yellow as an August sunset. I painted the bare ground with rainbows, mixing resplendents, yellow and red, lilac delights, coral ribbons, and Mount Hood, an old-fashioned white flower. Down the lip of the dell I scattered little waterperry, pinkish and fragrant, ten inches high; canarybird, slightly taller but still fragrant; and geranium, even taller but with a fragrance brighter than its white and orange blossoms. I don't know how long I lay in the dell. Clouds not minutes measured the day, and I started to leave only when the sun disappeared and a heavy mist began blowing across the yard. Even so, I didn't leave quickly, for while I lay on the ground a pileated woodpecker flew into the woods beyond the dell. Only once before, when I was a child in Tennessee, had I seen a pileated woodpecker, and I wanted to see as much of him as possible. His red head battering soft wood, he dropped from tree to log, flashing white and black. Only when he flew deeper into the woods and out of sight did I leave the dell.

Besides providing occasions to look at daffodils and woodpeckers, a still life frees one to write, not weighty books thick with the muscularity resulting from fast living, but soft books modest with easy observation. This spring I received a royalty check from the sales of a book published three years ago. "How much is it," Michael an inquisitive friend in the English department asked when I got my mail. Sixty-eight, sixty, I answered. "What," he exclaimed, "six thousand, eight hundred, and sixty dollars for a book which came out in 1985? Good Lord, what sales you must have had." "In three years," I said, putting the check into my wallet, "the book has sold fourteen hundred and seventy copies. The check is for sixty-eight dollars and sixty cents." The odd thing, and what I did not say to Michael, was that for just a handful of books a writer betrays:

himself, others, and the private decencies of life. Actually it may not so much be the individual who betrays, but the still life itself, its quiet demanding to be broken, its emptiness filled. Much as the painting over the sideboard seemed blank, until looked at closely, so perhaps only the unexamined life seems empty and quiet. When open spaces trail across the canvas of a day, one, more often than not I suspect, hurries to brush in flagons, grapes, pineapples, daffodils, woodpeckers, whatever, alas, falls before hand or eye.

A month ago I made a second trip to Nashville. Father was ill, and so when Mother suddenly had to have an operation, I flew down. Days were long and barren, and so I filled them in. While Mother slept hard, I sketched her room in the hospital, brushing in the bed, its body like the chassis of a fork lift, dials along bulky sides, and at the foot a clipboard hanging, covered with cold, frightening numbers; the television suspended on an L, high on the wall and leaning forward, almost intruding into the bed, white letters underneath reading "Patient Educator Channel 6"; beside the bed a table shaped like a C, one side open so the top could extend over the patient; against the wall a small chest with three drawers and ball feet, this time with no claws. On the chest was a beige telephone, a clear plastic envelope inside of which was the schedule for the television, a beige cup with a bendable plastic straw leaning out of it, and a box of paper handkerchiefs, bouquets of roses on the sides. On the floor was a brown wastecan with a clear garbage bag inside; behind it and to the side, silver and sticklike, stood a "tree"; hanging from it were plastic containers, tubes curling toward the bed, liquid running through them like roots. In front of the window was a second chest; on top was a pot of yellow chrysanthemums wrapped in green paper and blue ribbon. Beyond were Venetian blinds and the windows of other rooms. In hard rigor three straight chairs sat against the wall while two sprinklers jutted down from the ceiling. Near the door was a round thermostat with numbers too small for old people to read. I painted the room, I suppose, because I didn't want to see Mother on the bed, old and weak and suddenly dying, her cheeks waxy and sunken, her left arm cradled around a stuffed Easter bunny—a bunny which Eliza has now named Noodlely and which she keeps in her bed next to Kitty.

Although Mother's room was a dreary blend of blue and beige, someone had painted a fishing scene on the doors of the elevator in the hall opposite. Unlike the pictures at Frank's Bakery, the scene was not exotic, smacking of Reelfoot Lake and the local. While ducks dropped toward the water feathering their wings, the sun set in yellow bars. On the horizon two men sat in a rowboat, fishing, not for trout, I found myself thinking and noting down, but for bass or croppie. Alert to details, I sketched in the canvas of hours, studying the halls and listening to the conversations of strangers. Much as the painter of Mother and Father's still life meticulously sliced through pineapple and pomegranate with his brush, so I traced remarks with my pen. When I heard a woman in the hall describe a friend's trouble saying "her thyroid's down went out of berserk," I wrote it down. Late at night people often added details to my painting. During the long dying a nurse told me about her three miscarriages and Rosie talked about Mother. In November when Mother broke her hip and had the socket replaced, Rosie stayed in the hospital with her. Because she was taking a pain killer and on waking might have behaved irrationally pulling at her hip, Mother's hands were restrained. On coming out from under the anesthesia, Mother raised her head, looked around, saw Rosie, then noticed her hands were tied to the railings of the bed. "Rosie," Mother said, "get a pair of scissors and cut these ropes. I'm going home." "Miss Katharine," Rosie answered, "I can't do that." "Well, then, you are fired," Mother exclaimed, letting her head fall back on the pillow before adding, "again."

The morning after Mother's death I drove to Carthage, my father's hometown, to arrange her burial in a family plot. Suddenly it was a redbud and dogwood spring in Tennessee, and amid the cedars along the road, pinks and whites stood out washed and wholesome. The grass was greener and the light deeper and yellower than in Connecticut, and I dreamed about returning to Tennessee, to the past, to sprigs of redbud in vases and magnolias in bowls like lilypads, and to Christmases of cedar not spruce trees, soft sweet-briar Christmases of sunny winter days. I wondered why I stopped academic writing, forsaking the comfortable, otherworld of leather-bound books and musty knowledge. Far happier would I have been if the details of the present had slipped off me like thin paint, leaving only a blurred track behind. Far happier I would have been blotting the moment into cloud. Happier still dropping searing experience at the library door and spending life roaming the cool, serene corridors of old learning. No longer, though, was I a scholar; I was now an essayist, a person to whom observation stuck, unaffected by conscious scrubbing and scrapping. Beside the road I noticed a sign for the Mourner's Bench Baptist Church. "Once Saved, Always Saved," the sign proclaimed. "Doubtful," said my cousin Katherine who with her daughter Ann accompanied me. "I wonder what funerals are like at Mourner's Bench," I said. "I don't know about that church," said Ann who works at a florist's shop, "but we make some of the damndest palls imaginable for country burials. We just finished a humdinger. In the middle was a pink princess telephone made out of carnations. Written under it in big letters made out of white carnations was 'JESUS CALLS.' "

Although a still life makes one observant, it can also make life itself seem grotesque. Details slip out of context, and seem unnatural like wax fruit on a dining room table. Although the Nashville papers had already printed Mother's obituary, Mr. Dyer the Carthage undertaker asked several questions about Mother. "Why do you need this information?" I asked. "This is a small town," Mr. Dyer answered, "and every day, at ten in the morning, noon, and then again at four in the afternoon, the local radio station runs a program called 'Obituaries of the Air.' All obituaries as well as admissions and dismissals from the local hospital are read three times a day. It is the most popular program in Carthage." Later as we were leaving, I said, "Mr. Dyer, I do hope you got the right body." "Oh, yes sir, Mr. Pickering. Don't you worry," he answered; "I picked your mother up myself. The hospital ties a name tag to the big toe on the right foot, and I checked it twice." Most of the things I remember from my conversation with Mr. Dyer now strike me as funny: Mr. Dyer's calling coffins "the merchandise" and then later in the showroom as we examined the merchandise, his laying the green dress which I picked out for Mother's burial on top a modestly priced coffin and saying "the dress just goes with this casket."

Many of the observations which cling to memory I would like to bury deep in forgetfulness, but as the pomegranate seeds in the still life disturbed my sleep as a child, so some of the details of Mother's burial break my waking hours, turning consciousness nightmarish. Worst are the expenses, not yet blackened by the hard varnish of time, the cold practicalities they reveal numbing and final: two hundred dollars for embalming; seventy-five dollars for "other preparation of the body"; the same for "transfer of remains to funeral home"; "Immediate Burial," five hundred and eighty dollars; the coffin, a thousand sixty-five dollars; then the vault, the plot markers, tent and grave equipment, the labor of digging and filling the grave, and finally the tax at one hundred and thirty-eight dollars and thirty-eight cents, for a total of three thousand two hundred and eight dollars and thirty-eight cents.

Although chilling detail clings perhaps with greater tenacity to the still than to the active life, there is compensation. A still life nurtures imagination. Not sapped by the fretful drip of days, the imagination gathers strength, flowing and shaping realities beyond small fact. It even overturns death, creating not simply illusions but a truth greater than mere detail: that despite the grave there is still life. Just this morning I left the baked earth and hot, dry plains of grief. Ranging through foothills and shards of color, I climbed toward ridges yellow in the sun. In the distance stood tall mountains, their peaks white, not with ice but with warm milk, dropped from the udders of God's flock as they grazed across the heavens. Far below me in another world lay the shaley slopes and dried rivers of death, brown seams now lost in sullen heat. I climbed until I reached a valley golden with daffodils and blooming with birds. There across a blue stream sat Mother, a floppy straw hat on her head, her dress spread about her like petals, and her arms full of wild mint. "Sammy," she said, smiling. "Mommy," I cried and ran to her, the sky above me a bowl, fluted and gathering my joy like peaches and pineapples and pomegranates.

Bogs

This summer in the back house of our farm in Nova Scotia I found a toolbox which belonged to Vicki's grandfather. Sixteen inches long, eight and half wide, and eight tall, the toolbox had a red leather exterior, a heavy comfortable handle, and thick reinforced corners. Stamped in gold on one side was C. C. Johnson, Columbus, Ohio. Resembling a small, elegant trunk, the toolbox did not belong in a workroom, floor grainy with sawdust and ceiling caked with the nests of dirt daubers. As I ran my hand across the leather, still soft and unscuffed, I framed a world apart, turning joists into sleek closed cars with great white-walled tires and studs into ocean liners sliding light-heeled through waves like dancers through a waltz. Instead of resting on the solid girder of truth, my thoughts swung loosely about the cornerpost of imagination, and as I held the toolbox, I felt sheepish and silly like some amateur carpenter who raised a wall before framing openings for windows and doors. Later, though, I felt better, for I learned that Vicki's grandfather used the tools not for headers or trimmers but to build a way out of reality into dream. When his coal mines failed in the 1930s, he became estranged from his wife and growing depressed bought the toolbox and moving desk and bed to the attic, spent long hours alone making model ships: tern schooners, barkentines, and brigs. No matter how well crafted, though, a model ship is not strong enough to sail through years supporting the heavy cargo of a man's unhappiness. For a time Vicki's grandfather escaped land-locked Ohio, but then the winds of dream died, and becalmed, he went into the garage, and after closing the doors, climbed behind the wheel of that car with those great white-walled tires, turned the motor on, and sailed away.

The two sides of the toolbox opened into four trays, sliding smoothly outward above the well of the box like a butterfly unfolding its wings in the sun over a flower. The inside top of the box was lined with thick cloth while the trays and well were tin. The box was filled with tools—hand drills, files, ratchets, squares—things to be turned, twisted, grasped and inserted. In one tray were twenty-four bits for drills, each bit a different size; next to them were three boxes of flat head iron wood screws, manufactured by American Screw in Providence, Rhode Island. The tools themselves were heavy and hard, all made in the United States, in Philadelphia, and in Millers Falls and Greenfield, Massachusetts. I emptied the box onto the floor of the back house and examined each tool. I used my eyes more than my hands, noting places of manufacture and patent numbers. In my family the ways of hands with tools vanished three generations ago, and although holding them made me feel capable and confident, I couldn't identify most of the tools, much less use them. The only tool in my inheritance was a lawn mower. Seventy years ago my father mowed grass with it in Carthage, Tennessee, and I kept it for sentimental reasons. The mower is broken, and although I suspect repairing it would be easy, I don't know where to begin.

Tools of all sorts surrounded me as I sat on the floor of the back house: picks, shovels, hooks with straps attached, the blade of a plough, wooden mallets, and saws, some with blades shorter than a foot, others with blades six feet long. On the shelf above me was the rusty head of a broad axe, the type used by shipbuilders in the middle of the nineteenth century. Leaning against the wall was a scythe, the blade oily and black on the floor but the wooden handle curving above golden and voluptuously alluring. The scythe tempted me, and I imagined taking it outside and mowing grass around the barn. The moment of temptation passed quickly, however; I wasn't ready for mowing, only for thoughts about mowing, and even then I could not swing deep and clean. Because I knew almost nothing about tools, I knew little about bushes, grasses, trees—all the natural world dug, cut, or shaped by tools. I did know the names of wild-flowers, but now sitting in the back house, the mechanics of running a small farm surrounding me, such knowledge seemed aesthetic and empty. Moreover, identifying wildflowers had become faddish, almost like jogging. Having run through youth, my friends had reached early middle-age, and although surrounded by the prizes of wealth, had found themselves increasingly uneasy. Mantelpieces bright with Coalport and halls stately with Sheraton and Queen Anne could not, they suddenly realized, slow time and its cold

consort, mortality. Dissociated from permanence, or more impor-
tantly, the illusion of permanence, they turned toward nature, buying books about wildflowers, as they once bought knick-knacks for
corner cupboards, and planting gardens, much, alas, like mine—
not real gardens, muddy with weeds like original sin, but ornamental
gardens, filled with easy flowers: peonies, crocus, lilies, Iris, tulips,
and daffodils "naturalized."

I'm frightened of growing old, and for a moment there in the
back house, I felt the melancholy of Vicki's grandfather in the attic.
The little models of knowledge I crafted had run aground, beaching
me amid feelings of inadequacy and failure. I am not by nature
introspective, however; the mood passed, and I was soon sliding
light-heeled through the sand. As I looked about the back house, I
realized that I could never master tools. If I worked diligently, I
might learn, I thought, other things, not the practicalities of mudsills
and sole plates but things, which in their own ways, might be useful
to me. At the end of the fields behind our house and just before the
headland breaks off into the Gulf of Maine lie two stretches of
boggy wetland. In summers past I wandered around the edges of
the bogs but I never really went into them. This summer, I decided,
I would explore the bogs. What I saw would probably stir association and awaken memory. Hard hours in the bogs might, I hoped,
also teach patience and humility, resignation, consolation, perhaps
even hope deferred.

Our farm is in Beaver River, fourteen miles northeast of Yarmouth. From Route One, the coastal highway, the land stretches
back and down some four hundred yards through meadows, woods,
and bogs until it rises lightly, rolling upward into a drumlin headland
overlooking the Gulf of Maine. Formed some ten thousand years
ago, drumlins are the refuse of glacial drift. Elongated egg-shaped
hills are filled with till: silt, sand, pebbles, stones, and boulders, all
churned together. Tides off the Gulf of Maine have cut deep into
our drumlin, washing till away and creating a bluff sixty feet high.
During the summer, grasses, mints, flowers, and berries—cranberry, black crowberry, blueberry and wild strawberry—blanket
the slope of the headland. Every winter, though, storms scar the
headland, slicing vegetation away and letting rock and red clay spill
out. The drumlin begins at the southwest of our property, just east
of the old wharf at Beaver River. In the nineteenth century boats
were built at Beaver River: schooners, barks, and brigantines. Fifty

years later similar boats sailed through the imagination of Vicki's grandfather in Ohio. Today the wharf is a ruin. Sticking up through the sand on the beach are a line of trunk-like pillars, heavy stones still piled about them and thick iron bolts, jutting out and rusting. Much as time wears through family account, leaving a model here and a tale there, so Beaver River itself has washed into story. Houses have burned or been torn down; the businesses have died; and if it were not for the signs on the highway, the community would not exist.

Beyond the old breakwater and at the beginning of the drumlin is a mound, the remains of a brick kiln some two hundred years old. Every summer bricks tumble out of the mound to the beach, and my children collect them, along with colored rocks, bottle caps, and shotgun shells. Past the kiln the drumlin rises swiftly upward like the thick end of an egg, reaching its highest point directly behind the larger of our two bogs, a wetland surrounded by woods like a finger circled by a ring. For a hundred yards or so the drumlin runs level, but then it starts rounding slowly down, eventually sliding out to flat grazing lands just before Bartlett's River, the distance from Beaver River being just under a mile.

At the end of the first week in July I started roaming through the wetlands, beginning with the bog most accessible and most familiar, the one surrounded by trees and lying behind the high point of the drumlin. To reach the bog I walked southwest out of our kitchen and paralleling Route One crossed a small meadow and a stone wall into Ma's Property, a big hayfield, the edges of which have begun to tatter into alder and thorn. To my right two hundred yards away at the end of the field and across another stone wall, wood and bog began. In July and August, rainbows of flowers curved through the field: spikes of yellow swamp candle and purple fringed orchis, buttercups, blue flag, red clover, mallow both white and pink and along the walls meadowsweet and rose. Despite good intention, some mornings I got no nearer the bog than Ma's Property and returned home, not dutifully pregnant with patience and humility, but with flowers, blossoms tumbling riotously over each other in pagan fecundity.

Knowledge can limit vision and understanding. What a person knows often determines what he sees and thus what he appreciates. Because I recognized flowers, I saw little other than flowers when I began exploring the wetlands—not trees or mosses, not even bushes, just flowers. By the second week in July spring and early summer flowers had practically disappeared. Still, I found traces, lady's slippers, blossoms so dried and shriveled that the flowers seemed to have molted, hurrying color off to another stage of life, leaving only husks behind, veiny and nutbrown. In one spot I found twinflowers, pink bells nodding and seemingly too small and fragile for July. Under trees at the edge of the bog wood sorrel, starflowers, wild lily of the valley, and bunchberry still bloomed, the blossoms of this last cleanly white in a collar of green leaves like a diminutive earthbound magnolia. By early August its berries would be clustered and red, almost a ground holly and a harbinger of fall like the tall shafts of Clintonia, the berries coldly blue and sometimes solitary. By the middle of August summer had begun to unravel, and in the woods about the bog great patches of whorled wood aster straggled into bloom, the blossoms weak and raggedly gap-toothed like the season itself.

As I identified wildflowers, I began to notice ferns, at first only cinnamon ferns, great clusters of them arching up out of the moss, sometimes reaching to my chest. Often observation does not determine language; instead language determines observation. When I was small my favorite writer was Edgar Rice Burroughs, and on summer afternoons when thunderstorms rolled up the Pamunkey River then across my grandfather's farm in Virginia, I read the Tarzan books. While lightning cracked over our hilltop, splintering locust trees and bringing long limbs down across the boxwood, I heard nothing, for I was away in the jungle padding silently behind Tarzan like a shadow. Childhood reading rarely influences an adult's life. Despite all Kala's rough nourishing, I never wandered from books into life, placing my foot upon the neck of a vanquished enemy and roaring out the wild challenge of the victorious bull ape. Indeed the closest I have ever come to a jungle is my yard. On our return from Nova Scotia this summer, the grass was a foot high, and I did not try to cut it until after taking my lawn mower to Morneau's and having the blade sharpened. Still, since childhood a jungle of words has blown about my imagination, much like spores carried on the wind. Now in the bog the words fell and rooted and for a moment determined my vision. Looking about me I did not really see the ferns. Instead I saw darkness and disorder, red-toothed violence slinking low to the ground. Unconsciously I slipped into the language of conflict, thinking of conquering and taming, of shining order, hot and purifying, into the night. The foolish fit did not last long, and lacking a taproot in reality, the high words wilted.

The bog was fangless and sustaining a metaphor of conflict was impossible. In a southern wetland no matter how luminous the beauty, danger always coiled nearby in the mind: a diamondback twisted under a palmetto, a copperhead sunning on a rock, or a water moccasin, a curved black limb, heavy and thick on a bank. In our bog were no poisonous snakes, not even poison ivy. Unlike walking through a marsh in which each step releases gases and the smell of decay from the mud, the bog was almost odorless. Not flushed out by waters flowing through as in a marsh, acids build up in bogs, slowing decomposition.

Although cinnamon ferns grew in rich profusion around the bog, I soon found other ferns: crested and long beech ferns; netted chain ferns; sensitive ferns, veins prominent and so tightly woven through leaflets they resembled fish nets; marsh ferns, always seeming to dance, leaflets twisting in courtship over fruit dots; and then bracken, three leaves splitting out from, then tapering over a long, leggy brown stalk, reminding me of great blue herons, standing silent and stilt-like fishing in the tidal marsh south of Beaver River. New York and lady ferns became my favorites, the latter so peppered with fruit dots that its leaves seemed arrows of fertility and continuity. Almost like the sun itself, New York ferns grew yellow in the few open areas in the bog. After pushing hard through trees as close as turnstiles, then snagging thorn and alder, I came to associate New York ferns with clarity and soft rest.

Man is sadly flawed, however, and by the end of the summer I envied, almost resented the ferns' beauty. The delicacy and grace of their blades sliced into awareness and making me feel coarse, turned me toward simpler beauty. By August the luxuriance of the ferns seemed a fault, a kind of over-crafted Victorian ornateness, and in my mind I lifted ferns from the bog and transplanted them into a late nineteenth-century painting. I called the painting *Play*. It depicted a room in the Grand Seraglio in Istanbul. Two plump, round-buttocked women, their legs stretched through the foreground, lay on a pile of fat pillows and blue and red carpets woven into curious, dizzying designs. The women both wore veils long as camisoles and flimsy white pantaloons. Around the left ankle of one tinkled a bracelet of silver bells. Both women were busy, one winding a child's music box while the other puffed her cheeks blowing her breath over a small ivory bird. Against the right wall stood a large bronze griffin, baboons engraved on its front legs and wings swept back

over its shoulders like claws. On the other side of the room stood
a brass ewer decorated with hawking scenes, and a tall, golden
coffee pot, its spout beaked and engraved with leopards and then
fish with the heads of pigs. Towering in the background like columns
of papyrus stood two Nubian eunuchs. They wore black robes and
purple turbans, topped with the orange feathers of fighting cocks.
Their faces were blank and only their hands moved as they fanned
the air, sweeping great ferns back and forth, long ends tapering and
waving like tongues.

Learning to read the land was difficult, and although I recognized
most wildflowers and was beginning to learn the names of ferns, I
put the bog aside for some days in mid-July and read the easier
world of man. Two years ago boys from Beaver River built a hut
on the northern edge of the bog. To reach the hut one walked to
the highest part of the headland, then turned away from the beach
and pushed inland some seventy-five yards through blueberry and
sheep laurel, rhodora, Labrador tea, bay, fern, and alder. Hidden
by black spruce the hut consisted of two rooms, built at right angles
to each other. It had a full-sized door, two glassed-in windows, and
a linoleum floor. Inside were shelves, three beds, complete with
springs and mattresses, and four chairs, two folding and two stuffed.
What made the hut interesting was not so much the craftsmanship
that went into it but the building materials used. Although the boys
framed the hut conventionally with two-by-fours, they sided it with
signs, in the process stripping the roads for miles around Beaver
River. Some of the signs were small billboards advertising motels:
"Eaton's Cottages" and "Loomer's Camper's Haven, On Lake, 3
Miles East of Yarmouth." On the wall was a sign shaped like the
front of a barn, rectangular at the bottom then rising slowly up
through the roof to a sharp peak. In the loft of the barn were "Oxen"
and "Hayrides"; below with the stalls were "Wooded Camp Sites,"
"Free Hot Showers," and "Daily Activities." Part of the hut's ceiling
was a six foot square sign for the 4H Clubs of Nova Scotia. In the
center was a dark green four-leaf clover; a black *H* was printed on
each petal while a yellow ribbon circled the entire clover. Painted
under the clover was a band of light green bunting on which was
written "Nova Scotia." Serving as wallboard for another portion of
the ceiling was a six-by-three-foot sign. Baby-blue with thick white
letters in the middle wishing tourists "Aurevoir," it had been removed from a field just up the shore road along the French coast

near Salmon River. Tourists, actually, might have had difficulty finding their way up the coast, for along with billboards the boys used highway signs as building material: "Stop" and "Wrong Way" signs in red and white; markers for Route One, shaped like policemen's badges with the number one stamped in the center; in white letters on a green background a sign pointing the way to Beaver River Road and Cedar Lake; and then in black letters on a yellow background, a sign cryptically reading "1¼ Mile."

As decoration the boys nailed bottle caps along the rafters: one hundred and eighty-eight caps from bottles of Oland Export beer, one cap from a Heineken's bottle, and two caps from Schooner beer, one depicting a white sailboat fluffing across a smooth blue sea. Once a guest must have visited the hut, for alongside the beer caps was nailed a single cap from a bottle of Mountain Dew, "Caffeine Free" Mountain Dew. When the boys first built the hut, popular music interested them. Two years ago pictures of rock groups were glued to the walls, most having painted faces and looking more clownish than musical. A year can make a difference in adolescence, however; the boys had grown, if not up at least older. The rock groups had vanished, their places being taken by, as Francis my seven-year-old put it, "women pictures."

Before showing them the hut I took the children to the bog several times. Although I worked hard to cultivate an interest in wetlands, spading up excitement wherever I found it, the children's enthusiasm wilted rapidly, at least until they explored the hut. On returning to our house, they immediately began looting the back house, much as the boys from Beaver River looted the highway, and in the side meadow under black spruce and behind an English hawthorn and golden chaintree, they constructed a "clubhouse." Using tree limbs as roof and walls, they didn't so much construct as furnish. For a day they rolled wheelbarrows loaded with furnishings out of the back house and into the meadow. As house number Edward nailed a license plate to the hawthorn, a black and silver Nova Scotia plate for 1952 with the number "3·83·22" stamped on it. Inside the clubhouse the children crammed a washtub; buckets, both wooden and metal; bricks from the kiln at Beaver River; scraps of tin; a tire; the face of an old mantel clock, suns and stars in the corners and on the back written "Cleaned & Repaired June 26, 1876"; an ironstone wash basin, crazed and with a green strip running about the lip; thick iron spikes; a deflated beach ball; and the lid to a chamber pot, a muddily green design of willow fronds, windmills, and a warbler, mouth open and pursuing a fly. Some items the children found intrigued me: a small can, its side caved in but the label still readable and proclaiming Andrews Liver Salt Laxative "Effervescent"; a bootjack shaped like a cricket with long feelers; and then a charcoal burning iron, made by Cummings, Taliaferro, and Bless and with a tall chimney rising up and stretching away from the handle. Although the iron was rusty, I thought about cleaning it and carrying it home to Connecticut to use as a door stop or bookend. Because it was heavy and awkward, a "sure toe-breaker" Vicki said, I left it in Nova Scotia. What I did remove from the clubhouse and bring home, though, was a china cream pitcher, manufactured in Germany and sold as a souvenir in Yarmouth at the turn of the century. Not quite five inches high the pitcher was pink and white, and sketched on a medallion under the spout in front was the courthouse and Yarmouth's old Zion church.

Once the clubhouse was built and I had poked around and through it, carrying off the cream pitcher, I returned to the bog, not immediately, though, to the world of fern and flower but to the manmade. Running parallel to each other like tines on a rake, stone walls stretched from the back of Ma's Property down through the woods, stopping open-ended at the edge of the bog. A hundred years ago our farm looked very different. The woods didn't exist, and open fields ran from Route One all the way back to the wetlands. While some walls marked property lines, others bordered roads, one of which I discovered when searching for an orchard which disappeared forty years ago. Most of the walls, however, had been built, not so much to mark boundaries as to clear fields and make cultivation easier. The walls had not worn well; slumping over they slouched under the trees in long weary lines. Fishing had been more important in Beaver River than farming, and I wondered what crops once grew in what was now our woods. Mostly hay, I eventually decided, and maybe vegetables for the family table. Still I wasn't sure and felt not so much inadequate as illiterate. If I had known the language I could have read the walls like a book. The stones were not simply rough masses of till but biographies and histories. If I had had a different education, I could have seen beneath the stones to story and pieced out the hopes and struggles of generations.

Rarely does life mark the earth. Little lingers beyond death, except perhaps a couple of tales in soft memory or walls that no one can read. Even when we know the builders of walls we misread, razing personality as surely as a bulldozer clearing off the past. Before going to Nova Scotia this summer, Vicki and I and the children visited my father in Tennessee. While there I cleaned out Mother's secretary. Scattered through the drawers and amid canceled checks and income tax returns were little pebbles of living. Much as the children were to furnish their clubhouse with scraps two weeks later, so I picked up a handful of things. What I took away resembled matter thrown down from a wall by time, pieces of fabric shattered beyond repair and indeed beyond comprehension. From a shelf I took a set of six small books, each three and a half inches broad and four and three-quarters inches tall. Bound in blue and gold and printed in New York in 1841, the books belonged to my great-grandmother. Consisting of *Lady of the Lake* and *Lalla Rookh,* then four volumes of the verse of Milton, Wordsworth, Hemans, and Sigourney, the set was poetic and elevated, reading suitable for a girl growing up in the 1850s in a proper family in Franklin, Tennessee. Much as I saw stone walls in distant, contemplative, rather than practical terms, so I paid little attention to the contents of the books. Instead I studied the title pages. On all of them my great-grandmother had written her name, Nannie E. Brown. Each signature, however, was different. On two books she printed, her letters blocked and solid, the design broken into bands and diagonals and resembling the work of a schoolgirl on a sampler. On the other four books she practiced calligraphy, her script lyrical and light, looping around into roses then sliding upward through a bird perched over a deep open space, wings lifted to the edge of flight.

From the secretary, I removed two other very different volumes: one a bride's book in which Mother listed the wedding presents, four hundred and thirty-five of them, which she and Father received when they were married fifty years ago in Richmond, Virginia. The second book was a small address book, kept by Mother before marriage. In it were the addresses not simply of friends, but also of stores, complete with telephone numbers and names of sales staff. At DiPinna Miss Cahill waited on Mother while Madame Pettijean waited on her at Bergdorf-Goodman, Mr. Sidney at Robinson Shoeshop and Miss Rain at Jane Engle. I kept the two books, I suppose, for sentimental reasons. Like walls running through the woods in Nova Scotia, the books smacked of another era, one that through time's softening filter seems cleaner and not so cloudy as the present.

That explanation aside, however, the little and the neglected, indeed the odd, have long attracted me. From the secretary I removed the small, heavy plate used to engrave Mother's stationary. It stands now on the shelf of my study, the letters on the plate "K. R. P." being reversed and backwards. Near it are two other things I brought back from Nashville: a white enameled pin shaped like a bow, three-eighths of an inch high and five-eighths of an inch long. Written on the lower two ends of the bow are the letters W.C.T.U., standing for Women's Christian Temperance Union. On another shelf higher in the study is a silver case in a dark red linen cover. Like the pin the case is small, only a half inch deep, two inches high, and three and a half inches long. Inside is a kit for injecting insulin, a syringe and four needles of different lengths and thicknesses, manufactured in Germany and patented in this country on October 22, 1901.

I may be drawn to small things simply because I don't have room in my life or house for anything large. Like the woods in Nova Scotia my house is mossy and overgrown. Although I sometimes think about sawing through the clutter, cutting clean and making life simple, I don't have the strength or real inclination. Like most good husbands and fathers I satisfy myself by dreaming of square fields and new-mown hay, and then by treating little things as if they were big, rolling imagination through secretaries and back houses, picking out books and pins, irons and pitchers, letters and pictures. In an envelope I found four album photographs, one of children and three of young girls. Because the pictures were taken in Richmond—by C. R. Rees in 1869 and earlier in 1867 by Anderson at 1311 Main Street—the people in the photographs were probably relatives, Ratcliffes, Catlins, or Hornes. In the same envelope was a picture of a Victorian house, a patchwork of gables, cupolas, and balconies ponderously rising through three stories. Standing on the front porch were ten people, to the left two black servants, handkerchiefs bound over their hair and wearing long white aprons, to the right and down the steps five adults and three children, two of the children barefoot. Before the house ran a sharp picket fence while to one side and behind the house loomed a dark building, probably a barn. The picture had faded, and the house sat ugly and heavy in a yellow-gray fog. I don't like the house, and since I don't know the people in the photograph, I would not have kept it if I had not noticed the two barefoot children. They looked as if they would have made good playmates. When I was a boy, I spent summers roaming barefoot over Cabin Hill, my grandfather's farm in Virginia. Times have changed, though; my children are even farther from country things than I am, and they never go barefoot, not even in Nova Scotia.

I found many pictures of Cabin Hill in the secretary. Grandfather built a house there after his home in Richmond burned. Over the grounds he planted twenty-five thousand boxwood, and I found a picture of him standing in an open field, long rows of tiny box stretching behind him like ribbons. In another Grandfather stands with his arms outspread in front of a prize Guernsey, her bag swollen with milk. Although Grandfather owned a dairy and raised sheep, he was a florist with broad glittering greenhouses at Dumbarton and a store at the corner of Fifth and Grace streets in Richmond. In a drawer were two eight-by-ten-inch pictures of the store, taken by Deminti Studio in Richmond. Made from white rectangular stone blocks, the building resembled a big shoebox, a door and three large picture windows facing Grace, then around the corner on Fifth a door and another window. On the roof boxwood and flowering shrubs grew in long planters while ferns and ornate Italian vases overflowing with flowers filled the windows. The interior of the store bloomed. Bowls and pots of ferns and flowers sat on the floor or on wrought-iron, marble-topped tables which Grandfather bought in Italy. At one end of the store was the refrigerator for cut flowers. When at the store I often sat inside the refrigerator. A fan always blew and I tried to separate the breeze into cool, clean strands of fragrance. From Grandfather I inherited a love of flowers and maybe even the desire to write about them. In the secretary was the draft of a talk, "Flowers and their Relationship to the Happiness of Man," given by Grandfather at the Country Club of Virginia in 1947. Although the talk was, as could be expected, "flowery," with Grandfather declaring that "the love of land and garden" ran through "the blood of every southern man and woman," it was also earthy, its taproot drawing sustenance from humor and good sense. "I once asked a surgeon what he thought was the best thing for a patient after an operation, and the surgeon replied, 'flowers,' not," Grandfather wrote, "because the patient would be dead, but because flowers produce a mental picture which lifts a person out of suffering and appealing to one's love of the beautiful makes him temporarily forget himself." For my part I think flowers are "the best thing" for a patient's family if the operation fails. With flowers about a grave, tears seem natural, falling like green rain, watering deep and nourishing blue buds. This past June we took a bunch of yellow and white daisies to Mother's grave in Carthage, Tennessee. The sun had baked the hillside, and pushing the spike on the can of water into the ground was impossible. Seeing us struggle, Francis wandered away over a rise in the graveyard. When he reappeared his hands were full of plastic flowers: lilies, carnations, roses, camellias, and gladiolas. Without a word he dropped to his knees and arranged the flowers around Mother's stone. Then he stood and said, "I know they are not real, but Ree-Ree will like them anyway."

Mother's secretary itself was a kind of graveyard, the letters and pictures all stones marking time past and almost forgotten like the walls crumbling in Nova Scotia. On his death in 1948 Grandfather was buried in the family plot directly beneath the Ratcliffe stone. Six years earlier his son John, the father of Sherry my first cousin, had been buried in the plot. Although next to that of Grandfather, his grave was not directly under the family stone. "Sherry told me that we didn't treat her Daddy right," Grandmother wrote Mother late in 1948; "we were standing by his grave and I asked her why. She said we ought to put a big thing over him like we did his Big Ga. She meant the stone."

In the secretary along with the talk was a copy of a letter Grandfather wrote the editor of *The News Leader* on August 3, 1940. In the letter Grandfather urged Congress to arm the nation, asking if democracy was dead. "The stench of decaying France" was, he wrote, "fresh in our nostrils and the victorious totalitarians" were "trampling the dead and dying while making ready to destroy England." All the while Congress, he wrote, delayed appropriating money for defence and thinking only of getting elected sat idly by "listening for messages from Pressure Groups." Years earlier when he was ten, Grandfather recalled, his father told him democracy was doomed. Just a boy he paid little attention, but now Grandfather asked "ARE WE WITNESSING THE LAST STRUGGLE OF DECAYING DEMOCRACY?" Like Grandfather's greenhouses, warm and damp with flowers growing throughout the winter, the bog in Nova Scotia at first seemed a garden apart from the world. In it I thought to wander free from blighting fears about war and violence. I was, of course, naive. Even on days when the sun broke through the trees and ran across the moss in golden bars, fears for the world and my children hung black in my mind. At five o'clock one afternoon Edward and I suddenly pushed through some alders into a small, heart-shaped clearing. Like a yellow fleece swamp buttercups blanketed the ground. For a moment we stood speechless. Then Edward turned toward me with worry creasing the corners of his eyes and said, "Daddy, God must have invented all those army people with guns by accident."

Behind Edward's remark lay the shooting down of the Iranian jetliner over the Strait of Hormuz. Destruction and waste were much closer to us, however, than the Persian Gulf. Because the soil lacked nutrients and the waters were highly acidic, few animals foraged in the bogs. Even fewer lived in them. In the woods surrounding the bog, I expected, though, to see a goodly number of animals. Aside, however, from three or four red squirrels who buried caches of spruce cones throughout the woods, I saw few animals. Three summers ago grouse had raised broods along the wall bordering Ma's Property. This summer I didn't see or hear a single grouse. The woods had been hunted almost dead, and under the trees I found a score of twelve and twenty gauge shotgun shells. Hunters followed the old stone walls down toward the bog and then ranging out shot everything bigger than a fist. Still, I did see some birds, most small migratory foragers, though, not permanent residents: flocks of chickadees feeding quickly over elder and mountain ash, a robin dipping through the old orchard like a shadow, a black and white warbler turning up and down over limbs and across tree trunks hunting insects, and then a Lincoln's sparrow nesting on the ground amid thorn and alder at the edge of the bog. The bog itself was silent, suited more for contemplation than hearing. On windy days, though, black spruce rubbed against each other, making a pulling leathery sound. Often at high tide I heard the waves pushing rocks back and forth beneath the headland. Sometimes when there was no wind and the tide was low, I heard traffic on Route One, the bus to Halifax and then big ten-wheeled freightliners rolling down the French coast, loaded with gurry for fish factories at Short Beach and Sandford. Occasionally I heard birds, once the thick croak of a raven, but usually crows and gulls flying out over the headland. Sometimes I mistook the cries of the latter for the laughter of children, and thinking Francis and Edward were in the hut, I wondered how they slipped pass me. Sometimes in the woods, I heard white-throated sparrows, their high sweet calls, making me happy and melancholy at the same time.

The birds in and about the meadow beyond our kitchen porch outnumbered those in the bog. In the morning chickadees picked through the hawthorns, robins dug beneath the grass for worms, and flickers fed ants to their young while catbirds sat on the porch railing, occasionally dropping to the ground to search for bugs under the funkia. Moving through the horse chestnut down over the roses and across the grass to the maples and birch were warblers: black-throated green warblers, yellow, Nashville, and magnolia warblers, the eyes of the last shining out from a black mask of feathers, bold as those of a knowing matron at a costume ball. In the afternoon swallows appeared, flipping down over the eaves, then suddenly spurting off and upward before the windbreak. In late July I sat on the porch steps after dinner and listened to a veery calling back in the tamaracks, its song a silver spiral, trilling downward almost to stars like the evening itself.

During winter mice nest in our house and occasionally at dusk I saw mice hurrying through the meadow by the porch. Although I found the burrows and runs of small animals, I never saw a mouse in the woods near the bog. Sometimes balls of fluff seemed to fall out of my way and to tumble down holes. Still, I was never sure what I had seen. Rarely did I find anything when I investigated, and when I did, it was always a wood frog, itself camouflaged in black and brown, a piece of slate, damp against the moss. Under fallen limbs but more often beneath the bark of rotten trees, I found red-backed salamanders. Under one small triangle of bark were six, four ash-colored and two with bright red stripes running from their heads along their backs to their tails. The red-backed salamander often lays eggs in a rotten log, and those under the bark were probably females protecting young.

Most trees about the bog were black spruce or tamarack, but there were others, usually low and bushy: elder, its small white flowers bunched in sweet clusters; willow and paper birch along the walls on Ma's Property; red maple, alder, and mountain ash. Trees did not completely circle the bog. Flowing like a channel into the center of the bog was a thick inlet of bushes, many bright and fragrant or bearing berries: Labrador tea, the underside of its leaves white and furry; highbush blueberry; sweet gale; huckleberry, the fruit shiny and black in August; mountain holly; winterberry, and sheep laurel, dish-shaped flowers clustered pink and yellow around the stem like a display of china. Most of the tamaracks grew in relatively sunny spots, small clearings torn open by storms. The tamarack is the only conifer, evergreen, to shed its foliage every year, and its needles are softer and grow in tufts seemingly farther apart than those of the black spruce, giving it a green and delicate appearance. Almost like a dancer the tamarack sways in the wind, long twigs bending then floating melodiously like fingers interpreting mood. Most of the trees in the woods, though, were black spruce. Conifers like the tamarack and black spruce grow better in the thin, poor soil surrounding the bog than do hardwood or deciduous trees. Because its needles last several years, the black spruce has an added advantage. Not having to grow a completely new set of leaves each spring, it needs less nourishment than deciduous trees, including the tamarack. Additionally both the tamarack and black spruce can survive terrible cold. Within the live tissues of each tree are great numbers of minute, empty spaces. In winter liquids inside living cells seep out into the spaces and freeze there, thus protecting live cells from the cold.

Early in July thinking about seeing so preoccupied me that often I did not see, or if I did, I overlooked the obvious. Before I really looked at trees, I studied the lichens growing on them. In long pale yellow strands old man's beard hung from black spruce near the wet middle of the bog. Most of the trees there were small and a good many dead; partially uprooted they leaned against each other resembling aged mandarins, the lichens drooping like goatees unkempt and rheumy. Throughout the woods lichens covered the trees, some crusty and scalloped, others pitted. While some were brown and gelatinous, resembling jellied consummé, others were slate or pearl, wrinkled like lettuce growing in salad-like tufts over the bark. Still others resembled tiny elegant long-stemmed cups, green and red glasses for a fairy revel. Two different organisms, a fungus and an alga, grow together to form a lichen. The plant lives on the food manufactured by the alga from carbon dioxide and water, using sunlight for energy, the process schoolchildren know as photosynthesis. When damp, lichens absorb air through their surfaces. Because lichens are small and rootless whatever substances the air carries quickly accumulate in them. If the air is polluted, particularly with sulphur dioxide, lichens die or fail to reproduce. If lichens disappear from woods in which they once thrived, chances are good that pollution is the cause. In the bog lichens grew in bushy profusion, and the air blowing over the Gulf of Maine and along the coast was sweet and green, a flying meadow fallow with clean promise.

Although lichens thrived in the bog, black spruce had not done so well. The wetland was spreading and as the waters rose, many spruce suffocated from oxygen starvation. Others were diseased. Dwarf mistletoe and rust fungi caused witch's brooms, great mats of small bunched branches. From underneath witch's brooms resemble heavy nests and seem luxuriant, a sign of rich vitality. In truth brooms stunt trees and cause early death. Amid the beauty of the bog as amid the beauty of human life, I did not want to think about death and disease. I could not escape them, however, for they were, as they should have been, all about me. Legions of bark beetles attacked the spruce. When I peeled away the bark from rotten trees searching for salamanders, I almost always found traces of the beetles, galleries cut by grubs feeding on soft inner bark. Adult beetles bore through the outer bark and start the galleries; in them females lay their eggs, and once hatched the grubs eat their way along, forming new galleries. When a tree is attacked by beetles, it quickly exudes pitch, trying to drown the beetles and plug their entrances. Against a small number of beetles a tree is usually successful. If the number is large, though, the tree cannot produce enough resin to defend itself and is killed swiftly.Beetles were epidemic in the bog. Although a few trees thrived untouched, many more had been killed while all the others were marked by the struggle, yellow pitch streaming down the bark or hardened into brown clumps.

In the wettest part of the bog walking was difficult. Roots of the black spruce did not run deep, and those blown over in storms rarely fell flat on the ground. Instead they leaned over, trunks stretched out like fence railings and roots raised like the top portion of an open clam shell. In falling the roots lifted moss and rock off the ground with them, leaving gray holes beneath into which water quickly seeped forming small pools. Filled with humic acid the pools were dark and still, the water inhospitable to insect life and resembling strong tea made from cheap floor sweepings. When the trunks eventually broke and fell to the ground, moss covered them. The heartwood rotted, often leaving the shell of the tree running hollow under the ground. The shells looked like long hummocks of moss, and if a person doesn't tread lightly, he can break through and pitching forward twist a knee or ankle. Most of the trees grew straight up, but they could turn through many shapes. Blown by the wind the trunks of a few pitched sideways just above the moss and ran along the ground before they turned skyward, looking like the rounded curved butts of pistols carried by swashbuckling pirates. Other trees resembled candelabra, three or four limbs twisting out from the trunk and extending parallel to the ground for some feet before turning upward. Sometimes lower branches rooted themselves in the moss and started new trees so that in a sunny spot a ring of young trees grew around a dying parent. In parts of the bog black spruce were thick, and branches reached over the moss from one tree to another, grabbing and snagging, making me feel that I was going through a turnstile the wrong way. Irrationally I resisted backtracking, and when I first began studying the bog, I thrust ahead if I met opposition. I tore off rotten limbs and behaving like man mountain pushed over dead trees and made paths. A sensible person ought not to be bothered by turning back, however, and later I learned to glide around and under. I found animal runs, and slipped softly and chastely through the trees, dancing, it sometimes seemed, to melodies full and earthy.

Grandfather and Grandmother spent every winter in the Jefferson Hotel in Richmond. In January 1947 Grandmother wrote Mother that she was going to Cabin Hill "to see the baby lambs." "They have one hundred and five," she said, adding, "I wish Sammy could see them." I don't remember the sheep. As a boy I had eyes only for cattle. In Nova Scotia, though, I found myself echoing Grandmother and wishing I could see lambs. Huckleberry, sweet gale, alder, and highbush blueberry are overgrowing the meadow behind our house, and in early July when Vicki and I walked past it out to the headland, we often talked about clearing it, rebuilding the walls, and raising sheep. Much as I broke wide paths through the bog, so we discussed neatening our lives, moving to Nova Scotia and burning off the bushy undergrowth. We imagined square green fields and lambs prancing, firm gray walls and days whiter than washed wool. About the time I stopped pushing ways through the trees, Vicki and I stopped talking about moving to Nova Scotia and raising sheep. Something there is, though, in a person that wants to clear land and master life. In the back house I found a pair of iron tree clippers, a thick mass of bolt and spring, three and a half feet long with a beaked cutting edge. The field just northeast of our house once belonged to George Hall a neighbor and is known as George's Field.

In past summers we looked out from our kitchen window down across the field and the spruce, sharp like cut tin on the headland, to Black Point then over to the lighthouse at Cape St. Mary's, and on clear evenings all the way to Digby Neck. Washing dishes we saw sunsets break golden then slide slowly through pink into the deep, dark purples of night. For years, though, alder had grown along the wall bordering George's Field, gradually sweeping the long light into corners of the window. Unaccountably one afternoon I grabbed the clippers and chopped the alders down along the wall. Perhaps I reacted to the realization that I could never clear my life of undergrowth and raise sheep in Nova Scotia. Whatever the motivation, though, I worked frenziedly for two days, clearing over a hundred yards of alder from the wall.

The thickets of black spruce in the woods not only forced me to change the way I moved through the trees but they also changed the way I saw. Slowing, often stopping me, they pushed me past sentimental impressionism towards clarity and observation. If I did not immediately see relationships between things at least I began to see things themselves. The haze of mood blew away and lines became crisp and defined, not mottled or blurred beyond focus. When I watched the sunset out of the kitchen window, beauty was almost an emotion. Under the trees it was a still life: a bar of sunlight thrown between the spruce to break on a solitary blue flag and a small rotten stick, covered with slaty lichens, their surfaces not gray but speckled with silver in the light. The still clarity brought the flower almost to life transforming the old Indian story about the flower's miraculous nature from fiction to something akin to truth. The flower, the story relates, could change men and women who had been turned into animals back into humans. To restore a person a seed was placed beneath a fold of skin on the animal's forehead. The next spring a blue flag sprouted; in the center of its blossom was not a stigma or pistil, but a diminutive human being. As the flower grew the body of the animal withered. When it fell away in mid-summer, dry as a corn shuck, the person stepped out of the flower, fully grown and completely restored.

In the morning spider webs hung in the trees, soft and silver with dew. One day I spent half an hour looking at the web of an orb weaver, its foundation lines attached to a tamarack and the trapline running to an elder, sweet with blossoms. Resembling white scraps sliced from drawing paper by a child new to scissors, the webs of grass spiders sometimes littered the moss. In the windows of our house gray cross and foliate spiders, thick as thumbnails, weaved new webs every night. Vicki and I watched them weave, first stringing out dry radiating lines then circling about, spinning the spiral line, balls of sticky wet drops chained along the silk. We named the spiders: Jezebel, Ernestine, Abigail, Bella, Donna, and Family Friend. We saw them swell and predicted when they would make egg sacs. We knew their habits. Ernestine was careful and meticulous while Bella was sloppy. Beginning her web at dusk Abigail finished weaving before Donna started. Lights in the house attracted insects, and the spiders fed mostly on moths: loopers, inchworm moths, and occasionally a Virginia Ctenucha, its body blue with orange around the head and wings black and brown. Outside on the windows spiders seemed to flourish, they ate well and most were still alive when we left late in August. Life about the bog appeared harsher. Rarely were webs built in the same place day after day, and although the "House Araneas" often had to defend their webs against raiders, they looked free from parasites. In the woods I found a small orb weaver with a green worm attached to its back, probably the grub of a chalcis fly. The fly lays its egg on a spider; on hatching the grub buries its head beneath the skin of the spider and begins sucking out nourishment. The spider does not die quickly. Instead it remains alive, a slave doomed to hunt and provide food for its master the parasite. Not until it is ready to spin a cocoon does the grub set the spider free by eating its vitals.

In the bog there were no dangerous spiders, no brown recluse or black widow. If I brushed against a web and felt a spider catch on my neck I did not flick it aside, reckoning that if the spider made her own way off she was not liable to get hurt. At times I found myself wishing the bog were dangerous. Like strong coffee a little fear awakens and sharpens observation. Walking through the heath which spread out from the bog toward Beaver River was hot and frustrating. From their roots to their topmost leaves the shrubs tangled in great clots. To get through I tried to follow animal runs. Because the animals which foraged in the bog were small the runs were overgrown above knee level. And where foot led leg usually could not follow. To have neglected the heath would have distorted my view of the wetlands and so I forced my way into it. I always hoped to stumble upon animals, but because walking was always loud and rustling I saw no animals other than birds in the heath and the hours I spent there were dull. To keep alert I imagined hornets' nests, papery cones behind sheep laurel and white-faced hornets hanging inside like grapes. Not until I returned to Connecticut did I see a hornets' nest. Instead of being buried in bush, the nest was in the open, above a neighbor's front door and attached to siding and a plastic shutter. In Nova Scotia the only nest I saw was that yellow jackets built in the hawthorn just above the entrance to the children's clubhouse. No larger than a walnut, the nest, nevertheless, fueled an evening's discussion. For her part Vicki suggested boiling a tub of water on the wood stove. After I slipped the tub under the tree beneath the nest, I should, she explained, clip the branch on which the nest hung, making sure it fell into the water. Vicki is strong-willed and went so far as to begin boiling water. In the end, however, I knocked the nest off the tree with a long stick.

Mosquitos were a staple of the spiders' diet in the bog. Often they swarmed about me, so many that their buzzing sounded low and throbbing. Still, since I wore a sweat shirt and a sailor's cap, the brim pulled down over my forehead and the back of my neck, mosquitos did not bother me. Even when I stopped walking to examine something, I hardly noticed them. Only in late August when I picked blueberries were they a nuisance, forcing me to move quickly from bush to bush or to wedge myself under branches so they would have trouble biting me. Along with mosquitos moths furnished meals for spiders. In early July moths flaked from lichens in great crusts. Small with grays mottling into reddish browns, the moths may have been spruce budworm moths, the larvae of which feed on spruce, and when numbers are large enough can defoliate a forest. Under the alders in the heath were nests of red and black ants. Shaped like mounds or small, round trampolines, the nests were two feet high and over a yard wide. They were made from peat moss and had been built up to protect the colony from flooding. Egg chambers lay just under the upper covering of peat, and the ants were fiercely protective, at the slightest pressure swarming out over the mound in great hurried washes. In July spittlebugs were common in the bog. The nymphs of froghoppers, spittlebugs feed on plant juices. To protect themselves from predators and probably to keep from drying out, they cover themselves with frothy masses of white bubbles. Often the bugs were on sedges: hair's tail, cotton grass, or twig rush. I attempted to study sedges and rushes, not, I am afraid, very rigorously. Although I sat motionless for two hours watching gray cross spiders, ten minutes among sedges wore me out. On the last occasion in which I looked at sedges, I took Eliza, my three-year-old, with me, the unspoken hope being she would become bored and ask to do something else. Her father's little trooper, Eliza rarely lets me down. "Daddy," she said soon after I started examining sedges, "I have a dark in my throat. I want to go home." When a child has a dark in her throat, only a sadist would not respond. Home we went.

Because the meadow behind our barn is no longer ploughed, moss has spread into it. At the far edge of the field opposite the kitchen porch were buried three cats and a dog, the pets of Vicki's childhood. For tombstones Vicki selected flat rocks from the beach at Beaver River. On them she painted the animals' names in large white letters: Tiger, Sam, Bart, and Big Foot. Each summer she found the graves and repainted the rocks, at least she did so until we missed three straight summers. On our return to Nova Scotia, Vicki could not find the rocks. Moss had hidden them. Although I dug about at the edge of the field with a shovel peeling back the moss, I could not find the stones. The moss had moved quickly and frighteningly. In the bog it covered the stone walls, making me imagine them lumpy runs of giant prehistoric moles. Although I saw it every day, I avoided really looking at moss until late in the summer. Because it spread inexorably into the back meadow and had covered the walls and then those small emblems of Vicki's childhood, I associated moss with mortality and the fleeting nature of everything in life.

I had, of course, endowed the moss with attributes not its own. Finally, however, its beauty attracted me. The peat or sphagnum mosses rumpled across the forest floor in a rainbow of greens, some glowingly yellow, others shadowy and almost red. Dappled in the sunlight the big hummocks seemed to float, airborne above the ground. Feathery and softer than down, the mosses lightened my walks and later in the summer my moods. Instead of gloomily pondering mortality, I examined the mosses, trying to see if they did, as I read, grow from top to bottom. Some of the mosses held more than twenty times their weight in water and squeezing them like sponges I wrung out great droplets. On my hands and knees I crawled through the woods, marveling at the intricate tapestry of small leaves and branches: haircap with spikes like delicate yuccas, bushy sphagnum its spore capsules, diminutive stakes, red torches at the end. "Appreciation of the beautiful," Grandfather declared in his talk in Richmond, "brings out the best that is in us and adds peace of mind and happiness to our existence." Grandfather was right. Crawling across the floor of the forest I was happy. "Daddy, you want to be moss," Eliza said, "but when I grow up I want to be a ballerina, a fire engine woman, and a mermaid."

Toward the end of July the floor of the woods burst into bloom. Clusters of Indian pipes appeared pale under the conifers, their flowers demure and nodding like bridesmaids gathered for a forest wedding. Down the side of the blossom ten or twelve stamens stretched like snares, their ends creamy yellow. Like shy little girls in white summer frocks Indian pipes at first seemed too delicate for life. I longed to protect them, much, I suppose, as I long to shelter my children, watering innocence and hoeing out rough maturity. No matter what I do, of course, my children must grow hard and knowing and Indian pipes must age. By mid-August their bells had turned boldly upward, and their flowers had blackened, becoming fit companions for mushrooms rioting broad-hipped and fertile through the woods.

In truth Indian pipes and mushrooms and the conifers themselves were close companions, bound together literally and not just metaphorically. The mushroom is the flower of a fungus. In searching for salamanders I found fine thread-like filaments running beneath the bark of rotten trees. A network of filaments or strands makes up the body of a mushroom. An enormous number of strands branched through the forest soil. Some ranged upward through the tissues of rotten trees while others dug down to the roots of living trees. When they came into contact with a new root, they grew both around and in it, forming a soft case about the tip and then digging into the root itself, growing in the spaces between cells. What was formed is called a fungus-root, something beneficial to both tree and fungus. The fungus receives sugars while the tree, its fungus-roots stretching through a larger volume of dirt than short root hairs, has, in effect, greatly increased the absorbing surface of its roots, enabling it to pull water and nutrients from the soil with more efficiency and from greater distances. Most trees in a coniferous woods have fungus-roots; those lacking them usually do not thrive. For its part the Indian pipe exudes a chemical from its roots which attracts filaments from fungus-roots. Strands of fungus surround and penetrate the Indian pipe's roots, much as they do those of trees, thus forming links between trees and Indian pipes. From the Indian pipe the fungus-roots receive matter which stimulates growth. From the fungus the Indian pipe receives nutrients, some of which came originally from the tree.

Before July I could not distinguish a death cap from an ink cap mushroom, though somewhere I read and remembered that a paste made from the raw hashed stomachs of three rabbits and the brains of seven others was occasionally administered to people suffering from death cap poisoning. Although rabbits eat death caps without ill effect, the paste rarely saved anyone. In any case there were no death caps in our woods, and the only rabbit I saw was a snowshoe hare, brown in his summer fur, nibbling grass near the wall at the lower end of George's Field. Although the deadly death cap did not grow in Nova Scotia, other poisonous *Amanita* flourished, veils hanging down their stalks, occasionally as in the case of the white destroying angel, making them appear pure and delectable as church brides. Warty orange eggs of fly agaric pushed up through soil in clusters and rings, and then spreading their caps bloomed red and yellow, as lovely as daffodils. Fly agaric got its name from being used as an insecticide in the Middle Ages. To kill flies people set it out in houses, either ground up in a saucer of milk or with sugar sprinkled on the cap. Nervous about their contents Vicki and I don't use bug sprays, and I longed to try fly agaric out in the kitchen. Despite explaining to Vicki that using a natural killer like fly agaric could only be good, even better than a fly swatter made out of artificial rubber, I am afraid I wasn't allowed to run a test, not even a "closely monitored" one.

Although not permitted to experiment with mushrooms, I, nevertheless, brought quantities home from the woods. Often I displayed them on the porch as if they were fruits in a still life. Men, I believe, are drawn toward solitude more powerfully than women. Even the best husbands and fathers occasionally long for moments away from family and home. Alone in the woods I was wonderfully content. I forgot the irritations which made me petty and sometimes cruel, and after two hours of studying spiders or lying on the ground looking at moss, I returned home, happy and refreshed, and a better member of the family. I do not, however, think men high creatures. A few explorations did not last long, and on them, alas, I brought back some perspiration and only one mushroom. Six or seven inches tall with a thick stalk and a broad olive-brown cap, crusted with warts, the cleft-foot death cap was a strong, almost virile mushroom.

Thrusting up through the needles on the forest floor, and before the cap lifted up and spread out, the mushroom seemed ruttingly masculine. "Hey, hey, babe, what about this," I said rushing into the kitchen after a short visit to the woods and whipping out what I thought was a particularly impressive cleft foot. "My God," Vicki exclaimed, looking at the mushroom. "Harold must have died. What a loss." "Now," she said, a slight smile creasing her face, "I am busy with these raspberries. Why don't you be a good boy and go back to the bog for a while."

I turned and leaving the kitchen walked out on the porch, being careful not to let the screen door slam. For a moment I rolled the mushroom over in my hands, looking at it a bit wistfully I am afraid. At my age, though, all sorts of perspirations evaporate rapidly and I soon tossed the mushroom under the porch and sitting down on the steps began thinking about chickens. We picked the raspberries which Vicki was sorting just the day before at Sandra Phinney's farm in Tusket Falls. Edward and Eliza had never been to a working farm, and although they picked for a while, they soon disappeared, preferring to follow chickens about as they scratched and darted through the long rows of raspberries. When we had four quarts of raspberries and were ready to leave, I found Edward and Eliza in the chicken house, cackling over newly laid eggs. What a person sees one place often determines what and how he sees at another. As soon as we returned home from Tusket Falls, I set off for the bog. The day was foggy, and the fog blew through the trees in thick billows, resembling the feathers on Sandra Phinney's Barred Plymouth Rocks, black and white layers folding into gray. My grandfather raised chickens at Cabin Hill, and when I was a boy, I often fed them corn. Like Edward and Eliza I liked trailing behind them, watching them roll their heads about searching for bugs. Their mad, erratic dartings through the yard made me laugh, and I enjoyed hunting for eggs. Now sitting on our steps in Nova Scotia, my home in Storrs seemed sterile, and I imagined raising chickens, turning their names over in my mind like fat juicy drumsticks: Australorp, Buttercup, Speckled Sussex, Buff Brahma, Black Rosecomb, Golden Penciled Hamburg.

The mushrooms in the woods came in various colors: pink, cream, purple, orange, red, cinnamon, brown, violet, peach. When broken the tubes running down through the caps of some Boletes turned blue. Because its gills and cap were a deep burnt ochre, I named one mushroom "my lovely." Later I changed the name to "farewell my lovely." Identifying mushrooms was difficult, and often I made up names: red toe, leprosy, sesame, loaf, glove. The mushrooms came in all shapes from delicate fairy helmets to spongy, squat Boletes. The caps of some mushrooms were bigger than an outstretched hand. Other mushrooms did not have caps as such. White and pink, coral fungi reached up through the moss in branched almost salty racks. Pats of soft, yellow witches' butter stuck to trees throughout the woods. Sometimes mushrooms grew in demure groups of three or four, but often they bunched together in bright colorful fairy rings, orange and red. In another age when willows walked at night and birches stalked victims, leaves rustling like clothes on a corpse, fairy rings were useful. Inside a fairy ring one was safe from death and the clutch of cold, white fingers. Entering a fairy ring was done only as a last resort, however, for within a ring time was arbitrary. What seemed but a momentary reel inside the ring could roll out to centuries beyond, and once a man finished his dance and stepped outside the ring, he was liable to discover that his world had long since faded into dust. I stood in the middle of many fairy rings, always in the unenchanted day however. I longed to wander the woods at night and test the old charms. I never did, though, for every night I read to the children. Instead of striding into old magic I labored through a library, some of its shelves stocked with the marvelous, but a library, nonetheless, confined and safe: *Charlotte's Web, Pippi Longstocking, Dr. Doolittle, Mary Poppins, Paddington Bear, Peter Pan, The Princess and the Goblin,* fairy tales from sundry nations, and *Bunny Boy,* a book given to Vicki's father on his sixth birthday.

Mushrooms provided food and shelter for small creatures around the bog. Slugs pushed between gills; minute green worms chewed tunnels through stalks; spiders hid under veils; and squirrels and hares, and probably mice and voles also, nibbled the caps. Having read about mushroom poisoning—"evil-smelling diarrhea," "fatty degeneration of the liver," "cold sweats," "narrowing of the pupil," "slowing down of the heart," and death—I did not eat any mushrooms. Instead I smelled them. As could be expected most simply smelled like mushrooms or what one imagines mushrooms should smell like: a closed room, a musty wind, or moldy garlic bread. The aroma of some, however, startled me, bringing to mind sulphur water, lemonade, and mild paint. As I age and my eyes weaken, I rely upon smell more than ever before. On the ground caches of berries or nuts gathered by small animals often resembled droppings. When in doubt over what I looked at, I picked up two or three berries and after crushing them in my hand smelled them. Droppings, human or otherwise, have never bothered me unduly. Still, I doubt that ten years ago before marriage and three children I would have mashed and smelled berries without so much as a thought.

Near a wall grew the most aromatic mushroom in the woods. On first breaking through the dirt the mushroom grew four or five inches tall, its cap spread large and brown like a loaf of pita bread. As the mushroom aged the cap slumped down and moulding itself to the ground made the mushroom appear squat. The mushroom grew in heavy groups and seemed to mound up through the floor of the forest like the remnants of a primitive terrace. The mushroom may have been a brittlegill, perhaps the stinking brittlegill. What was certain, however, was that once the cap slumped to the ground, it turned blackly purple and aromatic, even becoming host to clusters of small, white mushrooms with bowl-shaped cups. When the big mushrooms first appeared and spread out like loaves, Edward and I used them for ammunition in a mushroom fight. At first we sailed them delicately through the air but then enjoying the battle we heaved them at each other in big, moist patties. Only after the mushrooms began rotting did their aroma become strong. Walking through the woods one day, I smelled them on the breeze. Almost overpowering theirs was the fragrance of doings intimate, and like a ram turned out to ewes I snuffed the air and found myself following the wind, stiff-legged. Once I discovered the source of the fragrance, I went on to other things, examining wildflowers and ferns. Alas, however, I never really left the mushrooms and so long as they were on the breeze, I circled around sniffing the air. For a while I was bothered by the mushrooms' attraction. When I first went to the woods, I hoped to experience, if not profound at least elevated thoughts. Profundity, though, is often abstract, and elevation implies distance. It just may be that the closest I ever got to Nature was there in the woods, mushrooms at my feet and my nose rolling in wrinkles like that of a ram.

Along with mushrooms I brought habits of behavior back from the woods. On rainy days I explored the house much as I explored the bog. On the floor of an upstairs closet I found an old wall telephone, made by Northern Electric and Manufacturing Company, the two bells on the front resembling eyes and the speaking tube a long nose. Stuck on the wall behind the medicine cabinet in the bathroom was a small piece of paper on which a child had drawn an insect. With great pincers near the tail the insect looked like an earwig, and at the bottom of the paper the child wrote in capital letters, "LONGUS BUGUS MAGNUS CUM PINCHO." Used as a bookmark in *The Captive of Nootka, or the Adventures of John R. Jewett,* published in Philadelphia in 1841, was a light blue, three-by-five-inch card printed for the Young Women's Christian Association at 40 Berkeley Street in Boston. "Permanent Board for young women under thirty years of age who are earning their own living, or preparing to do so, from $3.25 to $5.50 a week," the card stated, "room, light, heat and ten pieces of plain laundry included." I spent much time exploring books, and in the study found *Sailing Alone Around the World* by one Captain John Slocum. A reprint of a volume first published in 1900, the book itself did not interest me. On the title page, however, was a handwritten inscription, "For Vicki in honor of ocean voyages and other things. March 1974 with love from Peter." "Good Lord, you are mired down," Vicki said after I read the inscription to her, not even bothering to look up from the peas she was shelling, "you showed that to me last year. What's happened to your mind? Too much bog?"

My mind played odd throughout the summer, comparatively recent events seeming to slip out of memory while things which happened decades ago floated unaccountably to consciousness, so clear they seemed preserved in humic acid. I suddenly recalled one of the last times I shot dove. On a hunt many of the dove brought down are not killed outright but are only wounded. To end their suffering hunters snap off the birds' heads. Snapping off heads is unpleasant but necessary, and I had not thought much about it until I saw an acquaintance forcing his six-year-old boy to do it. The boy did not want to do it and cradling a wounded bird in his hands was crying. "Goddamnit," the father yelled, slapping the boy hard across the cheek, "you weak little bastard. Pull that head off."

Once while resting after forcing my way through alders to a clearing grown over with New York fern, I suddenly found myself out of the present and Nova Scotia and back in sixth grade in Tennessee. The summer had just ended; school had begun, and for an assignment all the children wrote about their vacations. I wrote about Cabin Hill and described the people I knew, a farm worker who drank and beat his family and the thirteen-year-old boy down the road who smoked cigars. I tried to write the truth, but the teacher thought I lied, and she made me stand and read my theme to the class. That night I wrote another theme in which I described boxwood and magnolias at Cabin Hill. The teacher liked it, and I got a good grade.

George's Field sloped gently down toward the Gulf of Maine. At the end nearest the headland was a stone wall, an old apple tree, and a thicket of alders and black spruce. Beyond the spruce was an open bog sunk into the ground like a washtub. The land surrounding the bog was raised, and on the far side ran quickly upward through heath then spruce and tamarack out to the high open headland. To reach the bog I walked northeast across George's Field, crossed a stone wall, and then circling wide to avoid the spruce approached through an old pasture, at the edge of which was the foundation of a barn, now overgrown with wild roses, petals at first red and then pink as the blossoms aged. Sometimes the fragrance of roses hovered just beyond the bog, misty and sweetly lavender like potpourri in the bedroom of a kindly grandmother. Beyond the roses the ground turned wet and stretched downward to the bog. In the damp, grew purple and ragged orchis. In August lady's mantle turned orange, and pinching up cut sharp facets in the dew balled in the center of its leaves. Over nearby pastures marsh hawks pitched and slid through the air, white rumps flashing. On the tops of distant spruce crows gathered and looked out over fields. The bog, though, was still and silent; aside from low bushes there were no perches for birds, and only an occasional sparrow dropped into the bog. The bushes themselves were shadbush, a few purple, gritty berries at the end of long stems. Throughout the summer I ate berries, great baskets of them. When I did not recognize a berry, I sampled one. If I liked the taste, I ate ten, after which I waited a day before eating more. If I felt fine at the end of twenty-four hours, then I returned and munched my way through the bush. Although I only tasted berries, I wanted to sample the soil under the moss in the woody bog. All the iron had leached out, and the soil was gray and probably free from bacteria. It looked like chocolate frosting, and although I scooped up handfuls, I was too much the product of tile and ceramic cleanliness to eat any.

I saw no animals in the bog. Winding through grasses at the margin of the bog, though, was a run ending in a burrow, probably

that of a snowshoe hare. Near George's Field was a small brown
pool. On sunny days an American toad, round and thicker than a
pile of pancakes, basked on a half-sunken post at the edge of the
pool. A dark oval surrounded by a gold ring, the toad's eye is so
striking that people once told stories about precious stones being
found within toads' heads. When worn about the neck, the stone
charmed away evil. Although the magical ability of the toad has
faded, some charm remains. Something is missing from a house
where no toad lives in the damp under the back steps. At Cabin Hill
my family and I sat on the steps after dinner, and watching the
toads, talked away the gathering dark. In Connecticut no toads live
by our door, and instead of sitting out the night, talk painting the
shadows, we drift into separate rooms and read or watch television.

On warm days damselflies hung like ornaments on the grasses
beside the pool. Curling their abdomens into black and blue half
circles, bluets turned over the water, attaching eggs to submerged
plants and sticks. White-tailed dragonflies, bodies pale blue and
wings banded with black, flew out from the bog to rest on the dry
raised road running past our barn through the woods out to the
headland. Dark patches like saddlebags on their back wings and
scarlet triangles chaining down their backs, Elisa skimmers glided
low across the bog. High up over George's Field big darners
drummed through the air. The darners never seemed to rest, and
finding an old butterfly net in the back house, I set out to catch one,
not before, however, leaping lightly before the kitchen window in
various poses: chin elevated, legs extended, and net held high and
delicately, its white cloth cupped and blowing behind me. Alas, as
I was unable to draw Vicki away from beet greens, so the darners
proved elusive, sliding off at right angles whenever I approached.
Despite being unable to catch a darner, I used a bit of dragonfly lore
I picked up. On returning to the house I found Edward hunched
over in the loft of the barn crying. I had left him with Francis playing
happily in the loft. While I chased dragonflies, they quarreled, and
Francis climbed down, and removing the ladder, marooned Edward.
Dragonflies were once called devil's darning needles, and according
to fable often sewed up the ears of bad boys. "And stitches through
the ears, big bloody ones, that's what you'll get," I said to Francis,
"if you treat your little brother badly." That night Francis fell asleep
with a pillow over his head; never again did he strand Edward in
the loft.

Not until August did I explore the bog behind George's Field. In part I stayed away because walking in the bog was more difficult than in the woods. A mat of moss, sedge, and leatherleaf floated over the bog; at each step the mat quaked and water seeped over my boots. In places the mat was thin, and twice I sank almost to my waist. At home I described the places, and whenever I went out to the bog, Eliza said, "watch out for sinkholes Daddy." The bog was not dangerous but I enjoyed imagining danger. Quicksand pitted the movies I saw as a child. Children were forever being rescued by branches extended like hands across the sand, while luscious heroines were pulled from watery death into marriage by faithful cowponies, lassos looped around saddlehorns. Villains fared worse, hands waving in wild despair before disappearing beneath the creamy, pitiless sand, after which a bubble of air burst leaving a small pock mark. I also neglected the bog because plant life there was not as immediately striking or seemingly so various as that in the woods. From the bog behind George's Field I took home only one mushroom, a bracket fungus called red belt. Growing on the side of a dead spruce it was eight inches wide and four and half tall. When wet the fungus weighed two and three-quarter pounds on our ancient Detecto bathroom scale. The underside of the fungus was yellowish, and its upper rings of growth were brown. A strip of red wrapped around the mushroom at the margin, a single thick lip seemingly pasted with make-up.

The most striking plants in the bog were carnivorous: sundews and pitcher plants. In late July the peat moss turned pink as leaves of sundew uncurled and opened like hands, long fingers with rounded or spatulate ends reaching upwards. Growing like hair around the end of each leaf were bristles of glands. They exuded a sticky liquid, turning the leaves into snares, making them glisten sweet and inviting. The leaves attracted small insects; once a midge or gnat landed on the plant, it rarely flew again. The liquid bound like glue to its feet, and the hairs wrapped like ribbons about him. In the morning light the sundew shined silver and pink, and its leaves appeared caked with honey. The plant was remarkably alluring, so much so that I sucked a handful of leaves, thinking they had to be sugary. Just like an insect I was fooled. Although I ran the leaves back and forth over my tongue, I tasted nothing.

Bog soil is generally poor, and plants may have become carnivorous in order to obtain nutrients. Unlike the small sundews which are not immediately noticeable, pitcher plants grew throughout the bog in prominent clumps, much like giant heads of lettuce, leaves unfolded and spread but still crisp. Nodding at the ends of stalks a foot and a half or two feet tall were flowers, yellow centers hidden behind curved green petals, the whole resembling a cup set in a saucer and then turned upside down. Beneath the flowers red and green leaves yawn up, swollen wide like big-lipped milk pitchers tilted on their sides. Sometimes called huntsman's cup, the pitcher also resembles a powder horn with one side pinched into a wing-like keel to hold it upright. Divided into distinct sections the leaf is a wonderful device for trapping then digesting insects. In the open lip color attracts insects while stiff hairs slant down, making descent into the pitcher easy and ascent correspondingly hard. Beyond the hairs is an area of adhesive cells; these stick to the feet of insects, increasing the difficulty of getting any sort of purchase and climbing out. Below this zone is the main body of the pitcher, smooth-sided and usually filled with rain water and digestive juices, a small pond in which insects drown. Below the pond the pitcher narrows and the digestion of drowned insects begins in earnest, aided by bacteria and, strikingly, by the larvae of a mosquito, untouched by the plant's digestive juices. Despite the danger, pitcher plants are homes of small insects; crab spiders hide under the petals of the blossom while another spider hangs its web across the mouth of the pitcher itself. The plants eat well. I emptied scores of pitchers; clotting the stalks beneath the pitcher was black, muddy matter wriggling with mosquito larvae. I was not tempted to taste it, but I poked through it, pushing recognizable bits of insects into small piles. Although the bog was so silent I often thought it dead, it, I soon saw, was alive with insects. I collected the wings and heads of flies, and the hard shells of beetles, most stained black but a few still glowing with color, red or dark blue. Indians supposedly used the pitchers as water dippers, and woodsmen put berries into them. Although I never drank from a pitcher, I filled them with blueberries. I didn't eat the berries without washing them carefully however. Worms and caterpillars don't bother me. I do not mind their crawling on me or on the food I eat. Yet the mosquito larvae thrashing about like *S*'s at the bottom of the pitcher unaccountably repulsed me, and I was careful not to eat any.

We left Nova Scotia for Connecticut in late August. Ten days afterwards classes began. Like the white strands of mushroom running through the ground then up beneath the bark of a fallen tree, wetlands get under the skin. From wetlands life rises into a person, making the dry spirit flower, and between classes I explored ponds and marshes on the university farm. In an hour and a half I wandered myself out of brooding and beyond anxiety and petty frustration. Contact with the earth strengthened me almost as if I were an alder, roots swollen with nitrogen-binding bacteria and nutrients coursing through summer wood. I walked along a farm road, a drumlin, Horsebarn Hill, rising on my right and a field running down through a marsh then up to the dairy on my left. Corn had recently been harvested on Horsebarn Hill, and crows, dove, and Canada geese gleaned over it, disturbed occasionally by hawks migrating south, most sharp-shinned hawks, and then by my family as the children gathered ears for the chipmunk living under our garage. Blue sailors; jewelweed, orange pendants swinging in the breeze; small white asters; goldenrod, yellow blossoms tumbling over in falls and stars, all grew beside the road. In the wet ditch under the barbed wire fence bur-marigold bloomed; along the fence running up Horsebarn Hill, velvet-leaf had gone to seed, its tall stalks brown with beaked, hairy seed disks, looking like cake dishes crimped and upside down. A quarter of a mile up the road, I turned toward the dairy and after climbing the fence, took off my tie and jacket and started down into the marsh. Asters and buttery birdfoot trefoil were scattered on the slope. Thistles had turned to down, and jimson weed bloomed, its blossoms white and purple trumpets, so pointed and plaited that they seemed to whirl like fireworks burning through bright circles. In the marsh itself cattails had shredded into seed. Walking was difficult and I sank into muck up to my knees. In contrast to bogs, water flowed through the marsh washing away acids and hastening decomposition by breaking down organic matter. As I thrust through the cattails, gases burst from the mud, sometimes in heavy round bubbles. My boots filled with water and mud caked my trousers, even squeezing its way into my back pockets. In my next class I resembled and smelled like a creature beached and rotting on the shore of some dark lagoon. What I looked or smelled like, though, didn't matter to me, for in the marsh I saw phantom crane flies, legs spread like hands before them and floating black and white through the air like seeds.

September

"She hath done what she could" read the inscription on the stone. What sort of man would want to remember his wife like that I thought as I picked out the letters under the lichens. A sensible, calm man, a resigned man at peace with himself and life's doings, a man in a September mood, I decided as I stood and stretched, marble tombstones running up the hill behind me. In May, buds breaking with promise and hope, the inscription would not have appealed to me. But August had just ended, and I, too, was in a September mood. Back from our farm in Nova Scotia, I was happy to be in Connecticut. Having been away for eight weeks, I no longer dreamed of an elsewhere. Instead, like "Sarah Elizabeth wife of Rev. Charles Morgan," I turned my attention from the distant towards the immediate and wandered through days satisfied to do what I could in my small yard.

The yard needed little work. The grass had practically stopped growing, and I mowed it only once. Still green, the leaves had not begun to blow from the trees and clump across the ground in heavy, damp mounds. I planted a few flowers, in the side yard, Iris near the Morrones' stone wall and along the front walk peonies, Ellen Cowley, Raspberry Ice, and Auten's Red. The planting was easy. My daffodils would not arrive until the middle of October, and for Iris and peonies I did not have to dig deep, levering up and carting stones the size of melons off to the pile in the woods. With little real work to do I was content to observe. What a person does in one place, though, often influences what he does in another. In Nova Scotia I spent the summer studying bogs. Now in Connecticut I studied my yard, not with the summer's long bright intensity, however, but with the blue calm of September, veiled and almost sleepy. Instead of puzzling my way through relationships between things, I only looked at things, sitting, for example, in a lawn chair in the front yard, watching dragonflies light on blades of grass, the chair, and sometimes my fingers. Small with red bodies and wings glinting yellow in the sun, the dragonflies were the last dragonflies of the year. In summer I would have hurried off to identify them in a guide. Now I just sat and looked, imagining them Chinese birds, lacquered and long-legged, fragile remnants of chalky dynasties.

Unlike the dragonflies which I had never noticed before, most things in the yard were familiar September companions: jewelweed, orange under the "No Parking This Side" sign; galinsoga, its minute toothed blossoms astonishingly hardy along the curb; and Asiatic dayflower, blue and yellow around the mouth of the culvert. Beside the drainage ditch grew lemony horse-balm, beggar-ticks, and yellow wood sorrel. Over an old bed of Iris were white wood asters and pink spikes of lady's thumb. At the edge of the woods was bergamot. Although the scarlet petals had fallen away and the cones were mouldy, the heads remained sweet and alluring. Behind it and down both sides of the yard, goldenrod hung in great yellow sheaves. Along the driveway some of Vicki's giant gaillardia still bloomed. In the blossoms lurked small, orange crab spiders, lower legs clamped to the cone of the flower while their top four legs curved deceptively upward like wayward yellow rays. While we were in Nova Scotia other spiders spun webs and laid egg sacs inside the screened porch. In September the eggs hatched and little strings of spiders hung down from the corners of the porch. Vicki didn't want to disturb "the nursery" when she cleaned the porch so she put the webs away as carefully as she did the furniture, folding each and its small spiders and mother into a soft dishcloth. Carrying the dishcloths outside she rehung the webs, one beneath a gutter low on the garage and another inside a plastic watering can under a mock orange beside the back door. Pressed against the leaves of the gaillardia were peepers, brown markings running across their backs like veins through a leaf. Wood frogs and peepers appeared throughout September, but I didn't see a single toad; toads have vanished from my yard, eradicated, I am afraid, by years of lawn mowing. At dusk the peepers began calling; later in the evening katydids joined them. Early in September a few cicadas called during the afternoon. By the middle of the month the cicadas had disappeared, and by late October the evenings had also become silent.

In early September the ferns in the little woods behind the house still thrived. Just the sensitive fern had begun to pale. By the end of October only the Christmas fern was still green, the others having dried brown, curling into themselves or turned yellow, ragged at the edges and looking like worn stained doilies. September is my yard's berry season, not, however, berries for a high summer's lust, purple and red on the lips, but inedible berries, berries like tombstones, marking time's passing and the end of appetite, awakening mood not hunger: orange bittersweet; the blackened flats of maple leaf viburnum; bunches of jack-in-the-pulpit, red above the periwinkle; Solomon's seal, curved like a harp, berries at the end of strings, hanging in the air like notes tingling through memory. In Nova Scotia the children roamed through the summer and meadows, devouring huckleberries, blueberries, and wild raspberries. We were back in Connecticut now, though; the weeks of freedom were over. September was a time of temperance and caution. I lectured the children about strangers and leading them around the yard told them not to eat berries, taking care to warn them about baneberry or doll's eyes, shining white beans at the end of pink stalks, thick and as binding as high, formal collars. I also warned them against mushrooms, particularly against honey mushrooms, humped in great yellowish masses at the base and up the sides of stumps. Few mushrooms grow in the yard or the woods, and aside from honey mushrooms, most were shelf fungi, fruiting on the woodpile in the back yard: turkey-tail, red-belt, birch-maze gill, and artist's fungus. Under a rotten mushroom in the woods were clusters of tiny dark beetles. When I shook the mushroom, the beetles fell to the ground, clicking lightly on leaves like a small, spring rain. In truth, though, I noticed few insects. Under a stone early in September I found three woolly bear caterpillars, predominantly brown but each with at least one band of black bristles. Later in the month, however, none of the woolly bears were banded; the caterpillars seemed to have rusted, becoming more orange than brown.

I worked some in the yard in September, digging plantain and dandelion out of the front and then pulling clearweed out of the pachysandra planted on the slope running down towards the Morrones' house. Although I did not accomplish much in September, I planned for October, staking out beds for daffodils and then on the last day of September buying eighty dollars worth of grass seed and fertilizer from Thompson and Sons in Mansfield Depot. Despite not really working in the yard, however, I started other activities. Neither enervatingly hot nor cold, September is my month for beginnings. I return from Nova Scotia full of energy and optimism; by the end of October I am worn out, sometimes angry, ready to retreat curmudgeon-like, damning practically everything as silly and futile. In the first week in September the children began school, and momentarily tolerant, I ignored the sudden deterioration of their language, the misuse of *lie* and *lay* and *there is* and *there are*. At dinner I smiled when they mentioned a restaurant they created called the Hungry Heinie. Specializing in Gourmet Poop Meals, the restaurant was noted for its beverages, especially something called Crazy Flush. Although I did not ask the chefs for the recipe for Crazy Flush, I contributed an item to the dessert board, Peeberry Pie, a seasonal dish served only in September. By October peeberries had disappeared along with my tolerance. After being away from Storrs for eight weeks and seeing almost no one outside family, I felt affection for groups of people and on meeting individuals, I wanted to hug them and say I was glad they were still alive. On a Thursday early in the month I went to a school board meeting, full of enthusiasm. A program detailing the teaching of "Refusal Skills" barely dented my mood, and like a grandfatherly sun, I beamed warm and benevolent throughout the evening. I agreed to talk and sign my new book in the university bookstore. At the signing I barely paused when a student asked me to inscribe the book to Paula and Mark, then write "Ain't Love Grand" before adding my name. For a dollar's royalty, no man with a hair anywhere near his heinie, I thought, would write and sign such a statement. Still, the leaves had not begun to riot, plugging gutters and rumpling across the yard in red gusts. Quiet September was in air and mood; I hadn't carted endless leaves off to the woods; back and mind did not yet ache in exasperation, and so I didn't raise a rake against autumnal lust. Instead I simply nodded, smiled, and inscribed the book.

In September I agreed to give several talks, in Simsbury, New Britain, and Mansfield. The only talk I turned down was in Chicago. Although the pay was handsome, the talk was in November, and I don't fly in winter. The Friends of the Mansfield Library wrote, asking me to make the after dinner speech at their annual potluck supper. After I agreed, the organizer of the supper telephoned and asked to meet me and discuss the talk. The organizer was a charming man, a retired schoolteacher, mild and understated. On the other hand, I can occasionally, even in September, appear flamboyant, if not uncontrollable, bobbing up and down when I talk and punctuating conversation with loud, nasal brays. After but a minute's discussion, the organizer appeared ill at ease. "You must remember, Mr. Pickering," he said, "the Friends are an older and rather conservative group." "Oh, nuts," I exclaimed, "then I won't be able to talk about my sex life." Almost as if I had slammed home a short right cross, the organizer's head bobbled back, then quivered for a moment. "And Mr. Pickering," he said, blinking and pulling his thoughts high to defend against any untoward remarks at the supper, "we do, of course, want your wife to attend our little gathering. Indeed, we insist that you bring her. We have heard so many fine things about her."

In September I attended a "Municipal Inland Wetland Commissioners Training Program," sponsored by Connecticut's Department of Environmental Protection. Despite my teaching English I attend few literary conferences. I have little use for ideas blown high and philosophic by people who can't identify the wildflowers in their back yards. I went to the training program to listen to discussions of hardpan and to learn to read maps. I wanted to know differences between soils: Leicester, Ridgeway, Wilbraham, Rumney, Walpole, and Whitman. I wanted to progress beyond reading books to reading the earth, to know that yellow soils are usually aerated and well drained while gray soils often lack oxygen and are saturated with water. At forty-seven, of course, I am a doubter, suspecting not simply method and philosophy but also facts, even those about dirt. Participants in the training program received a broadside of "Soil Facts," published by the National Wildlife Federation. Most of the "facts" were simple statements such as "Roots hold soil together and help prevent erosion." Some startled me, however. Spread over an acre five tons of topsoil supposedly creates a layer of new dirt no thicker than a dime. Although that statement brought a pause, what stopped me, making me resuscitate high school mathematics was the assertion that "one earthworm can digest 36 tons of soil in one year." Thirty-six tons, I wrote the National Wildlife Federation, is seventy-two thousand pounds. To digest that much dirt a worm would have to munch through 197.26 pounds of soil a day or slightly more than 8.2 pounds an hour, three hundred and sixty-five days a year, with no time off for cold weather, rest, sex, or to avoid robins or rain. "Only one big mother of a worm could eat that much dirt," I wrote, "one that had been raised on chemicals." "My advice to someone who found such a worm down amongst his crab grass would be," I said, "to take his leg in his hand and heist himself right out of there and down the road as fast as he could."

Along with filling my days with talks and programs, I did not neglect the children, signing them up for all sorts of activities: Eliza for dance on Tuesdays and Francis for piano on Saturday. At five Edward was too young for most community activities. For a long time, though, he had wanted to play soccer, and so I registered him for junior soccer, a league of twelve teams composed of first, second, and third graders, and then Edward the only kindergartner. Edward played for "Kathy John's," a sweet and sandwich shop at Four Corners. On his team were the sons of a local doctor, our Saturday mailman, the manager of a mushroom farm, the school superintendent, and the university president. The teams played eleven games over four weeks, Monday, Wednesday, and Friday nights at half past five. I took Edward to all the games and had a wonderful time. While Edward looped about the field, sometimes getting a foot on the ball, I looped about the sidelines, kicking words around. The wife of the president of the university is Swedish, and occasionally she encouraged her first-grader in Swedish. "What do you suppose she is saying," another parent asked me. "Kick the hell out of that little bastard playing fullback," I answered. "No," the parent said widening her eyes; "she's not saying that." "Yes, she is; I speak Swedish. But please," I said pausing to level out my eyebrows and straighten my nose, "please don't tell anyone. This sort of thing doesn't reflect well on the university." The soccer season ended on a cold mid-October night, not cold enough to chill my enthusiasm and that evening over cake and ice cream I agreed to coach a team next September.

For many animals September marks the beginning of the gathering season. In two days crows stripped the nannyberry beside the screened porch. A groundhog dug a burrow under a rock ledge in the back yard and spent late afternoons around the children's swing set, eating the seed pods of violets. A raccoon overturned the garbage cans in the garage and then when we investigated climbed onto the rafters, knocking lumber down on the car. Until an owl or a marauding cat got it, a chipmunk lurked by the back door, practically begging for kitchen scraps. Squirrels chased through the trees after each other and hickory nuts. For days gnawed shells fell down through the trees slapping into leaves like hard rain. In search of food animals wandered far from the safety of summer burrows, and their bodies began littering the roadside. I counted the dead animals, and even though I rarely drive, saw two skunks, one groundhog, four opossums, two mice, three chipmunks, three rabbits, five raccoons, three red squirrels, twenty-eight gray squirrels, plus, of course, many unidentifiable mounds. In September I, too, began gathering, not food for a cold hibernation but sustenance for a winter's writing. Unlike animals I take few chances. Long gone are those times when I roamed at night or darted across by-ways, pursuing sweet, dangerous thought. Now I stay safely at home with Vicki and the children. Early in September I glean over the mail which accumulated while we were in Nova Scotia. Usually I find a nourishing kernel or two. From Pennsylvania a man wrote succinctly, "I am afraid I have lost my youth. If you see it, would you please contact me." From Oregon a woman sent me a book of her poetry, declaring that we were soul mates whose essences had "comingled" on "the ethereal plane." On the ethereal level was about the only place we could "comingle" because the first poem in the book described the author's stitching up her lower regions.

I did not stay in Storrs throughout September. Early in the month I traveled to Boston to see whether or not I needed an operation on my back. I went the safe, or at least to me less frightening way. Instead of driving I took the bus. On my return I had a three-hour layover in Providence. I passed the time wandering about the bus station taking notes. Sometime this winter, I thought, I might want to put a bus station into an essay. Although modern, the station resembled a barn. In the center, which opened up almost like a courtyard, were one hundred and sixteen moulded blue plastic chairs, bolted together in long iron rows. Above, the ceiling spread, rising two stories to fluorescent lights and three fans, although heat and air conditioning came through big vents in the walls. To the left and directly behind the chairs were six columns, supporting a loft of closed offices. Screwed to each of three columns was a square of four telephones. Behind the columns and under the offices was a Bess Eaton Doughnut outlet, pressed against the back of the building like a stall. On the wall above the counter were two signs, the first stern, stating in black letters "No Change Without a Purchase" and the other lighthearted, suggesting in red that "A laugh a day keeps the doctor away." The two women working behind the counter wore cheerful red dresses and red and white caps, stuck to the back of their heads with bobbie pins. Coffee at Bess Eaton was expensive, cups selling for sixty, seventy-five, or ninety-five cents. While most of the doughnuts for sale were commonplace, despite the presence of sugary varieties called jelly stick, colored shot, and red raspberry, some of the muffins seemed, if not unique, at least a little out of the ordinary, peach melba being a favorite and Piña Colada, the muffin of the month. In the back center of the building was the ticket stall; funneling people towards it were two long raised planters, filled with wood chips and big-leaved green plants. At the end of one planter was a poster covered with pictures of missing children; at the end of the other was an advertisement for "Resorts International Casino-Hotel at Atlantic City." "Take a bus to Resorts Today," the advertisement urged, "And Strike It R.I.C.H." Along the right-hand wall of the station were cigarette and photograph machines, this last offering travelers the choice of one large three and a half by four inch colored picture or four small snapshots.

Next to the machines was a sandwich and magazine shop, managed by the same company which owned Bess Eaton. Unlike the open doughnut stall the shop was an enclosed room. Just inside the door was a poster for the Rhode Island lottery, "Lotto America." "Your Ticket to a Fortune," the sign said; "Picture Yourself a Millionaire!" Beside the poster was a small, squat machine with an opening in the front; for twenty-five cents one could insert an index finger and check his heart rate. "Relax Hand," the machine instructed, "And Don't Press or Wiggle." Next to the machine were racks of magazines, paperback novels, and newspapers, many of these last printing scandal and sensation. Appetites of sundry kinds dominated the headlines. While the marriage of a woman who ate a dozen bars of soap a day went down the drain, an overweight couple lost two hundred and thirty-eight pounds on a diet of love. An eighty-seven-year-old grandmother carried her sixty-second baby while childless "UFO Aliens" stole pets to brighten their endless journeys across space. Animals offered aliens devotion beyond the capacities of humans, and recently, one paper cited almost as proof, loyal bats fought fiercely to keep scientists from discovering the grave of Count Dracula. Beyond the papers and magazines, vending machines sold soft drinks and snacks: cheese puffs and tortilla chips. In a small ice box were sandwiches: tuna, pizza, egg salad, meatball, and steak and cheese, all made at J. R.'s Deli in Coventry, Rhode Island. For any sandwich that needed cooking a microwave oven hung on the wall. Facing the machines from the opposite side of the room were the cash register and two display cases. Practically filling one case was candy, most of it familiar and sounding old-fashioned: Snickers, 5th Avenue, 3 Musketeers, Oh Henry!, Baby Ruth, and Milk Duds. In the other case were an assortment of items, the sorts of things travelers might conceivably need: nail clippers, shampoo, camera film, cough drops, sun tan oil, deodorant, toothpaste and toothbrushes, razors, shaving cream, combs, cigars—White Owl and Garcia y Vega—and then beer mugs and shot glasses with maps of Rhode Island sketched on their fronts in black and white. On the wall behind the counter hung plastic kites with yellow eagles on the front, not one, the cashier told me, had been sold in a year. More popular were the sweat shirts, selling for $7.99 with Rhode Island flowing in white cursive script over a pink or dark blue background.

Resembling a shed attached to a barn, a short corridor opened off the waiting room near the doughnut stall. Along one side were blocks of square lockers in which one could store a bag for twenty-four hours for a dollar. Opposite the lockers were the bathrooms, the door to the men's room permanently bolted open. At the end of the corridor were two offices, one housing the Runaway Youth Project and the other Travelers' Aid. On the wall in the Travelers' Aid office was a big orange poster, black letters proclaiming "Consider Yourself Hugged." The difference between word and deed is vast. Instead of actually hugging some of the people who wandered through the station, it was more sanitary and probably safer to keep them a few syllables away, wrapping them about with words not arms. Actually the bus station itself was clean; although cigarette smoke hung low in the air like a dry cloud, there was no trash on the floor. A janitor and a tall security guard prowled through the waiting room, the one sweeping up candy wrappers and discarded newspapers, the other awakening seedy-looking sleepers by kicking them in the foot.

The guard was on friendly terms with a group of bus station regulars, retirees who met to drink coffee, discuss the news, visit, and then to bet modestly on the numbers. All over seventy the men looked like tailors and clerks, maybe printers from the *Providence Journal* across the street. They wore solid-color wash-and-wear shirts, V-necked sweaters, and gray or blue slacks. Two of the men wore jackets to old suits. The men had lost weight and the jackets draped shapelessly over them like heavy parkas on cardboard hangers. Although some of the men looked tired, their eyes damp and gray, most were lively, brightly holding forth about athletics, city government, and increases in health insurance. Several left when a man in a buttoned-down checkered shirt appeared and said that just around the corner a grocer was selling three pounds of grapes for two dollars. Although the men were often jovial, their presence upset me. Thinking about the journey which lay ahead of me, not the short trip back to Storrs but the long one to old age and death, I became melancholy, and turning away I began observing travelers, those passing through space not time, from Providence to Fall River and New Bedford, not from here to eternity. A hard girl in cowboy boots and spangles got on a bus for Springfield; an Oriental family got off, bustling about, grinning and merry. An older black woman with a kindly face and a suitcase and two large paper sacks sat down near me and smiled. Wearing horn-rimmed glasses, a wig, and a heavy sweater although the day was warm, she looked as if she should have been in Charlotte or Richmond, not Providence. In scarves and sweat shirts, college students talked together and moved through to the buses in groups of four or five. Most of them, as well as the better-dressed people in the station, left at one o'clock on the bus for New London, New Haven, Bridgeport, Stamford, New Rochelle, and New York. Despite the presence of the security guard, odd and battered people appeared. A teen-ager in jeans and white T-shirt smashed his fist into a phone and screamed, "but I haven't got any money." Every half hour or so a tall thin Rastafarian in a white shirt, yellow trousers, and sandals strolled through, hair falling over his shoulders in tight braids, speakers for his radio clamped down over his ears and the aerial sticking up like a silver finger. At noon a bearded man strode in, wearing a leather jacket, motorcycle cap with gold braid over the bill, round-toed black tennis shoes, and short, baggy trousers which gathered about his calves in rumples thick as bananas. Exuding the salty fragrance of dirt long-caked, the man was aggressively independent, and I labeled him "The Captain." After buying a ticket he sat down, oblivious to and somehow superior to his surroundings. Others in the station, however, did not ignore him, and soon in seats behind him gathered the soiled and the broken. Their movements were often furtive and nervous; rarely did they look straight ahead. Instead they rolled their heads to the sides, blinking jerkily as if they expected to be beaten if they stared at anything or anyone. Collecting characters in a bus station is riskier than gathering the names of wildflowers in a back yard. People watched as I walked about the station taking notes. Although I wore a coat and tie, most probably thought me one of the broken, and at the end of three hours when I stood to board the bus for Danielson and Willimantic, a tattered man darted up to me and holding his hands out, palms open almost in supplication, shouted, "I love you."

As I don't rush through the fall collecting material like a squirrel gathering nuts, so rarely do I wander through places like bus stations stirring the affections of strangers. Instead of my having to search out writing matter, material is brought to me. As soon as I returned from Nova Scotia, acquaintances began appearing at the door, minds loaded with nutty or odd things. Ralph, a twice-divorced historian, and if his stories are truthful, a much-wronged male, brought me a poster announcing "A Separated and Divorced Women's Support Group," sponsored by the university's Center for Marriage and Family Therapy. "Are you separated? Divorced? Thinking about divorce? Single parent?" the poster asked. "Thinking about divorce!" Ralph exploded when he handed me the poster; "these people ought to be sued for alienation of affection. They are the sorts of meddlers who ruined my marriages."

In September school had just begun, and after their vacations, friends in the English department were enthusiastic about literature, even to the point of suggesting subjects for my essays. "Have I got the topic for you," Pat said, bursting into my office early in the semester. "New Englanders write about meadows and islands; southerners about death and sex. Sam," Pat continued, "you are a southerner living in New England. Why don't you stuff some sex into a meadow or decapitate a couple of lobstermen? That way you would sell both north and south and make a bundle." "Quite an idea, Pat," I said when he finished, not listening, I am afraid, so much to him as to the trucks on Route 195, their motors pulling heavy and thick like old rope.

Most ideas brought to me resemble Pat's, and like a squirrel burying nuts in the fall, I stuff them away deep into a drawer and forget them. Occasionally, however, a person will bring or send me something so intriguing that it drives trucks from my head and brings paper and pencil to hand. My great-grandfather Pickering was born in Athens, Ohio. In 1860 he was a student at Ohio University. When the Civil War broke out, he gave up his studies and joined the Ohio Volunteer Infantry, later fighting in the big battles at Perryville and Murfreesboro. In 1863 he was stationed in Nashville, occupied by the Army of the Cumberland since 1862 and destined to remain occupied until the end of the war. Perhaps because I am a teacher and have moved about, family and place matter a lot to me, probably more than they do to people who have spent most of their lives in one location. Consequently I have written about my family and the Civil War, Great-grandfather Pickering and then those relatives living outside Nashville in Franklin, who fought for the South. At the end of the war Great-grandfather married a girl from Carthage, Tennessee, and after a sojourn in Athens to finish his schooling, he returned to Carthage and raised a family of, if not rebels, at least southerners sentimental about butternut gray and the lost cause. In September a stranger sent a package from Athens, Ohio; inside were two copies of *The Nashville Daily Union,* published on April 12 and September 9, 1863, respectively. "I have read your books," an accompanying letter explained, "and when I saw these papers in an odds and ends store, I thought about you. I remembered that you were from Nashville and that your grandfather, or was it great-grandfather, was from here in Athens. Anyway," my correspondent ended, "I hope you enjoy the papers. They look like fun to me."

For me the papers were more than fun. They were part both of the past of my family and the past of the world which nurtured me. I handled them carefully, and making them slow September reading, I meandered through them as I did the yard, stopping here and there, wondering then moving on. Each paper consisted of four pages, seven columns to a page, a page being twenty-four inches long and seventeen and a half inches wide. The pages were white, much whiter than papers today, and the newsprint was black and crisp and didn't blur through lines. The print was so fixed that it seemed almost classical, bespeaking truth and hard authority. The *Daily Union* cost twenty-five cents a week or a dollar a month to monthly subscribers. Provided it was paid in advance, one could purchase a yearly subscription for ten dollars. At the top of the first page, dividing "The Nashville" from "Daily Union," the paper's motto, a quotation from Andrew Jackson, curved upward in a half-circle forming a dome of words: "Our Federal Union: It Must Be Preserved." Beneath the motto a globe floated half-submerged in heavy seas. Stamped in heavy black letters across the face of the globe was "Our

Country" while above it an American flag fluttered from a tall pole. In the issue for April 12, a "Directory" filled the two columns on the left side of the front page. The directory was diverse, listing officers of the city, county, and military governments as well as assorted announcements and the numbers and locations of hospitals in Nashville and Murfreesboro. The city council was divided into sixteen standing committees, including, among others, those for schools, gas, pest house, slaves, and workhouse. The twenty-five hospitals in Nashville were located throughout the city, often, it seemed, in makeshift locations, in, for example, the Methodist church on Church Street, the Baptist church on Summer Street, in Hume and Hynes' high schools, in a Masonic Hall, in the Gun Factory on Front Street and the Carriage Factory on Market Street, and then in the Planters Hotel the "Officers Hospital." Filling the other five columns on the front page and then four more columns on the second page was a reprint of an address delivered in 1816 by a member of the Manumission Society of Knoxville, Tennessee. In the address the speaker argued that slavery broke natural and biblical law, was contrary to justice, and destroyed the sanctity of the family. "Let the chaste matron and the modest virgin look on the maid who serves at the table and reflect that before they could possess her every principle of modesty, truth, justice, humanity, and religion was violated," the speaker urged. "Let the Christian, let the republican look on the slave who drudges in the field and have the same reflection, and let all orders of society be roused to exert their influence to get our land freed from this God-offending evil. And you who are the ambassadors of the Prince of Peace, and the defenders and advocates of this holy religion cleanse your hands of this damning sin. Lift up your voice like a trumpet against it, lest the blood of souls be found in your skirts."

Opposition to slavery did not lead to granting blacks equality before God or the law. Indeed in urging the abolition of slavery the speaker before the Manumission Society argued that slavery harmed whites more than blacks. Slaves, he said, were "generally in a state of ignorance of God and moral obligation equal to the savages of the forest." Yet, he pointed out they were trusted to nurse and raise white children. Since "first impressions on our infantile minds" were "hardly ever erased," slaves shaped "the whole future" of children with, he stressed, disastrous moral results. For the *Daily Union* blacks were not and probably could never be the equals of whites and all talk of "negro equality" was sinister, a tool used by demagogues to stir terror and hatred, in the process fanning the flames of rebellion. "I am convinced," a correspondent wrote, "that some folks there be who are terribly troubled with negro mania. Some cry out that this war is being carried on only for the purpose of elevating the negro to a level with the white man—that it is a negro war, and a war for the abolition of slavery—some are afraid that the negro will be elevated to a platform with themselves, while others profess to fear that they will be put down on a platform with the negro. As a general rule when you find a white man that's afraid he'll be made a negro's equal, you will find the negro the best of the two."

In the *Daily Union* racial matters occasionally took up more space than war news. In great part, the paper implied, faults of the Emancipation Proclamation were to blame for local problems. In freeing slaves in states still in rebellion, Lincoln exempted Tennessee. Because Nashville was held by Union forces, slaves from Confederate states to the south fled to Nashville. As a result city officials did not know what to do. How in all justice, they argued, could they administer the law, forcing blacks owned by Tennesseans to remain in bondage while acknowledging the freedom of "contrabands," slaves who fled from adjoining states? Even worse was the problem of how to feed, care for, and "control" the "negro population," as Justice Brien of the Criminal Court put it in his charge for 1863. The contrabands, he declared, were "to the well-being of society as the locusts of Egypt were to the vegetation of that drowned country." There was little work for them and they were forced to become thieves, burglars, prostitutes, and vagrants.

If in 1863 the *Daily Union* could not or would not debate questions pertaining to racial equality and neither the government nor the military was capable of providing sustenance and shelter for free blacks, supporters of the Union were nevertheless able to accomplish the simpler, more propagandistic task of apportioning blame for the war. In almost classical terms the paper accused the rich of causing the war. "The great mass of the wealthy, especially wealthy slaveholders, have been traitors to their country," an editorial stated, valuing their property more than the Union. If they could have supported the Union without risking their property, perhaps they might have done so, the paper stated, "but whenever the issue was made whether they would give up the Union or their money, they preferred to give up the Union," trampling "upon the flag of their country to save a few negroes, a few acres of land, a few paltry dollars." Predictably the *Daily Union* argued that the rich had foisted the war upon the poor, people in "humble circumstances" with "no pecuniary interest in slavery." A letter signed W. J. Greer, the paper claimed, had been found on the body of a dead rebel sergeant. "I'll be d——d," the sergeant wrote, "if I don't think it's about time to stop killing off the poor white men that the rich may grow richer. I can't see what rights we have lost to make such a h—ll of a fuss about." "Alas poor fellow," the paper commented, "the 'killing off the poor white men' of the South is a part, and an important part of the rebel slave oligarchy. The non-slaveholders are growing too numerous for their safety; and they wish to get them out of the way and import slaves to fill their places. The scheme is progressing rapidly."

Although Nashville was firmly in Union hands, the countryside around was contested. During the week of April 12, Confederates captured the Murfreesboro mail and on the eleventh raided Franklin, twenty miles south of Nashville. Near Lavergne rebels captured a train, freeing prisoners after which they destroyed the locomotive and the cars. In columns called "The Latest News" and "By Telegraph," the paper printed accounts of battles and troop movements. On September 9 the paper published dispatches detailing skirmishes near Memphis, Louisville, and Trenton, Georgia. From St. Louis came the report that Quantrell was "about thirty miles from Kansas City on the Sinabar with about twelve hundred men." The *Daily Union* also printed excerpts from Confederate papers. On the ninth the paper published a column taken from the *Richmond Enquirer* of August 29. For some time a big battle had been brewing in east Tennessee as Rosecrans and Bragg maneuvered along the Cumberland Mountains and into north Georgia jockeying for position. The *Union* reprinted the column from the *Enquirer* most probably because in urging Bragg to fight the Richmond paper sounded desperate. Although "considerably inferior" in numbers to that of Rosecrans, "The Army of Tennessee," the paper wrote, "is now to have its opportunity to achieve as great, if not greater, fame than the Army of Virginia." "East Tennessee and our great inland lines of railroads," the paper continued, "are worth fighting for, and must be fought for. Gen. Bragg has given up just about enough of Tennessee; and with the army he now has, and in such condition, and driven to bay as he is, too, in the very heart of the Central

Mountains, it is time that he turn upon the Yankees who thus beard us in the fastness of our hills." On September 19, a dozen miles south of Chattanooga, the Battle of Chickamauga began, ending the next day in the rout of Rosecrans, only Thomas's stubborn rear guard and Bragg's ineptitude saving the Army of the Cumberland from destruction.

Amid the turmoil over slavery and the bloodletting on the battlefields, life, and death, spun along, solemn and silly by turns. For the month of August the sexton of the city cemetery reported two hundred and forty-nine burials: one hundred and fifty-one "U.S. Soldiers," four Rebels, sixty-nine citizens, and twenty-five contrabands. At Jenny Dorman's death at three months and nineteen days an obituary appeared in the paper. "This lovely blossom," the obituary stated, "suffered for a month more agonizing pain than its parents and friends thought ever a natural being could endure. Their consolation is the knowledge that she has been translated to bloom perpetually, where her sister preceded her, just seven months since, in the garden of the Lord." On the day of Jenny's death family marketing had been poor. "There was," the *Daily Union* reported, "but little beef or mutton to be had, and that of poor quality. Fresh pork was abundant, but its flabby, oily appearance was enough to disgust an honest stomach. The salad was indifferent, as was everything in the vegetable line. The first lettuce of the season made its appearance, grown by a distinguished jurist of this vicinity, and it went off like 'hot cakes.' " Although the market provided no vegetables good enough to be tossed about with the lettuce, the Recorder's Court furnished a couple of nicely seasoned anecdotes. Robert Williams, the paper noted, "had the misfortune to cultivate too rapidly his taste for 'Old Robertson,' and got himself into that state in which one feels himself 'Glorious, / O'er all the ills of life victorious,' and fell into the hands of the ministers of justice. He had to pay for his experience $3, and costs." Similarly Ann O'Conner was "charged with drunkenness." She owned up, the paper recounted, "that she had taken 'a wee drap too much,' but pleaded it was not intentional. She had not calculated properly the effect of the charges to which she had subjected herself. She had drank but three times, not more than three fingers at a time; but unfortunately the last time the pure spirit was adulterated by the addition of sugar and nutmeg. 'May it plaze yer honer, it was the nutmeg and sugar that made me drunk. If ye will let me off, I will go away from

Nashville—I will immygrate to Edgefield, and never more come back.' " In view of her promises and the fact that she had "mixed up her refreshments" with nutmeg and sugar, the Recorder let her off with costs. Charged with being both drunk and disorderly, Sarah Puckett "claimed that she had drank but little, but that the sun which was in the constellation of Capricornus caused her foundations to totter, whilst the position of the moon in the constellation Taurus gave her a propensity to butt." Despite listening to her explanation with amusement, the Recorder was "not satisfied that she had recovered from the effects of her potations" and, the paper reported, he fined her two dollars and costs. The Recorder seemed to deal mostly with drunkenness, although several people were charged with using hydrant water without a license while a soldier was sent to the workhouse for striking a woman, and Messrs. J. Peck, J. R. Davis, S. Pyser, and Mr. Peck "participants in a Hebrew fight" were each fined three dollars plus costs.

Unlike life, business often seems immortal, and advertisements and paid announcements filled more columns of the *Daily Union* than accounts of the war. On September 9, for example, the entire first and last pages and half of the second and third pages of the paper were devoted to advertisements. From the appearance of the paper, business in Nashville like the cannon at Chickamauga was booming. As the war led to the establishment of many hospitals, so it seems to have attracted doctors to Nashville. After practicing for thirty-five years in Pennsylvania and Maryland, Dr. M'Gill moved to Nashville and announced that as a "Botanic Physician" he was prepared to treat all diseases "to which the human family are subject." From Louisville but with previous experience in New York, Dr. King moved to Nashville and opened his "Dispensary for Private Diseases." Although he had practiced for thirty years, Dr. King was still vigorous, holding office hours from nine in the morning until nine at night. Dr. King solicited patients from commercial circles, claiming he could cure gonorrhea "without nauseous medicines or interference with business." Seminal weakness should be seen to immediately, he warned, for it undermined the constitution causing premature old age and "rendering the subject unfit for business." In his advertisement Dr. Coleman urged prospective patients to hurry to his dispensary and "Nip the Evil in its Bud." "All Chronic and Acute Diseases, Scrofula, Spinal Afflictions, Gravel, Hydrocile, Congenital and Accidental Phymosis" among others, he claimed, could not resist his remedies. Like his colleague and rival Dr. King, Coleman kept long office hours. On the theory that the early doctor got the patient, he opened his dispensary at eight o'clock in the morning rather than nine. For patients unable or unwilling to visit a doctor, patent medicines were available, the most widely advertised being "Dr. John Bull's Compound Cedron Bitters." No man was more "intimately connected with the history of the Materia Medica of the United States," an advertisement stated, than Dr. John Bull of Louisville, Kentucky. His Compound Pectoral of Wild Cherry was a "household word throughout the West and South" while in less than a year after their introduction his Worm Lozenges "attained a reputation as widespread as the continent of North America." Nevertheless, the "crowning glory of his life" is, the advertisement asserted, the "combination" which produced Cedron Bitters. As for the discovery of Cedron itself, that honor, the good doctor stated, "belongs to the native inhabitants of Central America, to whom its virtues have been known for more than two hundred years. Armed with it, the Indian bids defiance to the most deadly malaria and handles without fear the most venomous serpents."

Many of the announcements in the *Daily Union* pertained to things military or governmental. Over two columns in each issue were devoted to "Advertised Letters," a listing of the addresses of letters which remained unclaimed in the Nashville post office. The list on April 12, for example, consisted of the names of some eight hundred and sixty people and ten business firms. Advertised letters were subject to a penny surcharge the postmaster explained, adding that if the letters were not called for within a month they were considered dead letters. Army Intelligence announced opening an office in St. Louis "for the benefit of strangers" searching for sick or wounded soldiers. "Correct Intelligence will be given" for any soldier who enlisted "in the States of Illinois, Indiana, Ohio, Iowa, Michigan, Wisconsin, Minnesota, Kentucky, and Missouri," the announcement stated, "whether Sick, Wounded, Killed, or Taken Prisoner, and in what battles he may have been engaged, and where his regiment is stationed." Also available, the announcement added, was information about the condition of soldiers confined to hospitals in St. Louis, Louisville, Cincinnati, Nashville, Mound City "or any other hospital in the Western Department." The fee for providing the information was two dollars, whether one wrote to the office or called in person. In September the "Examining Board of

Applicants for positions in Colored Regiments" announced that it was in session, instructing potential applicants to present testimonials "to their character and capacity" from military officers or "well-known men of good standing." Under the headline "Declaration," Andrew Johnson, the governor of Tennessee, announced that three hundred dollars would be paid to anyone helping the state apprehend William T. Holmes and Andrew Huggins, the murderers of Robert Blair. Holmes, the announcement stated, was twenty or twenty-one years old, five feet six or eight inches tall, weighed one hundred and forty pounds, had light hair, a fair complexion, "one eye out, and blinked, uncertain which." Huggins was older and larger, thirty-five years old, five feet ten inches tall, and weighing one hundred and sixty pounds. He had "red hair, with beard on the chin, complexion very red, cheek bone high, rather quick spoken." At the end of the proclamation was a note stating that in addition to the state's reward of three hundred dollars Mrs. Jane Blair would pay two hundred and fifty dollars for delivering Huggins and Holmes "to the Sheriff of Davidson County." With bands of irregulars moving freely through middle Tennessee, so freely that the *Union* declared that the time was "fast approaching when every man in the county will be necessarily compelled in self-defence to arm himself," enforcing the law must have been difficult and often impossible. At a time when justice was often more a matter for low debate than a high ideal determining behavior, private citizens supplemented calls for law through practical action. Offering rewards they appealed to greed, that part of man's nature which remains green and vital long after commitment to abstractions like decency and justice has withered and blown away. "I will give one hundred dollars reward," E. W. Tealy, owner of the Eclipse Stable, advertised, "for the apprehension of a man named SIMPSON, who hired a Horse and Buggy from me on Wednesday morning, August 19th. Said Simpson is a young man about 6 feet high and wore a linen coat, and black pants. Fifty dollars reward will be given for the recovery of the Horse and Buggy. The Horse is a small light bay, about 7 or 8 years old, 14 hands high, rather long neck, and both hind feet white. The Buggy is nearly a new straight bed top Buggy, lined with blue cloth, and the front spring broke."

Under the heading "United States of America" in square, assertive, almost defiant type, the district marshall announced the confiscation of property, the owners of which were accused of "aiding, and abetting and promoting an armed rebellion against the Government of the United States." Much property was for sale in Nashville; H. G. Scovel who had an office opposite the state capitol seemed to handle most of it, taking out a full column of advertisements in the *Daily Union*. "Invest Your Money," he urged. "At no recent period in the history of the country, more than present, have surrounding circumstances indicated the wisdom of investing your money in something substantial. viz: Real Estate, a good Home Lot, or a Place for Business." Scovel was the John Bull of real estate salesmen, selling property as a cure-all for physical and moral ills. "Prolong Life," he advertised; "by the purchase of a Home Lot, for your own use, thereby avoiding those monthly, quarterly, and annual annoyances, such as RENT DUNS, which confuse, disturb, fret, and shorten life." "Soldiers, Clerks, Book-Keepers, Mechanics, Merchants, and Laborers," he wrote, "would do well to husband and apply their means to the purchase of good HOME LOTS, and thereby save their money, reap the advantages of enhancement in the value of their property, ward off the inducements and facilities for dissipation, and escape the *disgrace* and *ruin* incident to being caught in their snares and traps which are involving and destroying thousands."

As could be expected many advertisements in the paper were directed toward the military, individual soldiers and then sutlers who supplied the camps. From I. N. Rhodes a soldier could purchase a pocket album for a dollar and fifty cents and having the "portraits of his friends by him" could "refer to them in whatever scene of toil and danger" he was placed. For fifty cents Rhodes sold "a beautiful SOLDIER'S CERTIFICATE." Printed in four colors, it depicted "Cavalry, Infantry, and Artillery, marching in countless numbers into Dixie, with drums beating, colors flying, etc." Thirteen by seventeen inches with blank lines on which the soldier could write his name, "Company, Regiment, Officers," the certificate came "in an enclosed pasteboard tube," so that it could be mailed "to any part of the country without injury." For sale at Allen and Company on Cherry Street were "Books on Military Art and Sciences: Surgical as well as Tactical." Every Saturday *The American Soldier* was published, eight pages, Allen wrote, devoted to "the Maintenance of the Union Cause throughout the State of Tennessee and the United States, and early Overwhelming Triumph of the Union Army." Priced at five cents, each number contained editorials, "articles wide-awake to the crisis and fully up to its demands," and a series of instructive and thrilling sketches describing life in the British army and entitled *The Romance of the Ranks*. Several stores specialized in, as they usually put it in advertisements, "Fine Military Goods." At Derby's on College Street, officers could buy skeleton jackets, dark and light blue doeskin pants; staff, infantry and cavalry vests; "Fine French flannel blouses"; undershirts, "silk Lisle, Gauze, cotton, and woollen"; linen and cotton drawers; Angola flannel underwear; three thread socks; silk handkerchiefs; Castor gloves; rubber clothing; belts, "calfskin and enamelled leather"; "Burnside hats, and caps of every style worn"; as well as presentation swords, scabbards, spurs, gauntlets, haversacks, and folding military chairs and cots.

A. M. Landsburg prefaced his advertisement with a quatrain entitled "Sutlers of the Army of the Cumberland Rally." "May the *Rose* of England never blow," the verse began; "May the *Thistle* of Scotland never grow, / May the *Harp* of Ireland never play / Until the Stars and Stripes have won the day." After the quatrain Landsburg noted that he had "on hand a large assortment of Fine Wines. Also, a large lot of Ale, Beer, Oysters, Peaches, Cherries, Honey in Glass and Can, Pickles in Jars and Kegs, Spiced Tripe and Tongues, Nuts, Pigs Feet and Tongues, Condensed Milk, Figs, Dates, Raisins, Spices, Onions, Lemon Syrup, Dried Apples, Peaches, Rock Candy, Stick Candy, Fancy Candy, Cigars of all kinds, Tobacco, Sweet Owen, Rosebud, Silk and Cotton Handkerchiefs, Pins, Needles, Pipes, Boots and Shoes, Combs of every description, Good Stationery, and a variety of Yankee Notions, which we offer at the lowest figures."

Despite the war, grocers appear to have been well stocked. "Just Received," T. A. Atchison advertised, "a large assortment of groceries, provisions, and wines," consisting in part of 20,000 pounds of sugar cured hams, 10,000 pounds of breakfast sides, fifty barrels of coffee sugar, fifty barrels of Orleans sugar, thirty bags of Rio coffee, seventy barrels of Old Rye Whiskey, fifty barrels of bourbon whiskey, two hundred barrels of Chicago Stock ale, and one hundred cans of Catawba and Claret wines. Along with foodstuffs, many merchants sold liquors, advertising them in the paper and then indirectly filling the docket of the Recorder's Court. "Champagnes, Wines and Bitters, together with cigars, tobacco, shoes, and boots, and many other articles too numerous to mention," L. Block declared, "give us a call." "Choice Liquors, which will be sold low," ran another advertisement, "Fine Old Otard Brandy, 1840; Fine Old Pinet, Castillon & Co.; Brandy, 1846; Fine Old Bourbon Whiskey; Blackberry Cordial, 1850; Best Blackberry Wine; Ginger Cordial." Although A. Louis on North Market Street seems not to have sold liquor, his shelves were full as he advertised an eclectic assortment of foodstuffs, necessities, and luxuries, including dried beef, Bologna sausage, smoked herring, fresh salmon; western reserve, hamburg, and English dairy cheese; soaps, candles, starch, dates, almonds, macaroni, vermicelli; French, Kentucky, and American mustard; Cove oysters, lobsters, shirts, drawers, suspenders, "Fine and Dressing Combs," Meershaum pipes, "Writing Paper and Envelopes, Ink, Pens, and Pencils by the million," neckties, playing cards, butter crackers, ginger cakes, spice nuts, sugar cakes, "American and Imported" watches, and "Gold Pens with and without holders." Gold pens were popular, and E. L. Tarbox opened the "Gold Pen Depot," devoted solely to selling gold pens and silver holders.

Men may fight wars, but the real business of life is buying and selling, or so one could conclude from reading the *Daily Union*. Despite the war local citizens founded the Nashville and Northwestern Railway Company. Even the military sold things, the quartermaster's office advertising two steamboats for sale to the highest bidder, the *W. H. Siddel* wrecked near the head of the Harpeth Shoals and the *Charter* wrecked five miles above the shoals. Accounts of battles flow together into an indistinguishable whole and often are quickly forgotten. Partly because wars are ephemeral and business is enduring and, I suppose, because many of the advertisements in the *Daily Union* were written and put in the paper by individuals, the advertisements rang in memory long after the "loud yells of advancing rebels" faded into silence. On receiving a supply of Bay Rum, Joseph White, "Barber & Hair-Dresser," begged "leave to inform the public" and invite them to his shop at No. 37 Union Street. "We shall have here in a few days," the Lake Kingston Ice Company advertised, "three thousand tons of PURE LAKE ICE." Fielding P. Cook "respectfully" informed his friends and the public at large that his bath house at Sulphur Spring was in operation. "Persons wishing either a warm or cold sulphur bath," Cook wrote, "can be accommodated at any hour, day or night." "The next session of his school," Mr. Dorman announced, will "commence" on Monday, August 31. Was Mr. Dorman, I wondered, the father of Jenny who in April had suffered so much before dying? Most probably he was the girl's father. Neither her death nor that of her sister ended his life or occupation. Indeed like business, education continued during the war. Miss Fannie Bernard, "late of Cleveland, Ohio," offered "her services to the Ladies of Nashville, as Teacher of the Piano Forte." The Chegaray Institute, "A Boarding and Day School for Young Ladies" in Philadelphia, Madame D'Hervilly advertised, taught the English and French languages and literature, Latin, and "all the branches which constitute a thorough English education." Going north to school was not unusual. If family story is correct, my great-grandmother Eliza McClarin attended school in Philadelphia during the war, this despite her brother Robert's fighting and dying for the Confederacy.

At the Chegaray Institute, French, Madame D'Hervilly assured prospective parents, was "constantly spoken." At bookstores in Nashville English literature was more popular. Although Allen listed works by Dumas, George Sand, and Eugene Sue in his advertisement, he advertised sets of Dickens, Scott, Smollett, Lever, Marryat, Ainsworth, Fielding, Disraeli, Collins, G. W. M. Reynolds, and Mrs. E. D. E. N. Southworth. English drama was also popular in Nashville; in April *The Rivals* played at the "Theatre." The overture was from *Don Giovanni,* and the afterpiece was *The Toodles.* "This is a bill of fare of the most tempting kind," the *Daily Union* declared in a short appreciative review; "if there be one amongst our habitual playgoers, who can resist it, he may set himself down as at the point of losing his taste." Sheridan's play was not the only entertainment in town. Sprague's minstrels, cornet band, and theatrical troupe were appearing at the Odd-Fellow's Hall. "Comprising fifteen talented performers, including La Belle Louise, the charming danseuse and comedienne," the troupe ended the evening with a performance of *Black Statue.* In September *The Flying Dutchman* and the *Irish Tutor* were staged at the Theatre. The *Daily Union* thought this the "best bill of the season," adding, "We apprehend that there will scarcely be room in the theatre for the audience." By September the Theatre had a rival, the appropriately, if not imaginatively, named New Theatre. Ticket prices were the same, orchestra seats costing seventy-five cents, parquet fifty cents, and gallery twenty-five cents. Playing at the New Theatre was *Mazeppa; or, the Wild Horse of Tartary,* followed by the comic fare of the *Omnibus.* The New Theatre seems to have relied upon spectaculars, at least at first, heading its advertisement "Immense sensation to witness Mazeppa" and then ending, saying fifty young ladies were wanted for "the Corps de Balet. Apply immediately to the Box-Office." The spectaculars succeeded. For two successive nights Mazeppa "the great equestrian drama," the *Daily Union* reported, played to crowded houses. On Friday, the paper wrote, Mr. Miles, "the equestrian artist" and the trainer of Hiawatha, the lead horse, "is up for a benefit. It will, no doubt, be a rouser."

On the last page of the *Daily Union* for September 9, William Brownlow announced his *Knoxville Whig and Rebel Ventilator* would begin publication in October. "It was in that month, two years ago," Brownlow recalled, "my paper was crushed out, by the God forsaken mob at Knoxville, called the *Confederate Authorities*. I will commence with this hell-born and hell-bound Rebellion where the Traitors forced me leave off, and all who wish the paper would do well ought to begin with the first issue, as I intend that single paper shall be worth the subscription price to any Unconditional Union Man!" Strong words for September, I thought, as I lay the paper down, but then despite Great-grandfather, I wasn't an unconditional Union Man. I grew up southern and sentimental, believing, oddly, now as I look back, that failure taught a person more about life than success. From loss not gain came knowledge, first awareness of one's limitations and then later distrust of zeal. I suppose childhood in the South has made me a September person, a gatherer not a judge, a ruminator not an actor, a storyteller, not a preacher. Be that as it may, however, I did more in September than collect materials for essays. I began to shape some of the matter I had in hand.

Four years ago I started writing about our corner of Nova Scotia. First I described our farm, its buildings and fields, but then I wandered beyond the borders of truth and property into imagination and began peopling the countryside. Not long afterwards Bertha Shifney moved into my writings from Hectanooga, marrying Perry Weebe, a carriage maker in Beaver River. After Weebe's death Bertha married Worby Thursh, one of her husband's assistants. Thursh drank, and the marriage was not successful. Happily, though, Bertha was one of those women blessed to be widows. After an afternoon and evening of drinking with Otis Blankinchip on Otis's lobster boat, Worby answered a summons from nature and mistaking sea for sand tumbled overboard and drowned. Bertha gave Worby a good send-off. To lead the funeral procession from the Bay View Baptist Church to the graveyard, she hired Titus Raymond to play his trumpet and Abner Files to accompany him on the banjo. At graveside they played "Though Your Sins Be as Scarlet," "I Wish I Had Died in Egypt's Land," and as Worby was lowered out of sight into that better, dryer world, "The Healing Water" and "The Temperance Call." Shortly after marrying Worby, Bertha took out an insurance policy on him, and his sudden death, I am afraid, did not leave her so much inconsolable as wealthy. Once Worby was safely in that happy land flowing only with milk and honey, Bertha sold both the carriage business and the modest, little, one and a half story green cottage which Weebe built for her in Beaver River. Believing she needed a house appropriate to her means, she moved to Port Maitland and bought a large two story house on Cove Street across from the post office.

The house was not in good repair; the roof leaked; most of the paint had worn off, and some of the wood across the front was rotten. Bertha soon set the place to rights however. She replaced the roof, in the process adding to it an octagonal silo-like structure topped by a pointed, sharply sloping roof, resembling the sort of straw hat worn by Chinese peasants in rice paddies. To the front of the house Bertha added a porch, gingerbread resembling daisies, six petals clustered about a raised center, hanging down from lattices and rising up over railings. She replaced the rotten wood in front with a large square window, around the edges of which she planted a border of colored glass, green, orange, red, purple, and blue. Despite her new wealth and what soon became obvious, a desire not just for respectability but also for eminence, Bertha remained naive and countryfied at heart. Instead of white or cream like the other houses along Cove Street, she painted her home the colors of her favorite berries, the sides of the house the dark almost black purple of huckleberries and the trim the deep blue of highbush blueberries. The housepaint was her single lapse into display, however; Bertha was so concerned about reputation and propriety, that she refused to dry her wash on a clothesline outside but instead hung it inside on hooks in the attic. Although she could not play, she bought a grand piano for her parlor. Stacked atop the piano was sheet music, all of it religious, the first piece usually being "Jesus Paid It All."

Religion, Bertha believed, conveyed respectability, and she became an ardent churchgoer, attending both Baptist and Methodist churches, as well as all funerals in Port Maitland. Indeed she became a fixture at funerals, hiring Otis Blankinchip to drive her and sometimes attending two or three a day, some of which were as far afield as Cranberry Head and Norman's Lake. As time passed Bertha became known, not as she hoped, however, for her faith but for the wondrous statements she often made. Slemmons Ulery, she said, "went to bed feeling well but woke up dead." Erving Snook, she reassured her neighbor Clara Baw, "died suddenly but it won't nothing serious." Although Bertha's most memorable remarks pertained to death, she was also interested in birth and although she never had children considered herself an expert on child rearing. On hearing Clara Baw say she thought Gracious Chenoweth's little baby boy was spoiled, Bertha interrupted. "No, Clara," she said, "you are wrong. That baby ain't spoiled. All babies smell that way."

Initially because he felt guilty about Worby's falling off his boat and drowning and then later because he was a little simple and felt awe for anyone owning a big house and piano, Otis Blankinchip became Bertha's handyman, not only driving her to funerals but buying groceries for her and repairing her house. When Bertha went to Halifax to see a doctor about her adenoids, Otis took her to the railway station. On her return two days later he picked her up. When she stepped off the train, so the story went around Port Maitland, she wore a ring with a diamond in it as big as an egg. "Lordy, Bertha," Otis exclaimed when he saw it, rubbing his hands back through his hair, "Mercy me, is that a real diamond?" "It better be," Bertha answered handing him her valise. "If it ain't, I got skunt out of fifty cents." Although not bright, Otis was well-meaning, always willing to lend a helping hand, whether asked for it or not. One year after a heavy rain Canns Brook flooded and washed away so much of the bank below the little school at Beaver River that the schoolhouse needed to be moved back up the bank some twelve or fifteen feet. Because the school was small, Otis believed shifting it would not be difficult, and thinking to save the schoolmaster the trouble and expense of hiring oxen, Otis decided to move the building himself. Enlisting two of his fishing companions Jeremiah Gest and Gideon Tannehill in the good cause, he paced off five yards, back up the bank from the rear door of the school. When certain that his measurement was correct, he took off his jacket, laying it down as a marker, after which he strode around to the front of the schoolhouse and along with Gest and Tannehill began pushing. While they were pushing, the local wag, Demmick the undertaker passed by, and seeing what they were about decided to trick them. Without their noticing, he sneaked behind the schoolhouse and removed Otis's jacket. After they had strained and snorted for ten or so minutes, Gest spoke up, saying "Otis I don't think we are doing much good." Otis raised himself and putting his hands on his hips, stretched, and then after getting his wind back, set his mind to work. He stared hard at the schoolhouse door; then he turned and half-crouching sighted along his thumb down to the brook. "Jeremiah," he said, after a minute's hard, wrinkled cogitation, "You're wrong. I can see the building's moved, maybe as much as eighteen or twenty feet. Let's go out back and take a look." The three then walked around the schoolhouse. On turning the corner behind the building, Otis stopped and not seeing his coat looked puzzled, a frown creasing his brow. Suddenly, though, light broke in upon him; his forehead smoothed out, and he rocked up on his toes, his whole body nodding in awareness. "The devil," he exclaimed, slapping his hands together, "I knowed it. We've done pushed the school too far and buried my coat."

Bertha and Otis were good September companions, accompanying me on long walks when Vicki and the children were busy elsewhere. An in-between month, neither summer nor fall, September is a time for exploring the cracks between seasons. September is a walking month, a time for slow ambles and slow friends, a time for modest observation. After my morning class I walked over Horsebarn Hill on the university farm. The corn had been harvested, and only stalks remained, roots digging into the dirt like yellow bony fingers. One side of the hill had been left fallow and planted in alfalfa; beside the tractor road up the hill stood the brown husks of velvet leaf while here and there blooming white against the green was evening lychnis or thunder flower. The soil at the top of the hill was a fine sandy loam, red with iron oxide. Through the distance the hills rolled off in thick lumps, slowly flattening out and stretching up to the sky in a blue mist. By October sky and land were separate, the one still blue but the other now orange. Despite the low coughing of tractors in the valleys and the absence of corn, I think of October not September as harvest month. By early October I stopped walking Horsebarn Hill, and as the year suddenly began to spin downward so I roamed out of the Eastern Uplands down into the Windham

Basin, spending an afternoon picking pumpkins at Pleasant Valley Farm.

On weekends Vicki and the children accompanied me on my September walks. At Wolf Rock Francis and Edward hunted trolls while Eliza clung to my waist saying her legs had turned to ice cream. Early one chilly morning beside the Stone Bridge Trail near Schoolhouse Brook, we found a garter snake coiled in a loose eight. Not until I picked the snake up did it straighten. In afternoons we walked around the pond near the university police station. In mid-September wild mint was in the air. At the edge of the pond cattails were swelling and splitting. Joe pye-weed was going off, but the bushy asters, some white, others purple, were just beginning. Turning in through the willows were yellow warblers. Over the pond tree swallows dipped down then swung upward, white bellies flashing. One afternoon we counted six mockingbirds in the bushes about the pond. Like chips of paper thrown at some bright party, sulphers and whites tossed about over the flowers while viceroys and eastern swallowtails floated in and out of sight, orange and black. Hanging head down in the grass was a black and yellow Argiope, a grasshopper in its web. Edward and I watched it for seven minutes. I had not seen the spider since I was a boy living in the Sulgrave Apartments in Nashville. Hunkered down in the grass and sedges we saw traces of a small world: the footprints of coon, skunk, groundhog, and rabbit. Dragonflies slid around us in waves, mostly quick red skimmers and heavy eastern blue darners. I found a spike of nodding ladies' tresses, the bells creamy with fragrance. Nearby grew pokeweed, itself an in-between plant, some of its berries purple, others still green. On the far side of the pond goldenrod was yellow and thick with a wind of bees. Walking about the pond brought bittersweet thoughts to mind. Stacked nearby were hills of plastic pipes and great boxes of Dylite expandable polystyrene, materials for a new university telephone system. Half a mile away over a low ridge bulldozers were busy flattening land for a university development: parking lots and apartment buildings. The pond and four hundred acres of woods and farmland about it would soon become an industrial park, forced upon the community by university officials, cheerleading sloganeers "committed to excellence" and by experts biting after money like wolves. As I knelt in the grass showing Francis birdfoot trefoil and the last string or two of summery vetch, I thought about schooling and its betrayal of community. No longer did schools turn out people loyal to community or place, but professionals, glib men and women, small experts with guild loyalties. Such people flew into little towns from Indianapolis or Dallas, and after overwhelming instinct and history with fact and statistic, collected their fees, boarded their planes, and left the communities to sicken with their mistakes. In protest I wrote letters. No good, of course, came of them. I received replies thanking me for my "input" and saying my concerns were being passed along to the person in charge of "interfacing with the community." And that always was that. The bulldozers rolled on, toppling trees and slicing the hills away.

Such thoughts, though, were not for a September afternoon and a child kneeling on the ground, saying "Only God could make this. You couldn't Daddy." "No, Francis, you are right. I can't make trefoil, or even a difference," I said. I had slipped into a seam of melancholy running between and under all the seasons. "Come on," I said, pulling myself and Francis up; "let's go over to the gully." Staghorn sumac grew along the top of the gully, its leaves elegant lances and its fruit gothic red steeples. I picked a steeple. Short hairs covered it, and it smelled like cherry cough drops. Up the bank on the far side of the gully wound ribbons of wild New England asters, blossoms yellow and purple and in the late afternoon seemingly as round and as deep as coffee cups. Near the trees along one side of the bank grew sweet fern, shrubs arching over, heavy with awkward lobed leaves. "Daddy," Edward said pointing at the asters, "I wish we had some of those flowers in the yard." The next day I returned with shovel and boxes and dug up nineteen asters and for good measure two sweet ferns. I planted the sweet fern in the back yard near the periwinkle and the asters in the front, setting them amid some of their cousins, pink asters bought from Andre Viette in Fishersville, Virginia. My plants were lucky; they thrived. In October workmen felled the sumac and getting the land ready for the "park," smoothed out the gully, uprooting the asters and sweet fern. That, though, happened later. On this September afternoon we crossed the gully and, walking up the hill behind, climbed over the stone wall into the Storrs Community Cemetery. For a while the children played hide and go seek around the big monuments at the top of the hill. Eventually, though, they grew weary, and we started walking down through the cemetery toward home, pausing but once, before the tombstone of Sarah Elizabeth Morgan: "She hath done what she could." When September ends and the last winds blow cold and the final snows fall, how few of us, teachers and sentimentalists, fathers and mothers, collectors, tellers of tales, I thought, will have done so well.

Back from the Edge

Our farm in Nova Scotia overlooks the Gulf of Maine. Four hundred yards behind our house the land rolls up into a drumlin. Winter storms and tides off the Gulf have cut to the center of the drumlin, pulling its western slope away and creating a headland, towering bluff-like some sixty feet above the beach at its highest point. From the top of the headland the land turns slowly down, to the south running off to Beaver River and Green Cove and then to Port Maitland, distance pasting the houses square and white against an envelope of green and blue. To the north the headland first stretches lumpy and muscular like a long arm before falling away to a thin, scratchy finger pointing at Bartlett's River and the tall hill of Black Point beyond. On a clear day the waves fold together in silver and blue ribbons like Christmas decorations wrapped around a banister curving slowly up through a great house. Oddly, though, I rarely notice the waves now. When I walk out to the headland, I look down to the ground and the immediate rather than up at the water, flowing through space and over the unknown like a frightening abstraction.

Wildflowers and berries grow all along the headland, at the top and down the beach: evening primrose; yarrow, usually white but sometimes red; tall purple clover, the heads round and as full of pollen as hives; asters; and star chickweed, white in the deep grass. Not disturbed by the wind, roses grow spiny and pink along the lip of the headland; sheltered low behind are blueberries. Next to them lurk wild strawberries and cranberries. Beside the path my children have worn over the headland grow eyebright, cones of purple self-heal, and gerardia, its minute pink blossoms lasting but a day. Along a stone wall running back across a field away from the headland grow wild raspberries, the fruit small and tart. Not far from the wall out of the strongest wind are columbine and wild mint, fresh and crisp as the memory of young love. Growing all over the headland is yellow rattle, its pods dry and rushy with seeds by August. Lower down toward Bartlett's Beach the plants change. The roses grow bushier, and knapweed, water horehound, two-flowered Cynthia, and gall-of-the-earth appear. In the rocks at the other edge of the drumlin near Beaver River grow fox tail, lady's thumb, seaside goldenrod, mayweed, and sow thistle, its yellow blossoms fat and almost furry. Over the ditch beside the road leading to the beach hedge bindweed has spread. In the field just beyond are purple orchis and sweet everlasting, then creamy, green clusters of queen-of-the-meadow. On walks the children and I gather flowers, most for vases in the house but some to be pressed and brought back to Connecticut. With six rubber bands binding it tightly, a copy of *The Last of the Mohicans* published in 1919 by Scribner's sits on my desk, swelling bright more with the flowers my son Francis pressed this past summer than with N. C. Wyeth's illustrations.

When I look at the flowers growing over the headland, I often find things to fill hours and choke off disturbing thought, this past summer the pellets of an owl, gray fur wrapped about bones, some of them a yellowish chestnut color and resembling tusks. Because I had never seen a shrew except on television, the bones, I convinced myself, must have belonged not to a mouse but to a shrew, and, I told Francis, to a short-tailed shrew at that. Even when I looked up from the ground, I usually did not glance out over the Gulf. Instead I looked behind or inland to the side, back through the black spruce and tamarack toward the house or northeast across the pastures and pond at Bartlett's River. There in the low fields holsteins grazed, floating lazily above the land, it sometimes seemed, like elongated black and white balloons. Far behind them the spruce stood jagged and dark like the teeth of a saw against the pale blue sky—the whole still and muted, almost an artifact, a scene painted on the side of an old coffee creamer.

Years ago the sea was almost all in all for me, and I don't think I noticed the cows or paid much attention to wildflowers. Every night after dinner I walked out to the headland and watched the sun set. Often when the tide was out I strolled up the beach to Port Maitland. I walked as far out from the headland as I could, and sometimes on the way home, the incoming tide caught me on a sandbar forcing me to thread a way through rocks and rising water to the shore. When the waters broke above my waist, tightening my groin, I was excited, and instead of being chilled felt warm and alive.

Now after dinner I help Vicki in the kitchen; she washes the dishes, and I dry them, using a blue-checkered cloth for plates and saucers and then a white one for the knives, forks, and finally the pots and pans. Only occasionally do I stare out the window at the sunset. Sunsets now unsettle me. Too quickly the great bands of light drain away into stars. From all that orange and purple vitality, something, I think, should linger longer and as the stars cover the sky like the sand the beach, I turn back from the headland of thought and busy myself with the glasses and cups, dripping in the sink beside me.

This past summer I rarely walked alone on the shore. In fact I avoided the beach, only going there to watch over the children while they swam. Sometimes I swam too, but usually I sat beside a tidal pool and let scud and small shrimp nibble at the dead skin on my feet. Occasionally the children and I explored, searching for treasures along the high water line. Often we found interesting things: dead gulls, mostly juveniles; crab shells; leathery dried bodies of sting rays; white, sharp spines of fish; the shells of mussels and razor clams; and then seaweeds—dead men's fingers; kelp, long and green and resembling the tails of sea dragons, or so we said; and rockweed, air bladders swollen like small rough dirigibles. Along the foot of the headland wood had accumulated, much of it in thick, heavy, almost immovable piles. Great ten-by-ten-inch beams with rusty sixteen-inch bolts jutting out of them had broken off from the old wharf at Salmon River and washed ashore under the headland. Down the slope toward Bartlett's River were the remains of a small barn. It had, I was told, stood empty on the headland for many years. When the barn collapsed one winter, the owner, no longer having use for it, towed it beam by beam to the headland and tumbled it over. Amid the heavy lumber were sheds of driftwood, most shattered beyond function and recognition, but some still recognizable: crates for carrying fish, twelve inches high, twenty wide and thirty-two long with handles made from plastic twine at each end, and then lobster traps rounded like loaves of bread and narrow three and a half inch tin strips nailed along a side, each with a number, 44-361179 or 46-205590. The wood actually was useful, and twice during the summer I took a fish basket from our barn and after putting it into the trunk of the station wagon drove to the headland and collected kindling for the kitchen stove. The basket was big, its mouth some two and a half feet in diameter, so I did not remove it from the car. Instead I carted small loads of wood up the headland and dumped them into the basket, using a manageable cardboard box, one which once held "fancy grade" New Zealand apples.

From Port Maitland to Mavilette Park, just below Cape St. Mary's, a distance of seven or so miles, there are no houses near the shore, yet the rocks above high water lines and grassy slopes of headlands were littered with trash, all of it tossed off fishing boats. In places trash accumulated like driftwood, clinging together in lumpy mounds, bound in knots by thin strands of colored plastic twine: red, green, orange, blue, yellow and green, blue and white, yellow and blue, black flecked with white, and red, white and blue twisted together in rumpled lines. Lodged in the rocks like addled eggs fallen from the nests of big bumbling birds were scores of empty motor oil containers: Petro-Canada Super Plus, Irving, Kendall Super D, Quaker State, Havoline Supreme, Gulfpride Super Premium, Ultramar Super Plus, and Shell Rotella T and S. Most containers held a litre of oil; stuck in the driftwood sometimes, however, were blue plastic drums, usually holding twenty litres of Essolube XD-3-30 Engine Oil. Also scattered above the beach were containers for antifreezes, automatic transmission fluids, and bilge cleaners. On the front of a container of New England Bilge Cleaner a dory pushed across a spotless sea while the label for Sudbury Bilge Cleaner assured fishermen the product was "biodegradable," unlike, of course, the container.

The trash under the headland revealed something about life on inshore fishing boats. After topping the engine oil off and dropping the empty containers overboard, along with worn black gloves and rubber-soled shoes, fishermen ate, usually snacks, not full meals: eggs, peanut butter, chicken soup, boneless salt codfish, yogurt—once, at least, Dannon yogurt containing mixed berries—sausages or hot dogs basted with margarine, hamburgers spread with French's mustard, and then big platters of Brookfield cherry vanilla ice cream. During cold morning hours they drank dark coffee; sometimes they cut it with artificial "whiteners," but more often than not they used Cook's or Farmer's milk. When the coffee pot was empty, they switched to soft drinks, all sorts of soft drinks. Amid the rocks were caps to Mountain Dew, Schweppes Golden Ginger Ale, Pepsi—both the diet and the non-diet varieties—Country Time Lemonade, 7-Up, Hires Root Beer, Fanta, Big 8 Cream Soda; and Orange, Lime, and Grape Crush. For the children the most exciting discovery was a blue and yellow cap from Iceland with Egils written across the top and Reykiavik around the edge. Probably because they were breakable there were no bottles along the shore, and the single cap from a beer bottle was a red and white twist-off cap from a bottle of Oland Export. Despite the paucity of caps fishermen tempered their soda with beer, at least occasionally. Caught on the driftwood were many of the plastic holders which surround beer cans and make carrying six-packs easy. With round holes punched out of the plastic for the tops of the cans, the holders have lately received publicity from naturalists, magazines like *Audubon* and *International Wildlife* publishing pictures of dead birds and turtles, the plastic holders cinched tightly around flippers and wings. I picked up the holders and after carrying them back to the house, sliced them into small pieces. Although fishermen threw everything throwable overboard, many seem to have been neat in appearance. After snacking and smoking a cigarette, rolled by hand and made from Belvedere Cigarette Tobacco, they washed dishes in Dove or if their hands were not sensitive in Crystal White Octagon liquid detergent. On the way back to port they cleaned clothes adding KAO bleach and Downy Concentrate Fabric Softener to the wash. Near home some washed their hair with Life Brand Balsam Protein Shampoo while others shaved with Edge, doused themselves with Cuticura Talcum Powder, or rubbed away the smell of fish with Soft & Dri deodorant sticks. For the occasional rash, captains stocked Gold Bond Medicated Powder, an old standby sold since 1908 and advertised as "Everything You Need All In One Can." Not only did the powder cure the razor rash, prickly heat, jock itch, chapped hands, bed sores and itchy measles, but it brought "fast relief for" athlete's foot, wind burn, and for that occasional young fisherman, diaper rash.

The trash made me uncomfortable. It seemed the waste of an irresponsible age, an age so careless that it was destroying the future. But then I had reached that time in life in which the past promised more happiness than the future. Unlike the children I was unable to imagine possibilities for the trash. With life ahead, not behind them, though, the children started collections of bottle caps, shored up the walls of forts and castles with oil containers, and then at the top of the headland strung twine between lonely, rocky watchtowers. What I saw as signs of an ending the children used as blocks for beginnings. Edges, endings and beginnings, are, I suppose, personal matters, carved more in sand than stone. Certainly childhood sees and defines differently from age. "I am not grinding my teeth," Eliza said recently; "I'm just making music." "God causes earthquakes," Edward told me last month, "by stamping his feet." Where youth is bold and creative, age is cautious. Even the lies I tell are modest: writing that I made the short list for a college presidency when in truth I was considered for head of an English department or telling people that Vicki and I only put thirty-five hundred miles on the car each year when actually we put almost five thousand. When age, or at least my age, is unsure, pulling back from edges, childhood is confident, even assertive. One Sunday early in December Quintus Tyler who taught kindergarten in the Baptist church in Carthage, Tennessee, asked the children to draw Christmas pictures. Most of the pictures were conventional. Harriet Chism, for example, drew a manger with the baby Jesus surrounded by animals, and Billie Dinwidder drew the three wise men following the star to Bethlehem, riding, to be sure, not on donkeys or camels, but big, heavy Tennessee mules. Despite looking like they were heading up Battery Hill to plough rather than seeking the sower of good seed, the wise men were still the recognizable characters of biblical story, and Quintus praised Billie "for bringing Christmas home to Smith County." With yellow dots scattered like rain across the paper and green lines radiating out from the center of the picture, Quintus did not know what to make of Reba Droone's drawing. "Reba, my dear," he said, "the colors are lovely, but, honey, I'm not sure what you are drawing. What is it?" "God," Reba answered without looking up. "But," Quintus began, then paused and began again, "but you can't draw God. No one has ever seen him, not even Reverend Hackett. Nobody knows what he looks like." "Huh," said Reba, picking up a blue crayon and sketching something like an eye in the lower left hand corner of the drawing, "they may not know now. But they'll know when I finish."

On that December Sunday young Reba's confidence knew no bounds. In contrast doubt binds my speculations and even if I stumble near the risky edge of thought I pull back hurriedly. Story is almost the only thing which can lure me over the headland of certainty or taste, and in pursuit of a tale, I, I am afraid, rush heedlessly down slopes to revel if not in the trashy at least in the questionable. Just recently, Father told me a marvelous story, one, alas, which in the telling will undermine all my claims to sensitivity and high truth. That aside, however, it seems that Harry an aging bachelor had not seen his old friend David for some time. Concerned about him Harry drove to the Royal Oaks where David lived in Nashville and knocked on his door. When his friend answered, Harry said, "David, I haven't seen you for a long time, and I have been worried about you. Are you all right?" "Oh, yes, come in. I've got something to tell you," David whispered confidentially, beckoning Harry in and closing the door, "I've been circumcised." "Really," said Harry; "what kind of job did they do?" "Beautiful, just beautiful," David answered, shaking his head in appreciation. "Do you mind if I see," said Harry. "Certainly not, of course you can see," said David. "My word, yes, it is a beautiful job," Harry exclaimed some moments later, "why David, you look ten years younger."

Much as the refusal to recognize limits or edges can lead to originality, so descent into questionable taste sometimes produces story. In October I spoke to the Friends of the Simsbury Library. Because I talked on a Wednesday at noon, my audience was relatively old and genial, consisting primarily of retired people. In my talk I discussed writing essays and read selections from my books. One of the selections described May's breaking raucous and colorful across wintry Connecticut. In order to convey the month's lively vulgarity, I recounted finding a dildo while jogging one afternoon along the Gurleyville Road. Up until the moment I started reading it and then could not turn back, I wondered whether or not to use the selection. I suppose I began it because my talk had gone well and I assumed that the vitality of the selection would overwhelm its vulgarity, and indeed for some listeners this happened. Be that as it may, however, just the opposite occurred in my mind. The roughness of the excerpt embarrassed me, and I would have broken down if a couple of tweedy horsy women in the back of the room had not whinnied their approval and urged me to gallop on to the finish, bouncing on their croups and slapping their flanks in appreciation. At the end of the talk several people thanked me for coming to Simsbury and a few even purchased collections of my essays. Just before I left I was approached by two older women, both grandmotherly with gentle, smiling eyes. "I just loved your talk, and I must have one of your books," the elder exclaimed, "but I do have one question. What is a dildo?" For a moment I was silent, only able to push a hand over my forehead and through my hair. Rubbing the top of my head turned over a word or two, though, and eventually I said, pausing after each phrase, "Ma'am, I'm sorry. That is something I just can't tell you. You'll have to look it up in a dictionary, but I'm not sure you should." As I stumbled cloddishly along, her friend looked at me, her lips pursed in amusement. "That's not very good advice, young man," she said when I finished, "I'll bet the word isn't even in her dictionary."

Reading that selection in Simsbury was a little out of character. Generally I take care not to strain myself, mentally or physically. I plan work and readings so that I don't tear emotions or pull muscles. In the fall I do not rake until after all the trees have shed their leaves. As a result I don't start work until November. By then most of my neighbors have raked their yards two or three times, and on beginning to rake I always feel under pressure to rush quickly and neatly through the job. My yard, though, attracts leaves much as the beach in Nova Scotia attracts trash. Just when I have swept a corner of the yard clean, a current of offstreet wind washes a new mound of leaves ashore. To rake the yard in a single weekend would cramp both mind and back, and so I planned my work. After raking the leaves into piles I stuffed them into a plastic garbage can or tub, and carried them into the woods behind the back yard where I dumped them. This fall I began work on Sunday, November 6. I filled and dumped eleven tubs; on Monday, twelve tubs; on Tuesday eleven again, and so the work went, with days off for rain and meetings of the school board and at the university. Only once did I fill more than twenty tubs, and that was on Saturday the twelfth when I filled twenty-three. Since I was then in the back yard and did not have far to carry the leaves, the total time I spent working, a little over three hours, was about the same as I put in on the sixth when I worked in the front yard. Vicki's parents visited us at Thanksgiving, and I took a week off at that time to help around the house and also because I was tired of raking leaves. I finally finished work after breakfast on December 6; that morning I tidied up the front yard, filling two tubs with leaves that drifted mysteriously out of nowhere, piling under the yews and forming high-leaf lines around the pachysandra and periwinkle. In all I raked and dumped one hundred and thirteen tubs. I worked slowly, rarely disturbing the snowbirds who settled near me, combing mock orange and grass for food. Busy gathering and burying supplies for winter, the gray squirrels paid almost no attention to me. When I carted a tub to the woods, the nuthatches only twisted about slightly, eyeing me for a moment, before turning back to jerk through the trees, digging under bark for insects.

Once I was not so deliberate; spontaneous and a little unpredictable I wasn't quite so tediously safe or boring. Twenty-five years ago I escorted a tour of college girls through Europe. I watched baggage, paid bills, and, if the occasion arose, handled unforeseen problems. Until Rome the trip went smoothly, and I had few difficulties. As we left the *Sound and Light,* however, a girl ran up to me, and pointing at a man, shouted, "you have to do something." The man was a masher. His technique was to wave a derby hat in a girl's face and when she reached up to brush the hat aside, he grabbed her breast with his other hand. When I saw what he was doing, I snatched the hat from his grasp and threw it on the ground. Immediately he jumped in front of me and pointed to the hat and then to the top of his head, indicating that I had better retrieve the hat and place it upon his head. I walked over to the hat, paused, and then kicked it as far as I could, down through the crowd and off a small drop. The man raced after his hat, and the incident, I assumed, was over. In any case I soon forgot about it. Wandering through the Coliseum I remember the Byron Father used to recite to me. Instead of a lout I saw before me the Gladiator, "butcher'd to make a Roman holiday." I heard "the inhuman shout which hail'd the wretch who won." And then glancing high at the moon I saw "the stars twinkle through the loops of time." In walking back to the hotel with six or so of the girls my thoughts were still within that "magic circle" of mood and dream. The enchantment did not endure to the hotel, however. As we started down a deserted side street, I looked ahead. There in the middle of the sidewalk seventy yards in front of us lay a derby hat. Leaning against a car parked along the curb were the masher and three companions. Furious, I now suppose, at the shattering of my reverie, anger rushed through me. In a motion I jerked off coat and necktie and tore down the street, screaming obscenities. Startled, then unnerved, the masher jumped from the curb to pick up his hat. He moved too slowly, however. Before he could stand straight I was upon him, and grabbing him, I threw him over the hood of the car, the derby tumbling out into the middle of the street. Then spinning I turned to face the others, growling, it seems to me. Happily they didn't have teeth for a fight. Holding their hands in front of themselves, they backed away, saying "no, no." Within twenty seconds they had picked up their companion, gotten into the car, and vanished around the corner, leaving the derby on its back in the middle of the street, looking, I thought at the time, like a box turtle overturned by some cruel country boy. For the rest of the way back to the hotel, I basked in the girls' admiration, and, if the truth must be known, strutted a bit.

Strutting focuses attention on the individual; no longer do I want to be thought an individual. Nowadays I value anonymity and feel comfortable in crowds, not for me risky spontaneity or the sharp edge of thought. I even feel guilty and somehow exposed and ill at ease when the candidate I voted for in an election doesn't win. Something, I think must be wrong with me, not dangerously so but still wrong enough to disturb my tranquility. Surprises don't appeal to me any more. This Christmas, for example, I ordered my own present, a big, hardwood flower press from the Smith & Hawken catalogue. Assuming that most friends and family resembled me and did not want surprises, Vicki and I did all our shopping in catalogues, for everyone ordering flowers from the White Flower Farm in Litch-field, either paperwhites or an Amaryllis.

Instead of intriguing, the unique sometimes disturbs me, and rather than looking for differences between things I now search for similarities, believing that out of familiarity grow affection and appreciation.

This summer in Nova Scotia I bought an old painting, not for its artistic merit but simply because it reminded me of a place in Montgomery Bell State Park in Tennessee where I once swam as a child. On a bare hill in the left front of the painting stood a broken tree, blasted, it seemed, by lightning. Rushing down the slope behind the tree and diagonally from left to right across the picture was a stream of water, pausing only to pitch high over rocks in white fans of spray. Across the stream in the lower right hand corner of the painting a square tunnel bored deep into the dark under a hill. In the nineteenth century Montgomery Bell drilled a similar tunnel near his ironworks. The tunnel may have brought water to the smelter or led down beneath the hill to coal mines. As boys my friends and I didn't know and were too scared of snakes to explore the tunnel. Indeed swimming in the stream which broke through the hills and formed a bowl beneath the entrance to the tunnel was good enough. As a man I still don't know the use of the tunnel;

recognition, though, of the similarity between it and the tunnel in the painting was good enough, and I bought the picture.

Much as recognition drew me to the painting, so in writing I value conventional prose, its rhythms and thought crafted and elegant, smacking of centuries of polished civility. In November I recommended a friend for a position at Vanderbilt University. Two weeks later I received a response from Nashville. Instead of mechanically thanking me for the recommendation, my correspondent spun through academic matters to end graciously and lightly. "Do you know Fannie Estes?" he wrote; "she was telling me how much she had enjoyed your essays. She said she didn't know whether you or your father had written them, but she suspected it was your father because he is so witty. Sam, Fannie is eighty-four. She's had several strokes, but her mind is clear and sharp. I debated whether to tell her the truth or remain a silent coward and opted for the latter. I leave it to your father to do the honorable thing and disabuse her."

Out on the headland, framed by sky and sea, events stand sharp, almost as if they were cut in cold, hard iron. Inland, life is not so clear and flows into shadows, evoking the possibility of comforting interpretation. Turning away from headlands has influenced both my thought and vision, and as November folds into December I grow progressively uncomfortable. The bare forests seem to stretch into an interminable gray and smack of edges and the ocean. As a consequence this fall whenever I walked in the woods, I resisted the distant and focused on the immediate: hunting insects hibernating in tall, rusty shafts of mullein, watching starlings dot a bare oak like somber Christmas ornaments, or breaking bracket fungi off stumps and bringing them home for Francis or Edward to take to school for Show and Tell. The last fungus I found was a whopper, jutting out from the stump nine inches and measuring sixteen inches across at its broadest point. Of course the refusal to look down through forests has limited my vision and inhibited thought, forcing me into routine. Indeed the large fungus was the fourth I brought home since August. Still, as I age I value routine and the known more than ever before. In my essays I hesitate to create new characters, preferring the old instead, trusty rather than exciting companions. Rather than risking new encounters I prefer visiting with the familiar, imagining the same round splint box, ash bent and finger-lapped around a softwood top and bottom, the outside flecked with blue and inside, looking like fat, squat clothespins, two primitive hand-carved little men, remnants of Bertha Shifney's childhood in Hectanooga. I know the box well, for Bertha kept it on an end table in the parlor, and once when she was out of the room, I opened it and examined the men. Bertha spends a lot of time now just sitting in the parlor. Her legs swell and she doesn't get about so much as she once did. Still, unlike me, she hasn't lost her edge. One afternoon as she sat rocking in the sun on the front porch, a seedy-looking man with a red nose walked up from the wharf in Port Maitland and stopping before the fence around her yard, took off his cap and said, "Ma'am, could you do a little something for an old fisherman down on his luck." "Fisherman?" Bertha said, looking up. "Yes, ma'am," the man answered, "I followed the water for thirty-four years." "Well," Bertha said, waving him away after studying his face for a moment; "you don't look like you ever caught up with it." Not willing to be dismissed so abruptly and so empty-handedly, the man continued mournfully on. "Although fortune has not been kind to me, I want you to know that I was well born and am proud of my descent." "Huh," Bertha snorted, pushing the rocker back, "It seems to have been rapid."

In her younger days Bertha rarely missed a funeral or birth in Port Maitland. As she became progressively housebound, Otis Blankinchip, a drinking companion of her second husband, kept her informed on all local doings, funereal and parturient, describing christenings and swiftly bringing her news of fatal illnesses. Four hours after Gracious Chenoweth gave birth to twins, Otis was in Bertha's parlor. "One is called Asa and the other Jehoshaphat," Otis recounted, "and the amazing thing is they are so much alike, especially Jehoshaphat." Otis was a little slow, perhaps even a bit touched, but back from the horizon, deep in among the tamarack and the spruce, nothing is quite so simple as it seems, not even simplicity itself, and in the half light of fog and shadow, character stretches and rounds. One afternoon while a storm was sweeping down Digby Neck, Otis and two compatriots, Bankes Mowll and Hornus Roebuck, walked passed Captain Perry's house in Beaver River. In the yard a storm had pushed a big maple over, its top branches brushing against the roof of the house. "Look at that tree swaying," Mowll exclaimed; "it's really moving." "No," Roebuck answered after glancing into Captain Perry's yard; "the tree's not moving; the wind is." "Both of you are wrong," Otis said stopping in the road; "the wind and tree are still. The only thing moving is your mind."

Reviewers have labeled me a humorist, and that bothers me a little. "The heart of the wise," declared Ecclesiastes, "is in the house mourning; but the heart of fools is in the house of mirth." Laughter often seems public and open while mourning appears closed and comparatively private, hidden from view behind the shade of taste. By early December I had retreated to the inside of my house, turning away from wide hills and forests spread like fans. The brown smell of old books attracted me, and I stretched through days, the hours leafy and full, and becoming aware of, if not mourning, at least the brevity of life. In the short days of winter I looked through family Bibles, pondering the generations which have passed away, the darkened windows, and pitchers broken at the fountain. On the desk before me much of the time was a heavy, leatherbound Bible, printed in Philadelphia in the 1850s and some four inches thick, ten wide, and twelve long. Unlike bottle caps and oil drums along the shore in Nova Scotia, the Bible did not interest the children, and the slips of paper and mementos pressed between its pages seemed but trash to them. For me such trash was the stuff of imagination, maybe even truth, driftwood to kindle emotions, twine to bind the past to the future. Throughout the Bible were forget-me-nots of people and occasions long forgot: clovers, violets, asters, false Solomon's seal, shafts of lily of the valley, two leaves from a crab apple tree, an orchid once white but now foxed, snowdrops, a spike of barley, ferns and twigs tied by pieces of string, and then oddest of all half a piece of chewing gum, white as doll's eyes but still fragrant. The gum may have been a bookmark, for it was next to a plate depicting "The Finding of Moses." Surrounded by rotund, bare-breasted waiting maids and cooled by a servant waving a fan of ostrich feathers, Pharaoh's daughter knelt on a carpet beside a stream, reaching out into the rushes for Moses, big-browed with wisdom beaming from ancient eyes. In the background palms hung like Christmas pine on a mantel while against the sky a camel plunged forward, a waiting maid swaying on its back like a boy riding a dolphin.

How the Bible got into my family I don't know. When my great aunt Lula died thirty-five years ago, I found it on a bookshelf, brought it home, and have had it ever since. In any case despite the flowers the Bible recorded more loss than joy, raising the house of mourning over the shards of mirth. Lewis Gallaway presented the Bible to his wife, Myra Lenoir, on February 15, 1855, the day after they were married "at her Father's residence in Marion County, Mississippi." In December the following year William Lenoir Gallaway was born; fourteen months later he died. In March 1858 Robert Gallaway was born; fifteen months later he died. In August 1859, a third son Walker Lenoir Gallaway was born; twenty-two months later, he, too, died. In June 1861 Wirt Adams Gallaway was born. Then for five years birth and death ignored the family, birth most probably because Lewis Gallaway was away from home fighting, death, I like to think, because the war momentarily clotted his maw. Death is never satiated for long, however, and as soon as the war ended, he returned to the Gallaways, taking Wirt Adams on June 17, 1866, the little boy's fifth birthday. Six months afterwards Thomas Lenoir Gallaway was born; two years later he was followed by Murfree Gallaway. Murfree lived three years, dying in 1871. Thomas's death was not recorded in the Bible, and perhaps he lived beyond childhood. Him aside, however, the family did not continue; Colonel Lewis Gallaway died on January 25, 1869, and after Murfree's death two years later, the family account stopped, the long columns devoted to marriage white as tombstones.

Although Myra Lenoir's death was not recorded, I pieced some of her history together from odd clippings, put into the Bible, I think, by her daughter. Sometime not too long after Lewis Gallaway died, Myra married John Terrass a wholesale grocer and commission merchant in Nashville, Tennessee. She and Terrass had at least one child before Myra died in 1874, probably in November, for on the back of her obituary is a partial account of a case heard by the Chancery Court in Nashville on November 5, 1874. She was buried in Mt. Olivet cemetery in Nashville, and "the funeral ceremonies and services were most impressive," the paper recounted, adding that "those who knew the exalted worth of the departed realized in some degree, at least, the great calamity her death was to her family and friends." That her life had been sad, the obituary acknowledged, writing "Words are idle and weak with which to speak of her as we knew her, and a remembrance of her graces and goodness is more eloquent than any human language. Her patient resignation under her great suffering, her continued and unflagging faith in a life beyond and above this, speak to us now from her grave, and are more potent than a thousand sermons. Society had no brighter ornament. She was an untiring, faithful wife, mother and friend, never failing in her duty, in any of the relations of life, and when the full reality comes over us that we are never to see her again, we endeavour to bow in meekness to the sad, sad fate, but it is very hard to bear."

Myra Lenoir's Bible went to her daughter Myra Terrass. Near the end of the century, probably in the early 1890s, she married Henry May from Louisville, Kentucky. Except for a handful of clovers pressed between the pages devoted to births in the old Bible and an explanatory note in pencil reading "Myra Terrass May— These Four Leaf Clovers were found by me. Wednesday, April 15th," the Lenoirs like the Gallaways disappeared from the Bible, all the clippings suddenly referring to the Mays. Despite the change in family, though, family matters were similar, and in the Bible was a black-bordered invitation to the funeral of Mattie Lee May, buried in Elizabethtown, Kentucky, on June 25, 1895. "Yourself and family are respectfully invited to attend the funeral," the invitation stated, "at the family residence at 10:30 o'clock, to-morrow (Wednesday) morning. Interment in Town Cemetery." In the Bible were also newspaper reports, recounting the deaths of other Mays. Pinned together were two newspaper clippings. "Mrs. Katie Spoo, the wife of Mr. John C. Spoo," the top clipping read, "died at her home in this city after a long illness with typhoid fever." "Mrs. Will Morris," the second clipping stated, "died Saturday night at the home of her sister in this city of typhoid malarial fever. She came in from her home about ten days ago to attend the funeral of her sister, Mrs. Spoo, and was taken so sick that day that she was unable to return home. She was a Miss May and quite a young woman." Despite the preacher's warning that "the daughters of music shall be brought low," the "song of songs," pealing joy and hope, followed Ecclesiastes in the Old Testament. Although the Gallaways and perhaps the Mays also have withered and blown to dust, the rose of Sharon still blooms under the cedars of Lebanon. The black days of late fall aside, I planted a lily among the thorns in the Bible, pressing a forget-me-not between the pages of the Sermon on the Mount, two springs of purple statice around the stems of which I wrapped a piece of tape. On it I wrote "From the Christening of Eliza Pickering, February 9, 1986, in Storrs, at the White Church."

December is difficult. As Christmas approaches, tension builds and concerns cling to hours like driftwood to rocks. Instead of trying to solve problems which litter the moment—keeping the children sane and healthy, cleaning the house for visitors, calling to ask why our orders from catalogues have not arrived— I turned back from the bare headland of the present to tamaracks and recollections of Christmas past. There in the shadows as comfortable as an old armchair, I shape memory and grow warm and genial, so much so Christmas Day always arrives, red and green, happiness tinkling lightly like silver bells. The Christmas which came to mind first this December was that of three years ago, when Francis was four and Edward two. One gray morning late in November I found the "tell-tail" signs of mouse in the kitchen. Upset at having to clean the counters and then to throw away a stick of margarine and a box of raisins, a corner of which had been gnawed, Vicki asked me what we should do. A friend owned a Havahart trap, and after describing it, I told Vicki to buy one at Willard's. Having ordered a sleigh full of presents for the boys, Vicki hesitated, saying "Something like that will cost at least fifteen dollars, and that's a lot of money to spend on a mouse." "At Christmas," I said, "money doesn't matter." Later that morning, though, it did matter, and when Vicki telephoned from Willard's saying that a Havahart trap cost sixteen dollars and eighty-nine cents while a wooden trap only cost thirty-four cents, I told her to buy the wooden trap.

I made a mistake. The next morning Vicki refused to go into the kitchen until after I examined the trap. In it was a deer mouse. After prying the trap open, I removed the mouse, and taking it outside, threw it into some briars behind the woodpile in the back yard. Afterwards walking up the slope toward the back door, I sensed someone watching me, and looking up saw Vicki staring down from the upstairs bathroom window, her eyes, it seemed, rounder than those of the mouse. "What I want for Christmas," I said when Vicki came down for breakfast with the boys, "the only thing I want is a Havahart trap." That morning Vicki bought the trap, and after tying a red ribbon around it, presented it to me at dinner. No more mice visited the kitchen, and in December when we decorated the living room Vicki put the trap under the tree with the rest of the presents. On Christmas Eve I read "Twas the Night Before Christmas" to the boys, and after putting cookies and milk on the hearth for Santa Claus and tossing carrots out in the snow for his reindeer, the children went to bed, visions of Legos and toy soldiers in their heads. Vicki and I then wrapped a few last presents and shared the cookies and milk, after which I went outside to search for the carrots while she wrote a note, purporting to be from Santa Claus thanking the boys for the treats. By the time we finished it was midnight, and we were ready to settle down, as Clement Moore put it, for a long winter's nap. We fluffed the covers, turned out the light, and were drifting off to sleep when suddenly we heard noises above us, not, though, the prancing of reindeer on the roof but the gibbering of a team of mice in the attic. Down to the tree I flew "like a flash," and after removing the ribbon, filled the trap with granola and placed it in the attic on the floorboards over our bedroom.

The next morning we were up early. When Francis saw his stocking bulging over the fireplace, a grin ripe as an apple spread across his face and he said in amazement, "He came." Then noticing the empty plate and glass on the hearth, he almost shouted, "and he ate the cookies and drank the milk." St. Nick was, however, not our only late-night visitor. In the trap in the attic I found a Christmas mouse. Full of granola the mouse looked as jolly as Santa Claus after milk and cookies. For a moment I did not know what to do. Turning the mouse out into the cold on Christmas was almost unthinkable. Suddenly, though, I remembered the garage. Along the far wall stacks of old papers rose like mesas while swatches of insulation slumped into damp, yellowish dunes at their feet. In the back corner were two lawn mowers and then the garden cart, this latter filled with clothes and oddments: gloves, work pants, a Rice University sweatshirt with Snoopy the dog on the front, wearing sun glasses and impersonating "Joe Owl," boots, a tub of grass seed, the blue front wheel of a Charton "Babycycle," six empty plastic Tropicana orange juice containers, a wooden fish, flat and probably a flounder, two trowels, a rake, and four birds' nests found in the scrub near Mansfield Hollow Dam. Next to the cart was a child's desk bought at a tag sale for six dollars. On top were cigar boxes containing the children's treasures from Nova Scotia: smooth rocks from above the beach at Beaver River, shotgun shells, dried flowers, colored strands of twine, nails, and tarot cards from an old trunk in the loft of the barn. The garage was almost as cluttered as the attic, and attached to the house, it was just the warm place, I thought, for a Christmas mouse. So the mouse would have a big Christmas lunch, I emptied a cup of granola into a small yellow bucket Edward always carried with him on the beach in Nova Scotia. Then after tossing in a handful of raisins and a pecan praline for appetizers and dessert, I tilted the bucket over and put it under the cart. Next I brought out the mouse. When I opened the trap, he hesitated, and before scurrying away under a pile of rags, he cocked his head and seemed to wink at me, nodding almost like Santa Claus did before he vanished up the chimney that wonderful night before Christmas. "Won't he," Vicki asked when I told her where I let the mouse go, "Won't he come back into the house?" "Maybe," I said, "but it doesn't matter. Today is Christmas."

Whether the Christmas mouse returned to the attic I don't know. Although I have never admitted it to Vicki, I suspect he did. In any case, though, he left a North Pole of helpers upstairs. The next morning another mouse was in the trap. In fact by Twelfth Night I had caught fourteen mice. I didn't turn any of them loose in the garage, however. For three falls running, I had dumped leaves into the little woods some eighty yards behind our house, creating great soft hills of humus. The day after Christmas I shoveled away part of a big pile of leaves and then taking a crowbar, battered into the hard ground, shaping burrows and storage rooms. Next I padded the sides of the burrows with scraps of insulation and stocked the larders, two with cups of sugar and then the others with cereals, granola, of course, but then also, corn flakes, Rice Krispies, shredded wheat, and Cheerios. Finally, I rebuilt the pile scattering brush across the top, leaving only a "secret" door open to the outside. Afterwards whenever I caught a mouse, I carried him to the pile and opening the trap over the secret door, forced him down the burrow toward food and warmth. After Twelfth Night Vicki got tired of the mice and me, losing all distaste for wooden traps and urging me to buy a supply. "The burrows aren't working. You are catching the same mice again and again," she said. "If you don't believe me, band them," she continued, the subject melting the winter chill and warming her up a bit, "You could give them asinine names like the characters in your essays: Fudball or Gonad or something just as terrible." "Banning," I replied, "that's the most ridiculous thing I have ever heard. I could put signs saying NO MICE ALLOWED near all the sweeps under the doors and beside every crack in the foundation, and it wouldn't do any good. Mice can't read. But go ahead," I said stalking out of the kitchen, "It's your idea. Go ahead and try it."

My house is near the university farm, and I like to imagine myself a countryman. Of course I'm not one. A countryman would have solved a mouse problem with a cat. Buying a cat, though, would not have been right for the mice or me, and so I kept trapping until spring arrived and the mice moved outside. When Vicki told her friend Rita about me and the mice, Rita laughed and said I was silly. I don't think so. On that day when I go over the last headland and cross the last sandbar, when I pull myself over the top rung of Jacob's ladder and ring the doorbell outside the Pearly Gates, maybe someone will remember the mice. I haven't been much of a sinner, but then I haven't been all that good either, and when St. Peter and the angels look under my name in the book of Pickerings, they are going to discover some bad language and a little misbehaving. Perhaps, though, one of the old fellows in white will have a heart for me like I had for the mice. And when the toughies begin to talk about dildos and giving me the eternal hotfoot, maybe he will interrupt and say, "but what about those mice." I don't want much. I'm not interested in getting wings so I can fly down to the beach and see the sights. The golden streets don't attract me. All I want is a little crack under the gate, one big enough for me to scamper through, a burrow in a fat soft cloud, a bowl full of sweet, heavenly granola, and then every once in a while a little visit with Otis and Bertha, just to see how the nectar is flowing. Of course, if the big boy in charge is feeling generous, I wouldn't mind a few flowers to press, not all lilies either but flowers from the high headland: columbine, evening primrose, and then memory, its blue bells tangy with bees and its roots deep into the good, black earth.

Eyes On

The Maintrees were the most dogged, persistent family in Macon County. A hundred and forty years ago Uncle Zered Maintree fell, it almost seems, out of the sky into a crack on Goad Ridge. Sprouting, he pushed roots down through the hard granite, his seed splitting boulders and burning off hillsides, eventually washing down the ridge, hardy thickets of Maintrees growing thorny along Deep Hungry Creek over through Pinchgut Neck and across Shrum Hollow. Still, when Pocohontas Maintree set her cap for Horace Armitage, folks thought she overreached herself. Addicted to drink, Horace was rocky soil, even for a family toughened through long generations of growing tobacco under the bluffs along Goad Ridge. "Horace might have his faults," Pocohontas told friends, "but they ain't nothing serious. He's such a quiet man." "Honey," Aunt Huldah Mace said, "you best be warned. Trouble ferments in the still." Deafened by love, Pocohontas didn't listen. For a while after the marriage Horace behaved, but then, old habits hardly ever dying, he started drinking again, Aunt Huldah telling Pocohontas that nothing much could be done. "You was told," she said, "his better halfs always was pints."

Blood like alcohol will out, and Pocohontas didn't accept Horace's addiction without a struggle. Almost as if she were uprooting nettles, she laid hands and sometimes trowels and shovels on Horace, pursuing him through the streets of Carthage, down Main Street and along the Upper Ferry Road, even following him across the river into the shed behind Enos Mayfield's "Inn." For a while Horace wore the shattered gaze of a man standing on the edge of religion, but then like the lightning of the Word, inspiration struck and he was saved. Suddenly remembering that Pocohontas was frightened of snakes, he bought Long Jeremiah a six-foot black snake from Anable Tilly's widow. For years Jeremiah lived in the Tillys' barn, growing round and sleek on rats. After her husband's death, Mrs.

Tilly sold the farm and bought a house on Carnack Street in Carthage. Before moving, however, she wanted to find a good home for Jeremiah. The Armitage homestead was rambling and unkempt, just the place for rats, and after Horace assured her that Jeremiah could live in the basement she let Horace have him for almost nothing. A soft snake can, in some instances, turn away wrath. Once Jeremiah took up residence, discord vanished from the Armitage household, life dividing itself into that above and that below the basement stairs, the one sober and straight-laced, the other raucous and serpentine.

At dusk one cold February afternoon as Horace sat warming himself in the basement, snake at foot and mason jar in hand, there was a clattering noise, followed by wood splintering and coal dust billowing up from the floor. While driving down Back Street Dr. Sollows had swerved to miss Scarlet, Pocohontas's cat who lay sunning herself in the middle of the road. In turning the steering wheel, Dr. Sollows lost control of his car and bouncing over curb and sidewalk and through Horace's privet hedge slammed into the outside basement door, in the process shattering it and tumbling himself out and down the steps. Dazed, Dr. Sollows found himself sitting on wet concrete, splinters and dust over him like an eiderdown and a snake smelling like watermelon sliding slowly up his leg. "Where am I," he said feebly; "where am I?" "You are in my basement," came a husky, portentous voice out of the dark, "but don't try nothing. I've got my eyes on you."

Horace wasn't telling the truth of course, at least not all of it, for when the crash came he looked to his jar, gripping it tightly, not to the door. As much as the noise startled him, he worried more about drink than the apparition rising slowly from the floor, for he had seen lots of apparitions in his time and actually had grown fond of them. To a great extent we are, however, what we have our eyes on, be that mason jars or the boulders and red clay of Goad Ridge. Recently I have had my eyes on flowers; like moonshine they intoxicate feeling and I plant them in my writings, following no plan but letting them pull words through me, a blue flame hot and flickering but yet invisible. Beyond paragraphs tumbling like terraces nouns run down a hillside, tall and spiked, while verbs, bright hollyhocks, blow in the breeze by an old dry wall. Like wysteria and clematis adjectives cling to the side of a spring house, and adverbs, their *l*'s and *y*'s liquid and slippery, glisten like water lilies in a pool. Beyond are pronouns, some masculine but most feminine, peonies and hibiscus, white and lavender. Down the drive wind borders of conjunctions and prepositions, sometimes loosestrife and cowslips but more often than not ground covers: silver mound, rock cress, blue fescue, soapwort, and then lily of the valley, its white saucers fresh as clouds.

Words are annuals, their brightness alive for but a page, while the lure of flowers is perennial, roots thrusting deep below the snows of forgetfulness. Unlike matters bookish, for me the plants of the field smack of the eternal, and I spend hours spading up lore about flowers, much of it, appropriately enough, religious lore. When Christ was crucified, Spanish story has it, the deer in the mountains of the Iberian Peninsula wept, their tears hardening into bulbs as they fell to the ground. The following Easter the tears bloomed, daffodils blossoming like chalices, white and yellow from the Pyrenees to the Nevadas. For a year after the Crucifixion, the tale continues, all the butterflies which hatched in Spain were black, as if in mourning. Then that following Easter the butterflies blossomed with the daffodils. Those butterflies which sipped nectar from white blooms became spotted and streaked with white while those which fed on yellow flowers turned partially yellow, giving the world black and yellow swallowtails, daffodils of the air as they are sometimes called in the mountains about Cordoba.

Old lore blooms like a hidden garden, stone walls fragrant with jasmine and paths turning past iron fountains and sundials wrinkled with cherubs. As much as I enjoy twisting alone through thought, however, I spend more time in my yard, not by myself but in the company of others, usually my children. Last week we broke the frozen glaze over the ground and dug trenches around my daffodils so the February rains would not wash across the yard, cutting channels through our spring. Afterwards we went for a walk. Near Mansfield Hollow Dam I found bush clover. Against the bare sandy soil it looked brown; at home in the study, a green rug on the floor, it was reddish. This month I have taken the children on several walks, hoping they will learn to recognize ordinary plants in winter: mullein, cow cress, jimson weed, goldenrod, and asters, spindly and gray. Of course people see differently. Walking up Cullom Street one bright Saturday morning, Quintus Tyler noticed an unfamiliar plant at the edge of the sidewalk. Quintus was interested not only in the children he taught during the week at the Male and Female Select School and on Sundays at the Baptist church but in almost all things having to do with Smith County, its gossip and history, even its wildflowers. Seeing little Reba Droone sitting on the ground strapping on her roller skates, Quintus asked, "Reba, are you acquainted with this flower?" "Yes," she answered, standing up and pushing her feet back and forth. "Well, then," Quintus said, "to what family does it belong?" "The Chisms," Reba said, pointing over her shoulder to a small frame house before skating away to buy a Coke at Murrah's Drugstore.

Much as Reba saw the flower differently from Quintus, so my children see the plants I point out differently from me. Last week as we walked through a field below the university piggery, they hardly noticed the peppergrass, its seeds small hairy dirigibles, preferring instead to search for "beans," sheep droppings. Even when they look at the plants I show them, they see different things. For Francis how the seeds of burdock spread, hooked barbs practically grabbing the fur of passing animals, was marvelous. The knowledge contributed less to his becoming a gentle young naturalist, however, than it did to his becoming, as Vicki put it later that afternoon as she brushed a great clot of burrs out of Eliza's hair, "a brutal Hun." The Hun aside, the children are probably better off seeing things differently from me and my generation. Would that a change in vision could make a better world. Sometimes I think I keep my eyes on plants because I am too cowardly to look up and into the distance. "When I'm a big woman," Eliza said last night at the end of dinner, "I will let my children have lots of candy." Womanhood and children may not, I fear, lie beyond Eliza's today. At night I awaken and imagine rolling red balls of flame, daffodils turned to cinders and butterflies ash in the storm, dark funeral wreaths not garlands lilac with joy.

In part health is responsible for my pessimism. I have a spur and bulging disk in my neck and along with pain gloom radiates from my back. Instead of seeing possibilities for pleasure in experience, more often than not I see possibilities for hurt, indeed of danger, and so rather than expanding, I have contracted my world, withdrawing into the domestic and the local. From the physical often flows the mental, and I now avoid "new" ideas almost as much as I avoid experience. Awareness of my own frailty has made me aware of the frailty of others, particularly my children, and while my hand shakes, neck and back throbbing, I imagine disease, malice, and accident as brown-coated predators, waiting to gnaw a red way through my family. And so I keep my eyes on the children, pulling them close and reading to them every afternoon, this winter the seven Narnia novels of C. S. Lewis, and then *The Hobbit* and *The Secret Garden,* and now *Robin Hood.* At noon when she comes home from nursery school, I play with Eliza, nowadays Candy Land, a board game in which players draw colored cards from a stack in order to make their ways to King Kandy and his castle, a fluffy creation of ice cream cones topped with sprinkles and red cherries. The path to the castle is sweet, past Mr. Mint and the Peppermint Forest, over Gumdrop Pass, beside Grandma Nutt and the Peanut Brittle House, and lastly around Gloppy, a smiling chocolate monster bubbling up through a soft brown swamp. If a player is lucky, he draws a card depicting Queen Frostine, the ruler of a pink ice cream sea, and thus skips lightly by hazards such as Gooey Gumdrops and the sticky Lollipop Woods. The worst thing that can happen is to approach King Kandy and then draw a card with Plumpy on it, a furry green creature standing under a gingerbread tree covered with round purple plums. Plumpy's tree is only nine squares from the start; happily Eliza rarely draws Plumpy for I arrange our games so that she usually wins. Eliza is generous, though, and although she arrives at the castle before I do, she never eats all the ice cream because, as she says, she doesn't want her "daddy to go hungry."

For me, of course, the imaginary sweets at the Castle stale beside the real sweets of playing with Eliza. Although the pain in my back never goes away, life seems happier and kinder, in truth bearable, when I am with her or the boys. When I read the journal Francis wrote this past September in second grade, describing his summer vacation, the pain slides into smiles. According to Francis when we visited my father in Nashville, we ate at a country club which cost "five hundred trillion dollars" to build. In July in traveling from Portland to Yarmouth, we took the "fairy." In truth traveling with the children to Nova Scotia is magical, and when transformed by a small boy's spelling, the ordinary seems marvelous. Of an old bustle, Francis wrote, "We found in the top of the barn a thing that women put on thier fanys to make there dress stik out." Francis was particularly intersted in the functional: the wood stove in the kitchen, a buggy in the barn, and then the privy at the corner of the back house. Of this last he drew a picture, after which he carefully explained its use. Francis's explanation was so complete that his teacher wrote

"Yuck!" in the margin. What the children say and write brightens my days, and I turn their words through my mind like buttercreams. Of course not all they say is sugary. Two nights ago Eliza said, "Daddy, maybe we are windup toys and God and his friends are playing with us."

Pushing pain out of mind, I try to be cheerful. When the children are away at school or whenever there is no place for me in their play and I sense melancholy and selfishness begin to blow through me like a dank mist, I turn my eyes toward writing. I visit characters whose talk and dispositions are warm and summery. Often I sail to Nova Scotia and sit quietly in Bertha Shifney's parlor in Port Maitland. Bertha's speech is filled with oddities, and I jot them down, noting that she says "extracise" for "exercise" and "thoughty" instead of "thoughtful." Bertha had little formal schooling, and occasionally Francis's fairy waves a wand over her conversation, transforming weary nouns and verbs into glittering coaches and silver slippers. This past November when Otis Blankinchip asked her to explain the phrase "virgin soil," she answered, "that's dirt where the hand of man has never set foot." Otis himself is prone toward enchanted speech. Last week when Bertha asked him what caused Hornus Roebuck's sudden death, Otis said he didn't know, explaining, "Hornus died without the aid of a doctor." Generally after sitting for a while with Bertha and Otis, I excuse myself and slip down to Carthage and Quintus Tyler. I am particularly fond of Quintus because he is a teacher like me and also because plants interest him almost as much as they do me. Three weeks ago Quintus discussed the story of the Prodigal Son in his Sunday school class. "Amid all the music and dancing, the putting on of big rings and fancy robes," he said thinking about the elder son, "there was one who did not rejoice, who disapproved of the festivities and who didn't want to attend. Now class," Quintus said pausing, "who was this individual?" For a moment the room was silent. Then Billie Dinwidder, the son of Zadok Dinwidder, the owner of Bullock's slaughterhouse, raised his hand. "Mr. Tyler, please sir, I know," he practically shouted; "it was the fatted calf."

My friend Pat tells me that whenever he and his wife, Ann, travel he feels unaccountably warm and affectionate, even, he says, if they stay in a Marriott, cool with pastel silkscreens on pastel walls and ice machines at the end of every corridor. In my case, travel doesn't stoke the cinders of desire so much as it inflames observation, leading, alas, more often than not to red-faced absurdity. As soon as I step into an airport, currents of excitement blow ashes from my ears and clinkers from my eyes. Two weeks ago I flew to Nashville to visit Father. As usual I arrived at the Hartford airport eighty minutes before my flight left. After checking my bag I hurried down to the USAir waiting area at the end of Concourse B. Once there I sat down and opened Jane Austen's *Emma*. The book, however, was cover, and instead of reading I watched people and listened to conversations. Seated opposite me were two women, both awaiting the arrival of visiting family members. The women did not know each other and were dressed differently, one wearing a green sweater and bulbously tight green trousers, the other wearing a brown suit, a gold circle pin on the upper left lapel. Differences in dress, however, did not drop a stitch in the conversation, for the women were about the same age, in their mid-sixties, and had shared similar experiences. "I'm waiting for my youngest son," the woman in green began; "he's in the service and is coming in from Germany. The last time he came home," she continued, "he brought a girl with him, and they wanted to stay in the same room. I told them that if they wanted to sleep together they could go to a motel. I wasn't going to have that in my house." "What sort of person did they think I was?" the woman asked. "I've been a widow for three years and I don't sleep around, though I get plenty of offers, I can tell you." "I'm a widow too," the other responded, stiffening slightly then relaxing before adding, "but I don't miss it—any of it."

On the flight from Hartford to Pittsburgh, the man sitting next to me said little, busying himself by writing numbers in a looseleaf notebook. On a trip my vision almost always turns outward and although the man rebuffed all attempts at conversation, I wasn't put off, at least not from observation, and like lenses of varying strengths I rolled my eyes over him, looking beyond his gray suit and red and blue striped tie for something unique or out of place. Unlike beauty individuality does not reside in the eye of the beholder so much as it does in the intensity of observation. At first I noticed nothing out of the ordinary, but turning up the magnifying power, I found something. Tattooed on a fold of skin between the thumb and index finger of his left hand was a fly. The fold was as round and as plump as the weight in a window sash and the fly had grown fat and purple with age. On the next part of the trip, flight 409 from Pittsburgh to Nashville, I sat beside a large woman wearing a sack-like cream dress with a tree printed on the side, a thick brown trunk growing up from the hem to spread leafy and yellow under her left arm around her back and over her bosom. Well, I thought, buckling my seatbelt, this flight could be interesting, and glancing over at the tree, I scaled the trunk and climbed out along the limbs, hoping to discover a robin or bluebird hunkered low on a nest or, perhaps a squirrel high on a branch chewing on a nut. Unfortunately the tree was uninhabited and I wasn't able to find even a lichen, so in hopes of starting a conversation rather than an animal, I raised my gaze to the woman's face and said simply that the plane was crowded. When she grunted assent and then scowled formidably, I realized why the tree was empty. We did not speak again until the plane was well off the ground. Then while reaching for her purse which she had put under the seat in front of her, she brushed against my calf and muttered a perfunctory, almost begrudging, apology. "That's perfectly all right; that's much the nicest thing that's happened to me on this flight," I exclaimed, opening my eyes wide and turning my face like a moon toward her, before adding loudly, "so far."

The remark did not, as I hoped it would, bring the return of spring and twittering sweet conversation. Instead a wintry blast shook the tree, and silence fell like sleet. Despite the frost, however, the flight passed swiftly. Shortly after takeoff the stewardess served a snack, and I shifted my attention from the woman to food. The snack was served in a clear plastic lunchbox-shaped container. Inside the little box along with individually wrapped "entree" were a napkin, a spoon, fork, and knife—these three made from white plastic—and one loose cherry tomato. The main course was half a sandwich on French bread with sesame seeds on top. In the sandwich were bits of ham and turkey, a slice of American cheese, and a smidgen of parsley. Onto the sandwich I squeezed Grey Poupon Dijon Mustard, manufactured in East Hanover, New Jersey by Nabisco Brands. A product of Specialty Foods in Wilmington, Massachusetts, the salt and pepper came in ribbed, postage stamp size packets, one silver and red, the other silver and black. I didn't open the salt or pepper, but I did eat a four-ounce tub of Mott's Cinnamon Apple Sauce, flavored naturally and sold by Cadbury Schweppes in Stamford, Connecticut. Dessert was a Plantation Brownie manufactured in Lake Bluff, Illinois. Although containing artificial flavor as well as Thiamine Mononitrate and Riboflavin, the brownie, the package stated, was "made with Pure Vegetable Shortening," consisting, I read in another place on the label, of "Partially And/Or Fully Hydrogenated Soybean, Cottonseed or Palm Oil." I am afraid I skipped dessert. With the snack, though, I did drink an eleven and a half ounce can of "Very Fine" orange juice made from a mixture of water and concentrate extracted from "100% Florida" oranges and sold by New England Apple Products in Littleton, Massachusetts.

The next morning Father and I drove to Carthage. After visiting Mother's grave we parked on Main Street and got a cup of coffee in Murrah's Drugstore. Despite sitting peacefully, almost sleepily, in a booth, I was still a traveler, listening and observing. Behind us a woman sat alone at a table. When a friend joined her and asked what she had been doing, I heard the woman say, "Not much. I've been staying to home, cleaning and cooking. I'm just all mossed over." Later on the curb outside as we got ready to return to Nashville, an older man recognized Father then reminisced about by-gone days in Carthage and my grandfather, "the last of the good Republicans," the man said. The things I saw and heard during my trip were ordinary, but they entertained me and certainly were safer than the behavior of some folks, who misbehave once they get beyond sight of their own smokestacks. In Nashville I heard a story about the untoward doings of the Reverend Judah Sugg, a Methodist minister from Wartrace, Tennessee. The reverend, it seems, went to a big convention in St. Louis where he preached then got the pox. As soon as the meeting of the Ladies' Bible Forum adjourned on the Sunday after he returned home, Reverend Sugg drove over to Bell Buckle to discuss his problem with Dr. Cossey. "Parson, I'm afraid," Dr. Cossey said after the examination, "that I'm going to have to chop it off." "Oh, my Lord," the reverend exclaimed, "can't you do something else." "Parson, you got to understand," the doctor said, "the pox can kill you." For a moment the reverend was quiet, searching, story has it, for inspiration, high or low, in such an extremity it didn't matter where it came from. Finally he spoke, "Doctor, do you have to take it all? Couldn't you just save a little bit of it?" "Well, I suppose I could," the doctor said, rubbing his chin and studying things. "I suppose I could save you enough to knock around the house with, but," the doctor paused, "no more conventions."

In this account there is probably more tall tale, or perhaps more accurately, low tale than truth. I don't keep my eyes focused on the truth however; occasionally I even wander from both truth and propriety, though not I rush to add, in the way in which the Reverend Sugg strayed. Actually, despite growing older and more opinionated, I often have difficulty determining what is or is not true. At times I think that truth is not something a sensible person ought to bother about. As I age events in my past seem more dream than actuality, things done by another person, not by the me I now see in the mirror. Occasionally dreams themselves seem truth. Not long after Christmas I dreamed Vicki spent four thousand dollars one afternoon at the local mall. I awoke and for a moment, there in the dark, I was almost upset. But then despite the early hour truth dawned. Spending that much money at the East Brook Mall would be difficult. The shops are functional, not exotic, and the prices are modest, not high. The only expensive item I recalled was in Puppy Love, the pet store, a blue and yellow Gold Macaw, named Toby and selling for three thousand dollars. Supposedly the macaw could say "Good morning, rise and shine," a talent which would not endear him to Vicki who likes to sleep late and has banished alarm clocks from the bedroom, tolerating this husband only because he creeps quietly out of bed and turns the heat on downstairs before waking her.

Sometimes a dream lingers in the mind, enduring longer than most truths. For ten years I have been intrigued by a dream I had about a couple named Harry and Sally. Although she could be a charming conversationalist, Sally was shrewish and ill-tempered. Day and night she scolded Harry, rarely even letting him sleep in peace. Whenever he closed his eyes during a quarrel, she plucked his eyelids out from his face and pulled them up. One day after a particularly unpleasant argument, Harry exploded, and seizing Sally by the hair, dragged her into the basement, where he hit her on the head with an axe and then chopped her into pieces, all of which he tossed into the furnace. Thereafter Harry and Sally enjoyed, at least from Harry's point of view, a congenial, stable marriage. Whenever he wanted to talk to Sally, Harry turned on the thermostat, regulating Sally's mood and conversation by raising and lowering the temperature. Now that I think about it, though, I suppose Harry and Sally had not lived together long enough to grow close and comfortable. More than likely they didn't have children and Sally's attention was so focused on Harry that she became overly critical.

Like egg beaters children churn edgy intensity away. The sharp folds into the sweet, and days rise affectionate, a batter of duty and little moment, wholesome and wondrously sustaining. The Monday before Valentine's was Vicki's birthday and a school holiday. At breakfast the children and I gave her cards. Then I went swimming, after which I picked up a stack of freshman themes at the English department. At half past nine I met Vicki and the children at the Cup of Sun for birthday muffins. After eating our muffins we hurried home; at a quarter past eleven I had an appointment with a dermatologist in Willimantic to see whether a mole on my face was cancerous. It wasn't; in fact it wasn't a mole but a liver spot. On the way home I stopped by the Flower Sales Room at the horticultural school and bought eight chrysanthemums, four yellow and four white, big bushy football-Saturday chrysanthemums, the kind attached to badges which read "Go Commodores" or "Roll Tide." After milk, a peanut butter and jelly sandwich, an orange and an Oreo, we took a birthday walk around Tift Pond. The pond was frozen, and I walked out on the ice, not far, however, because Vicki said I was so fat that I might fall through, "fall through ice even a foot thick," she said. I did not stay on the ice long, and the only person who fell was Eliza who tripped on the path, breaking not ice but skin on her cheek. After the walk we drove to the mall and Vicki bought me a new red umbrella and the children boots for next winter, saving, she told me, thirty percent of the regular price. From the mall we drove to Tony's Pizza for an early birthday dinner. To celebrate Vicki had a draft beer, but since I was driving I shared a bottle of Coke with Edward and Eliza. Francis who doesn't like soft drinks had milk. For dinner we divided a big Greek salad with Italian dressing, followed by a large pizza, one half plain for the children and the other half covered with mushrooms, pepperoni, and black olives. The birthday dinner cost $15.85 plus two dollars for the tip. By half past five we were home and getting the children ready for a bath. At seven Vicki left for a meeting of the board of the Storrs Community Nursery School, and I read *Stuart Little* to the children and drank another Coke because the pizza dried me out. When Vicki returned home at 10:15, I was asleep, having spent a full and satisfying birthday.

Several large birch trees lay along the shore of Tift Pond, their white branches crooked across the ground like the bleached bones of prehistoric monsters, or so I told the children. During winter when the cold makes study appealing and television seductive, I force my eyes to the ground, taking two or three walks each week.

This past Saturday after ice-skating lessons and lunch at Jonathan's, a snack bar on campus, Vicki took the children to the Mansfield Library. Saying that the hamburger and french fries I ate for lunch had not settled comfortably, I begged off from the library and instead went for a walk. I began by exploring the marsh behind the dairy barn. Small creatures, probably mice, had fashioned nests under the cow manure around the edges of the marsh. I tried to pick up a pattie and examine a nest, but the manure was hard and frozen to the ground. After leaving the marsh I walked up and over Horsebarn Hill, crossing the field and road beyond and going down behind the piggery. There at the edge of the woods I stopped by the trunk of my "Owl Tree" and picking several gray, furry pellets off the ground opened them, pulling out yellowed bones and tusks. So far as I could tell, the owl only visited the tree at night, sitting on a limb and looking out over the small field below. Although I have never seen an owl in the tree, I looked carefully through its branches and through those of nearby trees. High in the sky above, I saw two red-tailed hawks riding the wind, and watching them, I forgot about owls. After the hawks floated out of sight, I walked into the woods and followed a dry stream, my feet making a crunching sound as my weight collapsed the broken, frozen soil. In a little while I pushed through the woods, coming out near a small white building that once housed the rope tow for the university ski club. The ski slope tumbled steeply down in front of the building. The gears of the tow had rusted red and yellow, and the slope was being overgrown, scrub closing in from the sides like folding window blinds. At the bottom of the slope was wetland. Over the next ridge and down across a corn field was the Fenton River. To have gone on would have turned the walk into a hike, and so I stopped at the wetland. Also, I didn't feel up to climbing the ridge; the day was cold, and the sky seemed to have holes in it, the wind blowing through them in long gray tunnels. Later in the afternoon as I walked home the sun came out, not warm and orange, though, but lemony and biting. So that I would look at the land about me and not drift along on abstractions higher than thermals, I collected plants to show to the children. I put them in a bag, a carryall with *Sewanee* stitched on the side in square white letters. The plants I collected were commonplace and despite being stripped of summery blossom and leaf were easily identifiable: chicory; hardhack; evening primrose, the seed capsules exploded and resembling spent shell casings; beggar ticks; dodder; yellow rocket, membranes from its seed pods waving white and silvery like small streamers; and avens, the burrs brown and solitary, almost aristocratic. Under the trees along the slope grew wild leek, its seeds round and hard and thrust upward in small black clusters. About the wetland were great patches of sensitive fern, spore cases branching out from the tops of shiny, khaki stalks and resembling the hair of an exotic princess, strands woven in dark beaded chains. I walked for almost three hours. When I returned home and settled down at my desk with books, magnifying glass, hot chocolate, and plants, I felt tired and wonderfully content. The lunch had vanished from my system, and the day seemed disciplined and focused.

Much of life passes indistinct and unfinished, and keeping one's eyes on anything for a long time is difficult, be it a birthday, a cold February afternoon, a dream, or even the past. The things I valued thirty years ago have changed, some growing more important, others fading from memory. Now I sometimes think life resembles an old porcelain doorknob. From a distance the doorknob appears white and solid. Up close, however, it is crazed, blue lines running through it, cracking it into fragments, almost as angular and as self-contained as dried mud in a riverbed. No matter how I try I'm not able to discover a pattern amid the lines. The doorknob itself blurs, and almost without knowing it, I begin to follow a particular line, neglecting the whole for a part. I write in much the same way, starting out with a large rounded topic, but ending with a single line, fragmented and unsatisfactory. Four years ago during a controversy about prayer in the public schools, I planned an essay on religion and society. Typically, though, by the time I began writing, the subject had shrunk to "Business Prayer," becoming derivative and almost topical. I was acquainted, I began, with few sinners aged six to twelve. Most sinners I knew really didn't get going "good" until after their schooling was over, at about age twenty-five. If Congress wanted to reform the nation, they should, I urged, begin with adults, not children, and make morning prayer a compulsory part of the business rather than the school day. For a while ideas came to me easily, but then I started thinking about exceptions. Airlines would have to be exempted from the law. No sane person would board an early flight for Chicago or Atlanta if he saw the pilot and co-pilot praying in the cockpit. An exemption would also have to be granted to the medical profession. If not, surgery would have to be scheduled during afternoons, for being rolled into an operating room and seeing the surgeon on his knees would, at the least, be unnerving. The more I wrote the less practical business prayer seemed. If prayer made honesty popular and honesty became everyone's policy, the economy would collapse. The legal profession would disappear overnight. Banks would fold like leaves on mimosa trees. At the end of each letter sent to prospective customers in which bundles of money were offered at "modest" rates of interest, a vice-president would feel compelled to write, "Ignore the enclosed advertisement. It is not for you. It will only bring you ruin and unhappiness." No longer would universities behave like snake-oil salesmen pitching education as the cure-all for the ills of society. Of course once educators told the truth, most universities, I realized, would close and I would lose my job. Suddenly business prayer seemed dangerous, if not un-American, and I stopped writing, concluding that prayer belonged just where the politicians said it did, in the schools with fat yellows pencils and big orange notebooks, as far as possible from adults and the world of buying and spending.

One social concern usually leads to another, and not long after putting the fragment on business prayer aside, I began a piece which I thought about calling "Mountains into Molehills." Man, I began, had grown too big for his britches, and if he could be shrunk, most problems facing the world—overpopulation, war, pollution—could be ameliorated, if not solved. The average five foot nine inch man weighed, I read, one hundred and seventy-two pounds while in contrast a man five foot two weighed one hundred and forty one pounds, thirty-one pounds or eighteen percent less. If people over five foot two inches tall were not allowed to mate, the size of humans would shrink rapidly, and with the decrease in size would come a corresponding decrease in consumption, or so I argued pointing out, for example, that urban sprawl would no longer threaten good farmland and that with little people would come little cars, something that would invigorate the economy as construction companies would spend decades converting superhighways into pathways. For a while I wrote almost thoughtfully, citing fact and statistic, but then I, as so often happens, got sidetracked and neglecting facts began to tumble words about. Expressions like "lowdown so and so," "pipsqueak," "pissant," and "obnoxious little twit," would, I wrote, suddenly become compliments. High seriousness would banish a book to the remainder house, and literature itself would cease being heavy and meaningful and would rapidly grow wholesomely lighthearted. Miss Muffet, Jack Horner, and Bo-Peep would replace John Henry, Mae West, and Paul Bunyan as folk heroes. With the disappearance of the tall tale and the big lie, truthfulness would be celebrated, and the world would become a better place as people would always be satisfied with "half a loaf" and a spirit of compromise would pervade society. Big shots and blow hards would become endangered species and civility would return to conversation as understatement would be celebrated and small talk recognized as an art. For pages I played, praising the small farmer and reducing the foot-long hero sandwich to the common man's four inches. But then matters personal intervened, as they often do in my writing, and reduced the piece to yet another fragment. "That's all well and good," Vicki said late one night after I described my idea to her, "but don't you think not allowing people over five feet two inches tall to mate might cause problems." "After all," she continued rubbing cold cream on her face before turning out the light, "after all you are over six feet and I am five foot eight."

No matter how I prepare my eyes for distant rooms, the doorknobs I seize roll inward, the crazed lines turning about themselves, instead of locks. Not long ago I began what I hoped would be a thoughtful piece on pride and self-knowledge. I started by criticizing the metaphor of the family tree, arguing that family trees caused untold trouble, provoking dissatisfaction and ambition, and then leading, as surely as apples, to falls as people forsook sturdy humility and attempted to hoist themselves up through their ancestors high off the ground. How much better and safer, and more reasonable, to have a family weed, I wrote, and then I paused. Hoeing around amid ground beetles and tumblebugs, I lost my way, or at least all elevated intentions. The crickets' serenades and the fireflies' festive lanterns made me forget the stars and the music of philosophy, abstract notes sounding across the far-off spheres. Instead I wandered the side yard, searching for a weed appropriate to my family. In the dell I found it, ground ivy or gill-cover-the-ground. Gill is a mint, albeit a humble one. Unlike pennyroyal, thyme, rosemary, basil, and marjoram, gill has rarely seasoned sugary verse or sweet recipes. "A low base herb," John Gerarde called it in the sixteenth century, which "creepeth and spreadeth upon the ground hither and thither all about." Like the Pickerings which have ambled unnoticed and unremembered through time, gill has an unobtrusive vitality.

Whenever it puts forth a pair of leaves, it usually sends down a tuft of roots, binding itself to the sustaining ground, far from the high winds of history. Blooming from April through July, the flowers are small and almost understated, occurring in whorls of three to six, light purple and speckled with dots of reddish violet. Like generations of good ordinary people never grafted onto a family tree, gill is useful in a quiet way. "It is," Gerarde wrote, "commended against the humming noise and ringing round the eares, being put into them." To block out humming or ringing, one need not drop gill into his ears. Almost any weed will silence those voices which urge a person to get ahead, be somebody, and cultivate an ancestry.

Gill was also good, Gerarde wrote, for aching backs and hips, and he suggested brewing tea from it, soaking half a dram of leaves in four ounces of "faire water." In hopes of getting some little relief for my own back pain, I tried the tea, gathering great armfuls of gill and boiling it in a stewpot on the stove. *Bitter,* alas, does not do gill justice. The taste makes the eyes bulge like onions and the nostrils flare like avocados. Still, in most things, taste is but a small fault. Once or twice I have been accused of questionable, if not poor taste. At a dinner party in Tennessee this last trip, one of Mother's friends said to me, "Sammy, Red and I just love your essays, but sometimes you are just so bawdy." For a moment I didn't know what to say, but then I thought of gill, a base herb, vigorous and sensibly low to the ground, and so I told the truth. "Yes ma'am, I know," I said; "but I just can't help it. I am bawdy." Absolutely perfect taste, I have decided since returning to Storrs, is for ambitious people who keep up with fashion and who prune their families into trees. It is not for people like the Pickerings who go modestly through their days, people who when the Great Lawn Mower cuts them off leave behind only a memory or two, minty and untrimmed.

Many people, I suspect, resemble me and have trouble keeping their eyes on a particular subject. Perhaps only people who see little see life steadily and see it whole. Such people have not sat with me in the crazed dark, talking to Horace Armitage and watching Long Jeremiah unravel over the coal. Of course it may simply be that I don't have my eyes on life but on words, and in seeing Golgotha and daffodils on the wings of butterflies, I'm cultivating a garden, filled with topiary as unnatural and artificial as any family tree. Be that as it may, though, I find it difficult to keep my eyes on things. Maybe being a teacher and having asked so many questions and heard so many answers has made it impossible for me to see things whole. Still, I'm not alone in my weakness; that other teacher, Quintus Tyler, resembles me. One Friday Quintus and Zadok Dinwidder found themselves boarding the early morning train for Nashville, Zadok to visit the stockyards and Quintus to have an impression made for a new upper plate. They sat together and conversation flowed smoothly from the Prodigal Son to the Republican Party. Just east of Lebanon the train passed a field spotted with fat black Angus. "Gracious," Zadok said, imagining rumps and loins, briskets, flanks, and short plates, "that's a fine herd of black cattle." "Yes, they are fine," Quintus answered, then paused before continuing; "at least they are fine from this side."

Near Spring

On the first day of March I walked through the woods in the back yard and turning south followed the cut for the telephone wires down to the small marsh next to the high school baseball field. Cattails and bulrushes grew along the third base line, and behind home plate I found horse-balm, water horehound, then a seed capsule from a single blue flag, mottled and brown and looking like an old leather football. The capsule had split and deflated, and the fibers which bound it together were white and stringy like rotten stitches. I started to pick the capsule and take it home, but I didn't. Winter no longer held me or the earth firmly in its grasp. Around the edges of the marsh ice had begun to melt, and I longed for the weeds of spring. Four days later down the slope of the long hill behind the cattle barn the children and I found pussy willow, swelling furry and silver. Turning north at the foot of the hill, we followed a brook through the woods, picking a way across the ice and through briar until we came to the bottomland alongside the Fenton River, part of the old Ogushwicz Farm. There in a wet spot between forest and field skunk cabbage bloomed, its red horns sticking up through the water, hooded and almost primeval. On fallen trees just above the wetland were clustered hundreds of small, grey puffballs, each with a hole in the end and swollen with spores. Two weeks later the puffballs were empty and liver-spotted, the sides having collapsed inward like the cheeks of an old woman.

The signs of spring excited us, and we roamed the field picking and collecting, the children filling their pockets with bits of clay pigeons, yellow and black, and then brass cases from spent rifle cartridges, the refuse of someone's winter target practice. Into a plastic bag I stuffed bracket fungus, mostly redbelt and oak maze gill, and then a score or so of goldenrod galls. In summer Indian corn had been planted in the field, and in the fall we gathered ears to hang on the front door and to feed to the chipmunk living under the garage. Now we wondered what animals lived beside the field and we searched for runs and burrows. Droppings were everywhere, deer and rabbit primarily. Near the skunk cabbage I found a newly dug burrow, wet mud pushed away from the entrance in piles the shape of walnuts. The burrow ran deep, and the piles were different colors, some black consisting of topsoil and others yellow from farther down. I showed the hole to Eliza, and after bending over to look into it, she straightened and said, "Daddy, we must be kind to animals, but I don't know what kind of animals we are."

At the end of the walk, we stopped at the university barns. The lambing was almost over, and we spent more time with cattle than sheep, looking at the young bulls, Hereford, Angus, and Simmental. I like to rub their thick necks and push their heavy heads, and so I called them. They came to me, as they almost always do, probably out of curiosity because my call is odd, beginning with a sound similar to that of a squirrel chattering then rising to a rolling high-pitched "hoo, hoo." Once we got home I sat at my desk and opened the galls. Most were empty; in two, though, I found fat green worms, the larvae of a small fly. Because the larvae could not live after the galls were opened, I felt guilty. I picked the galls, I think, more to teach the children respect for nature than to satisfy my curiosity. Certainly, though, I don't like destroying, and so as atonement, increasing life in one place where I lessened it in another, I ordered wildflowers for the side yard from Spring Hill, twelve Dutchman's breeches, six shooting stars, and eighteen lady's slippers.

Now that I think about it, I guess I saw the first sign of spring well before March, the day before Valentine's in fact and not on the air or along the ground but in the water at the university pool. The bathing suits worn by young girls do not resemble those worn by nice men's wives, with full backs and ruffled skirts. The girls' suits resemble skimpy exoskeletons. Hanging low over the thorax and cut away before the terga, they make wearers resemble insects, hind legs dangling out and down like those of crawling water beetles. While swimming that morning I noticed a girl with a bruise high on her coxa, so high that it was almost on the posterior epimeron. The bruise was round and mouth-sized. "Spring is on the way. I got close," Bhikhu said later in the shower, "and saw teeth marks, real teeth marks. The bruise was a Valentine's gift." I am too well-mannered and long in the tooth for nibbling. Still, I often hanker after candy, and on leaving the gymnasium and pulling my coat tight across my chest, I felt melancholy, remembering the wild sowings of springs past. How many more times, I wondered, would I see crocus push through dead grass, its leaves pursed and pressed tightly together like an arrow head. I had only just awakened, I thought, and begun to appreciate life. To leave now would be a waste and wouldn't be fair.

Like snow flurries at the end of winter, my chill mood quickly melted. For my family February began a happy, tiring season of birth, not death. Vicki was born in February, Edward in March, Eliza in April, and Francis in bright May. On March 8 Vicki took cupcakes to Edward's kindergarten class, white cakes covered with poppy pink icing and sprinkles. Three days later on Saturday we had a party for Edward at home. That morning I took Edward and Francis to East Brook Mall. First we went to Waldenbooks where I bought a birthday present for Andrew, one of Francis's friends. Francis had trouble deciding on a present so I selected *The Dinosaur Encyclopedia,* "A Handbook for Dinosaur Enthusiasts of All Ages." Next we went to Yummy's to pick up Edward's cake, a yellow cake with chocolate icing and purple flowers, costing $9.95. Vicki ordered the cake Wednesday morning; unfortunately the order went astray, and Yummy's had only two cakes on hand, a chocolate cake with chocolate icing and a white cake with whipped cream icing and strawberry filling. Vicki was upset when I telephoned to ask which cake she preferred, so much so that my face must have changed color. "Tell you what," the man behind the counter said as he watched me on the phone, "the mistake was ours so I'll give you both cakes for five dollars."

Edward's friends arrived at half past one and after opening presents and eating cakes and ice cream—their choice of chocolate, vanilla, mint chocolate chip, or any combination thereof—we played games: Simon Says, Pin the Tail on the Dinosaur, Steal the Bacon, and Musical Balloons, after which we tossed bean bags downstairs and hunted treasure upstairs. The sun came out, and at three o'clock the children went outside, and the boys chased the girls through the woods. I took Edward's "Devil Stick" away and so there were no tears or cuts. At half past three parents arrived to retrieve their children, and after packing Edward's friends off with candy, balloons, and prizes—model cars for the boys and little ponies for the girls—Vicki and I collapsed in the living room. "We need another car," Vicki said, "because next year I am going to take the kids bowling." "Another car would cost twelve thousand dollars," I said, "and I'm not about to pay that for a birthday party." "You better," she began, "or else this wife . . ." She didn't finish the sentence because Edward came into the room crying. He had lost the snow plough off the front of a toy truck. Half an hour later I found the plough in the trash in the kitchen. Later that afternoon I mended the box which contained the marbles and board for his new set of Chinese checkers. Before dinner I spent twenty minutes searching for a diminutive man in a red helmet, the driver of "Mega Star," an amphibious vehicle armed with a "4X1G" rocket and decorated with a yellow hawk's head and jagged silver triangles resembling sharks' teeth. By evening Vicki was too tired to think about another car, much less dinner, so I got a pizza at Paul's, and, splitting a bottle of Miller "Genuine Draft" beer, we ate pizza and munched cake. Two days later I put the remnants of the cakes outside on the woodpile for the crows.

In March school activities resumed. The parents' club stretched after its winter nap and scheduled a night of bingo. I donated books as prizes and spent the evening eating fudge cake and drinking decaffeinated coffee. In order to pass the budget the school board began meeting every week. When the vote finally came, I was lying flat on the floor, the muscles of my back balled like pearls on a string. "And then," my friend Neil said, "you got up only to abstain. You should have stayed on the floor; that would have been more appropriate." Money like spring was on the wing, though, and the school budget was the only expense from which I abstained. One afternoon I drove to Munson's candy factory in Bolton and sent Father six pounds of dark chocolate creams. Bulb catalogues arrived, and I ordered two hundred and eighty-four dollars worth of daffodils. Then I bought a piano for Francis, the purchase accomplished with my usual financial wizardry. Last fall Francis began piano lessons. Because he liked them and showed some skill and because I am musically illiterate and, like most fathers, want my children to rise above me, I suggested to Vicki that we buy a piano. In February we drove to the Piano Warehouse in Bloomfield. Before going I decided to buy a used piano and limit my spending to a thousand dollars. Like buds on a Japanese magnolia in the warm sunlight, my determination soon expanded, blooming in fact into a new Walter piano and three thousand dollars. Despite the sudden expansiveness, however, I remained crafty and tight. "Vicki," I whispered, "don't buy now. Let's go home. In six weeks the price will drop, probably by about five hundred dollars." Six weeks later the owner of the Warehouse telephoned. A sale, he told us, was about to begin, and we could buy the oak upright which we had looked at for twenty-five hundred dollars. "That's splendid," I said, winking at Vicki. Right there is where I should have stopped. Oak in a piano or any kind of furniture does not appeal to me, however, making me imagine the back rooms of hardware stores and roll-top desks stained by soda bottles and cluttered with nails, crumbs from cheese crackers, pencil nubs, and a silver sardine can, the top peeled back and the inside stuffed with cigarette butts. "And the other pianos," I continued, "have they come down too? I am especially interested in that dark cherry model." "Oh, yes," the owner answered; "they are also on sale, and you can get the cherry Walter for thirty-two hundred." "Terrific," I said; "that's what I want. Bring it out here and I'll have the check waiting." "Well," Vicki said later; "you're a shrewdy. By waiting six weeks for the price to drop five hundred dollars, you spent two hundred more. Thank goodness you kept your mouth shut at the school board. If you had started talking, there's no telling what you would have cost this town."

"Horseshit," I said and left the house. My response, I am afraid, was a little bold, but in March about the time the robins reappear and mockingbirds begin to sing, I become assertive. When I read about the spraying of pesticides on apples, I dumped all our apple juice down the drain, without Vicki's permission. The next day in the shower at the gymnasium, I said, "I poured the apple juice out last night. I hope all you fellows did the same." Basketball is the subject of most shower room conversations. In general basketball fans are not enthusiastic environmentalists, and when I stopped speaking, a man turned to me and exclaimed, "Poured the apple juice out! Don't be ridiculous. To get cancer you would have to eat twenty-four thousand apples a year for seventy years." "Oh," I said; "that's fascinating, but could you tell me more? What difference would it make in the numbers if a person ate only winesap or delicious apples? This is important," I continued, seeing the man look at me in an odd way. "I eat lots of apples to facilitate the easy movement of my bowels—mostly baldwins and cortlands, in the mornings and evenings you understand, and I wonder." I got no further; the man cursed, in the process breaking one of the Ten Commandments, and closing up his soap dish and grabbing his towel left the room. *Assertive* may be the wrong word. Last week I talked to my great-aunt Lucille; she is ninety years old and in poor health. "I asked that damn doctor yesterday," she said, "if I've got all these ailments, why I am alive. He said I was stubborn, but that's wrong. I'm contentious." Aunt Lucille is right. In March members of my family grow contentious, rather than assertive or stubborn, and contentious not simply with death but about apples.

In March I began to range out, pontificating on things about which I knew little and then roaming across the landscape. Two weeks after the children and I found the skunk cabbage, I telephoned Neil. Like groundhogs we spent the winter isolated and in hibernation, and it was time, I told him, that we dug out of domesticity. The next morning we scurried afield, walking in the woods behind the university farm for three hours. Ours was the walk of good friends. We discussed our children and wives, and the misbehavior of acquaintances. We wondered about the changes middle-age brought to marriage and speculated about the future. Comfortable and relaxed, and conventional, we were men with no secrets—well, perhaps one, a secret kept not from each other but from our wives. Before starting the walk we bought big ice cream cones at the university Dairy Bar. The bar had run out of chocolate, and Neil got almond joy and I got mocha chip. We followed the route the children and I took earlier except we crossed the bottomland and getting onto the Nipmuck Trail walked alongside the Fenton River. The ice had pulled back from the middle of the river, retreating to shelters under hemlocks and becoming loose and grainy like shavings dropped from a snowcone at a baseball game. After a while we left the trail and pushed back up into the hills through the woods toward the old turnpike. Stone walls curved cold across the hills, from a distance gray and resembling lines of pebbles tossed high on a beach by a big tide. The trees were bare, and instead of new growth I noticed decay, black knot canker on shrubs and stumps pocked by woodpeckers.

Not seeing signs of spring disappointed me. That night, though, almost as if she were trying to make me forget my disappointment, Eliza turned into a hothouse garden, washing herself with Vicki's cologne and then climbing into our bed and falling asleep. The fragrance must have affected us, for the next morning Vicki bought five pots of plants at Shop Rite, three of hyacinths, purple, white and pink, and two of daffodils, small orange and yellow tête-à-têtes.

For my part I visited the greenhouse behind the Torrey Life Sciences Building. The greenhouses were divided into rooms, some large, others small, some damp and hot, others dry and cold. Twisted over the door outside the orchid room was bougainvillea, its blossoms pink and papery. Inside the room orchids were planted in clay pots or grew in hunks of bark suspended on screens. Despite the heat the room smelled like teaberry, and colors floated like rainbows in the air. A purple flower reminded me of high school dances and girls in stiff white dresses. I shut my eyes when I smelled it, and for a moment Randle and I swayed together again, youthful and cheek to cheek as the band played "Good Night Sweetheart."

Beyond the orchids were tables of mints: rosemary, thyme, savory, sweet woodruff, chamomile, lamb's tongue, southernwood, Jerusalem sage, hoarhound, and English lavender. Along a wall were tanks thick with carnivorous plants: Venus fly traps, bladder worts, pitcher plants, and then sundews, some resembling frying pans and others brooms. Beside a stream above a pool grew a fern garden, lacy and green; next to it was a mangrove swamp. Hanging from rafters were blossoms of angel's trumpet, long and thin like delicate orange post horns. Brunfelsia bloomed nearby, resembling a gay checkered harlequin, some of its blossoms blue and others white. Just beyond, the rich vanilla freshness of gardenia sweetened the air while the blooms of cassia glowed in the sun like scarlet powder puffs. Accustomed to woods as bare as the white aisles of a Congregational church, I was ready for signs of spring, not a lush equatorial summer. Soon I observed little, and colors and fragrances folded into each other, losing their individuality and appeal. I did not want to leave the greenhouses, so I shut my eyes and ran my hands over plants. For a while the leaves tickled my senses, but then I groped about mechanically, sensing only the familiar: saws, needles, hooks, paddles, brushes, and fans.

After leaving the greenhouses I paused to get my seasonal bearings. Not only did the cool March wind feel good on my face, but it awakened me, and looking up, I suddenly saw three small houses on top of the Life Sciences Building. In a dozen years at the university, I hadn't noticed them. Feeling curious and a little assertive, I decided to investigate. After riding an elevator to the sixth floor of the building, I opened a door with "Insectary" written on it and discovered some five hundred aquariums, all afloat with algae and small fish from Mexico. Relatives of the guppy, the fish were not so interesting as the people studying them. One woman, I learned, was an expert on animal droppings as well as fish entrails. She could identify all the animals in New England by their scats. Just recently, she said, a local police department called her into a case as a forensics expert. An intruder, it seemed, broke into a house in the middle of the night. The intruder made so much noise that he woke the owner who screamed then telephoned the police. The scream so frightened the intruder that he suffered an "accident," shortly after which he disappeared. On arriving at the house the police found no sign of forced entry, only the accident, and not sure of what they had on their hands and the owner had on the floor, they called in the fish expert. "I picked up a piece," she told me, "and passing it under my nose took a whiff and then said 'possum not person.' "

As the white-throated sparrows appeared in the yard, so I began to chirp. Winter is too cold and summer too hot for waggery, but March is just right. The account of the opossum amused me, and when I got home, I telephoned the English department. Recently the university received some bad publicity. In going over the university's accounts, state auditors found that some moneys which should have been deposited in the state-controlled Research Foundation had instead been placed in the Connecticut Foundation, a private organization run for and by the university to get around the cumbersome state bureaucracy. Although there was no real wrong-doing, for a few days the air was rank with rumor. The English department itself kept an account in the Connecticut Foundation. In the fall the department collected twenty-five dollars from each member. Deposited in the foundation, the money bought gifts for secretaries, paid for the Christmas party, and sent flowers to funerals. When I called the department, I lowered my voice, stuttered slightly, dropped the *s*'s off my words, turned all *th*'s into *d*'s, and like a child scattering grain in a chicken yard cast agreement between subject and verb to the wind. Understanding what I said was difficult, and struggling to get at the words behind my pronunciation, people paid little critical attention to my sanity. "This is Mr. Mahmoud Burruti of the state auditor's office," I said coughing into the phone when the secretary answered; "let me speak to Mr.-Mr.-Mr.-Mr. Hankin." There was a pause then a voice said tentatively, "What did you say your name was?" "Mah-Mah-Mahmoud Burruti of the state auditor's office. What's the matter with you people," I yelled, then breaking into a bullfrog-like boom, belched an answer, "The earwax?" After a pause and some hurried footsteps and whispering, the head of the department came on the line and said, "This is David Hankins, Mr. Burrunder, what can I do for you?" "The first thing is to irrigate the ears. The name is B-B- Burruti-Burruti of the State Auditor's Office," I said. Before he answered, I then asked if it were true that the English department had an account in the Connecticut Foundation, adding that from the state's perspective the account looked like a party fund for "whiskey, Doritos, the onion dip, and that stuff, the boys and the girls." For a second the phone was quiet, then David said, "Mr. Burruti- Burruti, we do have an account but you must understand." "Understand!" I interrupted, "oh, yes, I understand. I'll understand you right now. There is enough corruption in that foundation to fry your ass, and that of your wife, and fry them, not in the nice Crisco but the goose grease." And here the audit ended as Mr. Burruti experienced a cardio-vascular guffaw and dropped the phone on the floor.

In the middle of March I received a letter from the "National Council on US-Arab Relations," asking if I would be interested in spending July in Tunisia. I was a lover of things Arab and little would give me more pleasure than visiting Tunisia, I said when I telephoned the council. But, I explained, I was a son, a father, and a husband, and my pleasure fell at the end of a long list, behind those of family—wife, children, and parents. Instead of Tunisia, I would spend my July on our farm in Nova Scotia. In fact I had already booked passage on the ferry from Portland. Not only that but I had begun thinking about Nova Scotia stories and the inhabitants of our little area along the Gulf of Maine, from Port Maitland to Beaver River. This past summer, an old man told me why there were no poisonous snakes in Nova Scotia. Once, it seemed, poisonous snakes were widespread. They disappeared only after deer began eating them as worm medicine.

In the past parasitical worms were epidemic in Nova Scotia. One yellow, spotted variety plagued deer in particular, first breeding in the animals' intestines and then after maturing crawling up to the animals' mouths where they attached themselves to the roof. Hanging down like curtains in front of the throat, they seized food before it could be swallowed, causing whole herds of deer to starve. Because snake venom was an effective antidote, killing the worms if it were sloshed through the mouth, deer began hunting snakes, thrusting their muzzles into the ground and blowing hot air down into dens.

Attracted by the heat the serpents crawled toward the entrances of their dens; as soon as they reached the surface, the deer seized them, crushing them between their teeth. The snakes tried to strike back, swarms of them attacking sleeping deer. Unfortunately for the snakes, the deer were immune to their venom, and rolling over and thrashing about killed scores of snakes, after which they ate them. Following such a struggle the heads of a few snakes remained pinned to the deer. To rid themselves of them the deer went into the ocean and, standing still, let crabs clamber over them and pluck out the heads for food. I repeated this story to a neighbor. "So far as it goes," he said, "the account is accurate." However poisonous snakes still lived in Nova Scotia, he said, explaining that they were never seen because they spent their lives underground. After the deer killed vast numbers of them, the remaining snakes grew wise and refused to leave their dens. Instead of coming up and out of hibernation in the spring, they dug deeper and making long tunnels began feeding on mice, moles, and shrews, even blind cave fish. The spruce didn't lose leaves during winter, he cited as proof, because the breath from the numbers of serpents underground warmed the trees' roots, turning them into evergreens.

In thinking about the story of the opossum and the intruder, I wondered how the fish expert came by her knowledge. Curiosity, I decided, a good, hearty curiosity, must have started her sniffing. Long gone were the days when one could get occupational experience as a gold-finder or honey dipper. Of course being a plumber back before the time of the indoor necessary house could distort as well as educate the sense of smell. Certainly it did peculiar things to the nose of Bankes Mowll who years ago took plumbing jobs in Port Maitland when fishing was poor. One afternoon after a hard day's work behind the school, Bankes ambled into Gawdry's Store just as a drummer was trying to sell Gawdry a line of perfume and bath powders. Bankes approached the counter and started to ask for something but then before saying what he wanted, Otis Blankinchip recounted, he turned a complete circle and fell out on the floor, his head just missing a keg of pickled fish. "The saints preserve us," Bertha Shifney said, "what was wrong?" "Oh, it won't serious. Bankes was just overcome with the fumes," Otis explained. "I went outside and picked up a handful of horse manure and held it under his nose and he come round right away."

As spring drew near, Nova Scotia sprouted in my mind, characters budding and blooming, a few of the earliest bright as marsh marigold but most as strong and as rudely horned and red as skunk cabbage. One day a wagon suddenly appeared outside the old, abandoned, one-room store on Straddle Street in Beaver River. Driving it was a large woman with one leg, Mother Noon as she introduced herself. In the back of the wagon were a bed, two tables, four chairs, some decorations, and stock for her store, Noonday as it was called by local people. No one knew Mother Noon's real name or where she came from. She was dark, and some people thought her a gypsy, others a Spaniard. A couple of folks claimed they knew her family. Gracious Chenoweth told Bertha Shifney she was a Watrous from Tupperville while Idella Shoup declared her to be a Purshull from Bridgewater, saying she had lost her leg in the great train wreck at New Minas. These last two claims obtained a little credence because Mother Noon was well spoken and appeared to have been a person of substance at some time in her life. Above the counter of the store she hung an old fireboard, three feet high and five feet long. On it was painted a gold grasshopper, a halo over its head and a blue ribbon around its neck. Written on the ribbon in black letters was "God's Harp." Over a shelf on one of the side walls she hung a small painting, one that provoked more controversy and mystification than the grasshopper. In the painting a naked woman sat on the back of a toad. The toad was shiny and green and had an orange eye as big as a teacup while the woman was small and so hunched over she looked like a pink nut.

Mother Noon sold herbs and dispensed folk wisdom and remedy, and Noonday was a jumble of pots, boxes, baskets, and jars. By the door were two baskets filled with dried mice and the bills of woodpeckers. To prevent toothache she recommended eating two mice a month while bees, she said, never stung anyone who approached them with a woodpecker's bill in his hand. She sold honey, only late fall, or ivy honey, however, because it was grainy and woody and supposedly good for digestion. Behind the counter she kept earthworms in a box stuffed with damp moss. She treated burns with a salve of oil and ground up worms, and every week changed the moss to keep the worms clean and healthy. At the other end of the counter was a jar of leeches, great horse leeches for piles and blood blisters. In two other jars were spider webs sold for warts and weddings. If a web were rolled into a ball and then put on top of a wart and set afire, the roots of the wart would be killed and the wart would wither away. For warts any web would do. For weddings only webs of the house spider sufficed. If a bride drank a glass of wine containing the web of a house spider on her wedding night, she would, Mother Noon assured prospective suitors, become a frugal, patient, hard-working wife. In a woodbox on the porch were the bleached skulls of mares who had foaled. In spring farmers bought them and buried them in the fields to insure good crops. Despite the oddities Mother Noon made most of her nostrums from the ordinary plants of field and woodland: sorrel, hawkweed, tansy, canary grass, rhubarb, lupine, yarrow, thistle. Of course like all good merchants she responded to the community and for a price accommodated her lore to individual needs.

When Jeremiah Gest suspected his wife Honoria of forgetting herself with Gideon Tannehill, he consulted Mother Noon. She suggested two remedies, Bankes Mowll later told Otis Blankinchip. If Jeremiah dried the pizzle of a red bull and then dissolved it in wine and got Gideon to drink the mixture, then, she advised, Gideon's "obscene part would lose all vigour." If, however, Gideon couldn't be persuaded to drink or Jeremiah had difficulty finding a red bull, Mother Noon said Honoria "would come to abhor venery" if her loins were rubbed with the blood of ticks, removed from the right ear of a spotted dog. Experience shapes the individual, and what impressed Bankes most about Mother Noon was not her solutions for matrimonial problems but her skill in purging and plugging— in short her ability as a plumber. In his professional life Bankes had observed many unique specimens of the crawling creation, but they were nothing, he told Otis, compared to the worms Mother Noon flushed out of the inhabitants of Beaver River. She kept the best of them in jars on the shelf beneath the painting of the woman on the toad. In one jar was, Bankes described, "a great black worm with black hair, five feet long, and big as a crane." In another was "a worm with red hair, standing straight up and long as a hand, both ends pointed like a nib." Next to it "wrapped about a ball of phlegm" was Bankes's favorite, "a very plain worm with a green head that was smooth and about the bigness of pen with a body that was downy and a tail that was crooked like the half moon."

I'm a poor plumber and a worse fisherman, and I don't have Bankes's interest in worms. Still, March has been hard on me. I'm not in good shape and all this roaming over the university farm and talking on the telephone has worn me down. Since Valentine's Day,

I have suffered through two colds, a sinus infection, and the hives. I wouldn't mind Mother Noon's prescribing a potion to buck me up, not though, I hurry to assert, one of her love potions made out of the gall of a cat and the seeds of wild cucumber washed in vinegar. After three children and a pleasant decade of comfortable domesticity, neither Vicki nor I could endure a hard-core marriage. Daffodils, though, are pushing up in the dell; woodpeckers are knocking in the back woods; spring is almost here, and I would like some of the winter to melt off my head. According to Mother Noon if I boiled the ashes of "tender earthworms" in oil and then rubbed the mixture into my scalp, all these "hoary hairs" would disappear and then folks passing by on the road might think there was a drop or two of life in the old boy yet.

Celebrity

Twenty years ago my father attended the Swan Ball, a dance held to benefit Cheekwood, a center for the arts in Nashville, Tennessee. Arriving shortly before Father a newspaper reporter and an accompanying photographer settled into place at the foot of the long spiral staircase near the entrance to Cheekwood. "When anyone important appears I'll tell you," the reporter told the photographer just as Father started down the stairs. "I took my time on the steps, and the girl looked at me," Father said later, "but the camera didn't click." Rarely has a Pickering been thought newsworthy, and although I have written hard for fifteen years, few cameras have pointed my way. What attention I have received has usually been inaccurate or embarrassing, lending itself more toward notoriety than importance. Last fall I spoke at a potluck supper sponsored by the Friends of the Mansfield Library. The crowd was large, well over a hundred people, brought out in part, I am afraid, by a flyer announcing that the speaker was the author of children's books and a religious novel. When my mother died two years ago, her obituary stated that she was a native of Hanover Courthouse, Virginia, the daughter of the late Mr. and Mrs. John L. Ratcliffe, the wife of Samuel F. Pickering, and then, horror of horrors, "the mother of the noted essayist Samuel F. Pickering, Jr. of Storrs, Connecticut." My God, I thought, what will people think? I imagined old friends at breakfast tables flipping through their papers and stopping to read Mother's obituary. "Jesus, Varina, look at this," I could hear Jeffrey saying; "Sam's trying to sell books on his mother's grave." "Huh, that doesn't surprise me," Varina would answer, taking the paper away to read it; "he always was an SOB. He may have fooled you and those friends of yours for a long time, but he never fooled me."

In February I received a letter addressed to "Samuel Pickering, Jr. WRITER," *writer* being printed in red and circled by two black lines as thick and gloomy as mourning bands. Inside the letter was a note reading "God loves you very much. You are precious to Him" and then a tract entitled "A Rock Through The Window." "Your heavenly Father," the tract stated, "wants to deal with you as His beloved child, not as a guilty delinquent." I had spent a quiet, and in this world what passes for the same thing, a moral winter, indeed a quiet last decade and so I paid little attention to the tract. Still, the sender might have known me better than I knew myself. In April I traveled to a conference in Arkansas to discuss "Parents and Children in Southern Autobiography." The conference was solemn, and the talks and audience thoughtful, at least they were until I spoke. As I climbed the stairs toward the stage, a noisemaker began wailing, the sound rising shrill then snapping off in a cackle of laughter. For late morning the audience seemed oddly alert, and I wondered why until I reached the lectern. Spread open there was a *Playboy* magazine, the centerfold pink and creamy and looking like a mound of overly ripe cantaloupes. For a moment I paused, taste buds pricking delinquently; but then buckling appetite about with thought, I closed the magazine and began lecturing. In truth I did not pause long, for at forty-seven I was not the trencherman I once was, the boy who long years ago ate seventeen ears of corn at one sitting. Indeed since marrying Vicki I have bought groceries at Shop Rite, avoiding natural food stores and in matters personal preferring the institutional and the packaged to the organically grown.

Recently attention paid to my writing has changed slightly, becoming at times almost serious. In an article a writer mentioned my "aristocratic impulse." "Too bad," Vicki said when I read her the phrase, "too bad it's only an impulse." In March the wife of the president of the University of Connecticut interviewed me for a newsletter published by the regional arts council. At the Middle School one Saturday morning we met in her new silver Subaru station wagon, and she taped our conversation while our children practiced soccer on a nearby field. Last winter Bill Berry, an old friend, wrote an essay recalling his days in the graduate college at Princeton. He sent me an early draft in which I often appeared as aggressive and frivolous, once eating a lunch of flowers in order to startle the stuffy and the boring. Still, Bill also recalled that I often ate with "a severely afflicted friend who had great difficulty eating and speaking." He said I befriended those less fortunate than myself and while my friend struggled to speak I "focused on his face and understood the words that most did not watch form." Until I read Bill's draft I had forgotten those meals but I was glad he brought them back, for what seemed insignificant twenty years ago now struck me as important. At eight, Francis my older boy is ashamed of me. Indeed I sometimes think he despises me. Perhaps someday, I thought, he will read Bill's article and decide that maybe, just maybe, his father wasn't so bad. Alas, Bill's editor made him cut the article, and when the essay appeared, the lunch of flowers remained, its stems coarse and silly while the meals with my friend had been mowed and had fallen away to be lost in the mulch of time.

Family stories matter to me. I want my children to have a sense of their history. I hope they will be able to think beyond self and see themselves as part of a community, not simply of a present but of the past and of a future. If they recognize the influences of the past, perhaps they will see ties in the present and realize that they have responsibilities for the future. And so for me, the most important attention my writing has evoked has been private, not public, appearing in letters, not magazines. On the jacket of my second collection of essays was a sketch of my father's home in Carthage, Tennessee. While browsing through a bookstore in Nashville, a woman from Carthage saw the jacket and recognized the house. She bought the book and later wrote me about my grandmother "Miss Frances" and recounted the history of the house: that Miss Frances sold it to the McDuffees in 1950 and that in 1976 they sold it to the Gammons who moved it off Main Street down the hill toward the river, after which they built a grocery store on the site. In that second collection of essays I mentioned attending Ransom School in Nashville. When a neighbor on Eastwood read that, she sent me a copy of the Ransom School Song, noting that we were fellow alumni. The song is innocent and optimistic. "There is no school like John B. Ransom School," the song bounced along to the tune of the "Washington and Lee Swing."

> We do our lessons 'cording to the rules.
> We can read and write and cipher, too.
> And we do just what our teachers tell us to.
> We have a Mothers' Club that's hard to beat.
> They gave us sidewalks so we keep dry feet.
> They gave us flower beds and shade trees, too.
> Shade trees, too—Ransom sch—ool.

Among the essays in the book was a sketch of Father, and after reading it a woman who worked for the Travelers Insurance Company in Nashville wrote me. She wanted, she explained, to tell me "how he appeared to the clerical workers." She never met him outdoors, she recounted, when "he didn't remove his hat." The staff benefited from his "gentlemanly instincts," she recalled, saying, "One of the first things I ever heard about him was that he would never say anything improper to a lady or allow anyone else to," noting that "this was mighty valuable protection in the days before corporations had sexual harassment policies. He was all the protection we needed, and if you had a problem, you went to him. Some of the managers were afraid to make waves, but he wasn't."

This past June I received a letter from the press which was publishing my next book. "Here," it read, "is another marketing questionnaire that we'd like to have you fill out for *Stiff Life*." Unfortunately Father's gentlemanly instincts have run shallow in me, becoming at best only impulses, and I wrote back that although I was flattered I had not lost the reputation of my vigorous younger days, the title of my book was more detumescent, *Still,* not *Stiff Life*. Although I did not recognize it at the time, the letter was a harbinger of raucous days of attention and celebrity. In April I received a letter from Tom Schulman, a former student of mine at Montgomery Bell Academy in Nashville. I myself attended MBA, and before going to graduate school and just after leaving Cambridge, I returned and taught English there for a year. I was twenty-four and Tommy was fifteen, a sophomore. The students were bright and generous, and I had a marvelous time, but the year like the meals with my friend at Princeton had dropped out of thought until Tommy's letter reminded me of it. He had written, he said, a screenplay "inspired in part by your teaching" and he urged me to go to the film, saying I would enjoy seeing "how what you taught affected at least one of your students." The name of the movie was *Dead Poets Society*, probably a zombie film I guessed at the time, appropriate enough, I thought, for the teaching profession in which being one of the walking dead was often more an asset than handicap. Still, I was proud of Tommy. I liked him enormously at MBA, and happy that he was doing well, I wrote and told him so. When he replied that being my student "had a profound effect" on his life and that I "reached out with an approving smile and an unconcealed joy that inspired self-confidence and happiness," I was touched, so much so

I kept the letters, not for myself but for Francis in hopes, of course, that someday he would see them and think better of me.

The end of the semester rush of papers and examinations began, and I soon forgot about the movie. The second week in June, however, Bill Weaver, my closest boyhood friend, telephoned from Nashville, saying there was a rumor going around that I was the model for John Keating, a character, he explained, in a movie about a prep school and played by a comic actor named Robin Williams. Years ago, I told Bill, I taught Tommy Schulman the screenwriter at MBA, but, I stressed, the film could not contain much of me. "Well," Bill answered, "I'm going to the movie tonight, and I'll let you know." Late that night Bill telephoned. "It's you," he said, "all your mannerisms, and I have called the paper." The next day a reporter from the *Nashville Tennessean* telephoned and interviewed me. I repeated to him what I told Bill: that whatever there was of me in the Keating character had to be small, and he assured me he would dig about thoroughly before writing a story. Several days passed, and then on June 22, a half page article appeared in the *Tennessean*. Headlined "Robin Williams, meet Dr. Sam Pickering, Jr.," the article had pictures of Tommy and me in the upper right corner, and then down in the lower left, taken from the MBA yearbook for 1966, a picture of me sitting cross-legged on my desk, reading and declaiming. That morning the telephone began ringing, mostly friends from Nashville wanting to discuss the movie. Because my children all had chicken pox when the movie showed in Willimantic, I hadn't seen it, so I took the occasion to renew acquaintances and ask about family doings. One man said he was soon leaving with his children for a vacation on the dude ranch where Hemingway wrote *A Farewell to Arms*; another's older daughter was working on Cape Cod while the younger went to sailing camp in North Carolina and his son studied language in France. That night a cousin called, and when she said, "I can't tell you how proud I am," I suddenly realized that matters were out of my control. This past spring three literary agents wrote, asking to represent me. Knowing that I often described my children, one sent a picture of his daughter, a smiling brown-eyed little girl wearing a blue dress and eating a chocolate bar, actually a Hershey bar with almonds or so it appeared when I examined the picture under a hand lens. Although I am sweet on Hersheys and children, I declined the agents' offers to represent me, explaining that I valued controlling my affairs more than I did money.

Now caught up in the popularity of *Dead Poets Society*, I was losing control. Moreover I started doubting my teaching. Tommy was not the only student to write last year. On my desk was a postcard from Portugal. "Played a little in Metro Station in Lisbon with a couple of Rastafarians," George wrote, explaining that he planned to work his way across Europe as a street musician. "Now," he continued, "I'm sharing a room in the home of a sweet old Portuguese couple with an insane German girl. The day we got here after renting the room she says that maybe it's not good that we sleep in the same bed and the next day on the beach she is lying there next to me, completely naked!" What sort of effect, I asked myself, had I had upon George. Whatever it was, it smacked more of lecterns in Arkansas that it did of profundity.

The following day I received only one call from Nashville, an invitation to attend the MBA spaghetti supper. Both the Willimantic and Hartford papers, however, obtained copies of the article in the *Tennessean* and interviewed me over the telephone. I wasn't home when the reporter from the Hartford paper first called, so she talked to Vicki. Whom had we told about the movie, she asked. On Vicki's saying "No one. Sam had nothing to do with the movie," she paused then asked, "What is it like being married to an eccentric?" "Eccentric," Vicki responded; "Sam's not eccentric. He's normal, very normal, so normal in fact that he's abnormally normal." That, I am afraid, ended the conversation. The following day, though, articles about the movie and me appeared in both the *Willimantic Chronicle* and the *Hartford Courant*. In the English department late that afternoon a colleague greeted me, saying "you are certainly becoming notorious. I went to the podiatrist today to have my ingrowing toenails chopped out, and when I told the receptionist I taught at the University of Connecticut, she asked 'Do you know Sam Pickering.' " I smiled; no longer did I have the leisure to think my way into doubt or embarrassment. On the twenty-eighth Vicki and I and the children were leaving Storrs for our farm in Nova Scotia. Little chores clogged my hours, and I didn't have time for celebrity. The chimney on the house was collapsing inward, and that morning Mr. Brown examined it and estimated the cost of repairs. Mr. Brown was a fine mason, but he wasn't young, and when he talked to me, his false teeth slipped. Pushing them back up into the roof of his mouth, he explained, "I forgot to put the cement in this morning." "Oh, Lord," I thought, "suppose he forgets to put the mortar between the bricks when he rebuilds the chimney." At lunch Vicki informed me that only one key to the house was left. For most people getting keys is easy. Our house, though, was once owned by the university and the locks on the doors take keys, the blanks of which are sold only to the state. To obtain new keys necessitates obtaining a work order, and work orders are issued only for state buildings, not private houses. "I'm sorry. I don't know how you can get new keys without replacing all the locks on your doors," a sympathetic woman told me. "I leave for Nova Scotia the day after tomorrow," I said; "I can't replace the locks." Four hours and six telephone calls later, I had nine keys, too many for Vicki's liking but just the right number I think.

That night while I was gathering things to be packed, a reporter from the Associated Press called. Saying he had read the piece in the *Courant,* he asked to interview me. I explained I was leaving for Nova Scotia in two days but said that if he could be at my house at two the next afternoon, I would fit him in between getting a haircut and mowing the grass. He arrived on time, and we spent a genial hour and a half talking first about teaching, then about writing, and finally our children. Just after he left, his photographer appeared, and for thirty minutes I posed around the yard: on the front stoop, leaning against a hickory tree, and finally on a rock near the children's swing set where mosquitos dropped on me like leaves in the fall, big mosquitos with black and white, candy-cane, striped legs.

The next morning we left for Portland and the ferry to Yarmouth. Although the drive was only two hundred miles, the trip took six hours. We stopped to let the children run about, and I drove slowly, never faster than fifty miles an hour. Last summer I did not pass a single vehicle, and this year I passed only two: a rusty Pontiac creeping along the shoulder of the road, its exhaust system dragging on the ground and then near South Portland a pickup truck towing a wagon carrying a yellow race car with the number forty-seven painted on it in blue. Because I drive in an eddy, letting traffic sweep around me, the trip was almost easy, and I spent time thinking over the interviews which I gave and the articles which discussed the *Dead Poets Society* and me. I felt ashamed. The film was Tommy's, not mine, and a stronger person would not have given the impression of wanting something for nothing by allowing himself to be interviewed. Even worse the life I had shaped and the little things I achieved seemed lost. Instead of being the books I wrote or the family I cherished, I was a creature of publicity, a nice person because the articles were generous, but a creature, nevertheless, fathered by a newspaper and nurtured by an ego. On the positive side I said nothing harsh and actually corrected a misrepresentation. People had not stopped at identifying John Keating as me but had rushed on into error by assuming the head of Welton to be Francis Carter, headmaster of MBA in the 1960s. As the head of Welton was a fiction so was his conflict with Keating. Mr. Carter was a close friend, a man whom I admired and whose family I have loved for years. Rick his son took my little boys to see their first movie, a story about a mouse named Fievel, and since Mother's death, Rick and his mother have hovered over Father, bringing him presents and inviting him to their house for meals.

Once or twice the articles made me smile. In the *Tennessean* a former student said that when my class studied Poe's poem "The Raven" I stood a boy on a chair and told him to flap his arms every time we came to the word *nevermore*. I did not remember that class, but I was lively and young when I taught at MBA and giving students the bird sounds like something I might have done. I remembered standing on desks and in waste cans. One day I went outside and taught through the window. I did such things not so much to awaken students as entertain myself. If I had fun, I suppose I thought, the boys would have fun, too, and maybe even enjoy reading and writing. In the *Tennessean* Gus Kuhn a member of Tommy's class attributed high purpose to my antics. "He really wanted us to think, to find our own voice," Gus said. "It's interesting that I never knew his political orientation—he just wanted us to find our own ways." Although I did want the boys to think a little for themselves, it is no wonder Gus did not know my political leanings. Even today I am not sure what they are. Some mornings I think myself more liberal than anyone I know; by afternoon I often think myself more conservative than anyone. At a school board meeting in May another member called me a Communist. When the chairman of the board said that name-calling, even in jest, was out of order, I interrupted. "Oh, no," I said, "that's the nicest compliment I've received in months. Of course," I added, "if he had called me an Episcopalian, there would be gore on the floor." Although the newspapers rarely quoted me exactly, they got down the sense of what I said correctly. Actually their changes often brushed and smoothed me over. When I said that I no longer climbed through windows to teach outside because my present classroom was on the second floor and I might fall down and "bust my ass," the reporter wrote, "His classroom is on the second floor now, making leaps through windows unwise." Only the Willimantic paper left me linty and rough of tongue, and I was chagrined to read that Keating's being a sympathetic character pleased me because "I'd rather be known as a nice guy than as a son of a bitch."

Once we reached Nova Scotia, the movie almost slipped out of mind. Our farm in Beaver River seemed beyond celebrity's schedule, the ring of the telephone, and events hurrying over each other into meaninglessness. The landscape was mild: blue and green and yellow. Near the front fence the golden chaintree bloomed. Cedar waxwings searched for bugs in the spruce windbreak while warblers hunted through the alders. Wildflowers glowed like small suns; in the side meadow: buttercups, cinquefoil, hawkweed, moneywort, and daisies, white and yellow and looking like morning. In the hedge of roses behind the well cover hung bittersweet nightshade, petals curled up and back into purple turbans and their centers arrowheads dripping yellow. In the damp by the stone wall stood swamp candles, budded and blooming in the imagination. Along the lane toward the bluff were two-flowered Cynthia and in low spots blue flag, brightness streaming back through the petals into the stem. Along the bluff grew yellow rattle and great stalks of evening primrose while lower down in the rocks at Beaver River sow thistle was beginning to open. The calm, of course, was deceptive for beneath and behind the yellows lay purple; in the meadows vetch and clover, its heads as big as biscuits. In the stony foundation hole of the old house on Ma's Property were clumps of knapweed while behind the outlet at Beaver River beach pea sprawled garish and luxuriant. Around the pond rose shafts of pickerel weed, still narrow and green but certain to swell into bloom.

For two weeks time slowed and I busied myself with important things: at dusk and dawn studying shrews, during the day teaching the children to shoot bows and arrows and throw boomerangs, at night reading to them, first *Caddie Woodlawn* and then *The Twenty-one Balloons*. One morning, though, as I cleared Japanese knotweed from around the barn, levering up masses of damp, orange root, thick as hams, the calm burst into celebrity, purple and spiny as bull thistle. The first batch of mail had arrived from Storrs. "I've only carried that *Hartford Courant* article around for three weeks telling every one, 'I know this person,' " Alice began and I winced. Alice's letter was one of many from former students. Occasionally the letters were not addressed to me but to Sam Pickering "Media Sensation" or "Personality." One man assured me that he had not used an exclamation point since taking a course with me seventeen years ago. School superintendents and principals invited me to address faculties and "to share," as one administrator put it, "some of your ideas about motivating and challenging students." I replied that I was not an educational theorist but just somebody who happened to teach, "a guy with a nice wife, three small children, an aging father, and a six-year-old Plymouth station wagon." Two people wanted to know how to become an essayist. Lost friends surfaced and described former wives and new loves. Strangers told stories about their school days. Three people said that although I might be the model for the character in the movie for them the real John Keating was one of *their* former teachers. A goodly number of letters contained clippings from local papers. I was relieved to see the captions of the articles were not sensational. Typically they read: "Meet the Real John Keating," "Eccentric Instructor Inspires His Students," "Model for 'Dead Poets' Hero Sees Himself as Ordinary," and "Professor Shrugs Off Comparisons to Lead Character in 'Dead Poets.' "

Much as fireweed and purple orchis seem part of July's lavish train so telephone calls accompanied the mail. A man in Ohio asked me to become an honorary member of a Christian Dead Poets Society. I agreed although I didn't think the society would be popular. My children would prefer to join a Little Scorpions Club and would have more fun frolicking, I suspect, with Aunt Eppie Hogg and the Terrible Tempered Mr. Bang than with a schoolhouse of preachers. The director of a library where I read my essays last winter telephoned and asked to speak to "Professor Keating." From Oklahoma a woman volunteered that during the past four and a half years the right side of her brain, the creative side, had grown while the left, the mechanical side which controlled such things as mathematics and duties domestic, had shrunk. As a result, she said, "I'm a pisspoor wife." The telephone was in the kitchen, and all my conversations were public and thus open to interruption and editorial comment. During the discussion with the woman from Oklahoma, Edward, my six year old, tugged on my shirt and looking up asked, "Daddy, what is sex?" Covering up the receiver, I said,

"It's the way men and women make children." The answer satisfied Edward, if not perhaps his mother who dropped a beet on the floor, and I was quickly able to return to things brainy, if not intellectual. The moderator of "Straight Talk," a television program produced in Virginia Beach, Virginia, invited me to appear on the show. I declined but I did have several radio interviews. I was in our peat bog when a woman called from a station in New Haven, Connecticut. When Vicki said I could not come to the phone, explaining "He's in the bog," the line was silent. Finally the woman asked when I would be out, and Vicki said, "Probably in an hour. He never gets out of the bog any quicker." Vicki does not like to answer the telephone, especially when it is for me. This past spring I was at Northwest School talking to the principal when a bank officer called to discuss Mother's estate. "He's not here," Vicki said when the man asked for me; "he's in the principal's office." "Sam," the man said after reaching me the next day, "when I hung up I kept wondering what the hell you had done at your age to be sent to the principal's office."

The Associated Press article fathered several offspring. This second group of reporters were invariably curious about my philosophy of education. What they wanted was not real philosophy, problematic and deep, but aphorism. I tried to say what I believed, but everything sounded sappy. In one paper I declared that the end of education was to learn to learn, "to make decent men and women, to learn how to change your mind, to say 'I was wrong.' " "It's to be moral," I explained, adding, "I'm moral in my life, but not in my thoughts." For the interviews I changed my personality, becoming saccharine while actually I am often acerbic. At the end of this school year a student said to me, "No one can accuse you of prejudice. You've insulted every group in the country. You even insult yourself. It's a marvel you don't get in a fist fight with yourself." Eventually I reacted against the interviews and purged the sugar from my system by writing crude notes about academic matters. When a professor asked permission to quote a letter I had written about the environment, I made a single stipulation. "You can quote the letter," I wrote, so long as you don't begin, 'That turd Sam Pickering states.' "

Occasionally reporters contacted my friends. One old buddy supposedly said, "Pickering has single-handedly revived the familiar essay, a genre of the Romanticists of the first half of the 19th century." "Now," I told Vicki when I read the piece, "I have finally found an article that's right on the money." Of course I didn't agree with everything published. According to the *Richmond Times-Dispatch* my cousin Sherry said I met Vicki when I was a graduate student at Princeton and her father was head of the English department. Vicki was "thirteen when she first met Sam," the paper stated, "thirteen years later when she was twenty-six they married." Lest people fear to trust me with their small daughters, I must now say that I did not know Vicki until she was twenty-one. I am absolutely trustworthy around little children and everything sweet except chocolate cake. Because Mother was from Richmond, the *Times-Dispatch* wrote about her family, the Ratcliffes. Ratcliffes are often odd although I don't think they are quite so individualistic as the newspaper implied. Sherry, the paper said, remembered Mother "wrapped only in a sheet on hot nights in Hanover when the family ate on the screen porch. She would say, 'Pass the bosoms,' And Sam's father would answer, 'Say chicken breasts, Katharine.' "

As the telephone rang and letters poured in, the order of my days and thoughts unraveled. I watched for the mailman and waited for phone calls. I became crass and tried to figure out how I could use the movie to turn my books into best sellers. Not even reality stopped my scheming. I shrugged off the royalty statement for my second book of essays. In two years, the press wrote me, the book had sold eight hundred and fifty-five copies, and during the past year there were thirty-four more returns than sales. Sometimes I even convinced myself that Disney Studios, the makers of the movie, owed the family a trip to Disney World. When Father came to Nova Scotia in mid-July and I told him that I was fed up with being a celebrity, he laughed and said, "Don't take it seriously. Just have fun. I have." Great numbers of people spoke to him on the street, he recounted, and friends whom he had not heard from in years wrote letters. Last week on the elevator in his apartment he met, he said, an acquaintance and her eleven-year-old granddaughter. "Mayellen," the woman said, introducing the child to Father, "this is Mr. Sam Pickering." "What," the girl gasped; "Sam Pickering! Why you are famous." Indeed the nicest thing the movie did for me was to give Father pleasure. No only that but it made conversation between us easier, and soon after Father arrived in Nova Scotia, we left the movie behind and talked about family. I learned that when Father was a boy he had a horse named Donald. During his sixteenth summer, Father worked on the highway as a water boy. The spring, he said, was a mile from the construction and as soon as he brought water up to the road he had to turn around and fetch more. He carried two buckets, for white men one with a green stripe on the outside and for black men one with a red stripe. Everyone worked ten hours a day and was paid twenty-one cents an hour, except men who were paid a bit more because they furnished teams of mules. Father told me many stories about Nashville. Leslie Dickerson, he recalled, once visited a country girl at her home in Una and stayed too late in the parlor. "Sister, is the company gone," the girl's little brother called down from upstairs. Embarrassed and slightly nervous about having overstayed his welcome, Leslie instructed the girl to tell her brother that he had gone. "Well, then," the voice came back from above, "Ma says to pee before you come upstairs. The pot's full."

Although the movie brought father and son close together, it did not have the same effect upon wife and husband. Celebrity did not heighten my appeal, and whenever I tried to kiss Vicki in the pantry, she practiced what I call the "embrace domestic." She placed her right hand flat against my chest, the heel of her palm just below my breastbone and her fingers stretched out full length toward my throat. By straightening her arm slightly, she was able to repel all unwanted familiarity. In truth Vicki found celebrity a nuisance, something which changed a useful and perfectly good house cleaner and plate dryer into an inefficient dreamer and speculator. In early August an assistant to the president of the University of Connecticut telephoned and asked me to speak at the Convocation in September. Last year's speaker was a Nobel prize winner, and I didn't think I could refuse. "I'm honored to be asked," I answered, "and as a servant of the university I will be glad to speak." "Great God from Gulfport," Vicki exclaimed after I hung up, "Servant of the University! That makes me want to throw up." "Look Vicki," I said, "I may have been blinded by publicity for a while, but I haven't been taken in." Then I left the house and going to the bog picked leatherleaf in order make tea for Vicki's upset stomach.

A week later we left Nova Scotia. Waiting at home for me was a letter from a man who knew nothing about the movie but who had read my second collection of essays, the one that sold eight hundred and fifty-five copies. He, too, attended Ransom, and he enclosed a copy of the school song, observing that for best effect it required a minimum of six monotones, three breaking tenor voices, and a trio of shrill sopranos accompanied by a hollow, resonating piano, all to be performed in a room decorated in "School Board Brown." I want to write more about Ransom. Before starting, however, I must do two things. First I must address the Convocation. I am going to begin with one of Father's stories. While attending the funeral of his cousin Rushton in Pleasant Shade, Tennessee, Clovis Hurlburt saw Byron Pogue, son of his old friend Peevy Pogue. Byron worked for the undertaker in Pleasant Shade, Lonnie Fedge. Sometime after he returned to Nashville, Clovis met Peevy on Union Street, just outside the Trust Building. After chatting amicably about the influenza and railway fares, Clovis mentioned Byron. "Peevy," he said, "I saw Byron in Pleasant Shade. He works for Fedge the undertaker, doesn't he? I could have sworn you told me he was a doctor." "A doctor, good Lord, no," Peevy exclaimed; "I said he followed the medical profession." I resemble Byron, I will say in my address; I am not the real thing. I am just a follower, not even of the medical profession but of that lesser thing publicity. I offer no cure-alls for the ills of society. All I have ever done is cope: digging about here and there, once or twice unearthing something interesting, but more often than not simply burying my errors. Then as soon as the Convocation ends, I am going to jump in the car and go see *Dead Poets Society*. I wonder if John Keating really resembles me. If he does, I'd like to stand and say, "that's me." Of course I won't. Despite the occasional hankering, Pickerings aren't the stuff of celebrity and avoid spiral staircases and cameras, preferring instead to wander the fields and bogs of old farms: leading small children by the hand, brewing remedies for weak stomachs, and painting days yellow and purple.